DUAL LANGUAGE
Teaching and Learning in Two Languages

SONIA W. SOLTERO

DePaul University

PEARSON

Boston ■ New York ■ San Francisco
Mexico City ■ Montreal ■ Toronto ■ London ■ Madrid ■ Munich ■ Paris
Hong Kong ■ Singapore ■ Tokyo ■ Cape Town ■ Sydney

To José,

my source of inspiration, encouragement, and affection

SERIES EDITOR: *Aurora Martínez Ramos*
EDITORIAL ASSISTANT: *Katie Freddoso*
SENIOR MARKETING MANAGER: *Elizabeth Fogarty*
EDITORIAL-PRODUCTION ADMINISTRATOR: *Paul Mihailidis*
EDITORIAL PRODUCTION SERVICE: *Chestnut Hill Enterprises, Inc.*
TEXT DESIGNER: *Karen Mason*
COMPOSITION BUYER: *Linda Cox*
ELECTRONIC COMPOSITION: *Peggy Cabot, Cabot Computer Services*
MANUFACTURING BUYER: *Andrew Turso*
COVER ADMINISTRATOR: *Kristina Mose-Libon*

For related titles and support materials, visit our online catalog at
www.ablongman.com.

Between the time Website information is gathered and then published, it is not unusual
for some sites to have closed. Also, the transcription of URLs can result in typographical
errors. The publisher would appreciate being notified of any problems with URLs so
that they may be corrected in subsequent editions.

LIBRARY OF CONGRESS CATALOGING-IN-PUBLICATION DATA

Soltero, Sonia White.
  Dual language : teaching and learning in two languages / Sonia White Soltero.
     p.   cm.
  Includes bibliographical references (p.) and index.
  ISBN 0-205-34381-3
     1. Education, Bilingual—United States.   I. Title.
  LC3731.S665 2004
  370.117'0973—dc21   2003050283

Printed in the United States of America

10 9 8 7 6 5 4 3 2 1   08 07 06 05 04 03

Contents

7 BUILDING AND MAINTAINING A MODEL PROGRAM   127

APPENDIX A CHILDREN'S LITERATURE AND PREK–8 PUBLISHERS   143

APPENDIX B STAFF DEVELOPMENT VIDEOS   151

APPENDIX C PROFESSIONAL ORGANIZATIONS AND RESEARCH CENTERS   155

APPENDIX D INSTRUCTIONAL SOFTWARE   157

Boxes

Figures

Tables

Preface

Given the increasing number of students who enter schools speaking a native language other than English, it is clear that attending to the unique conditions of language minority students is the responsibility of all educators. For students with limited English proficiency, suitable approaches geared to their particular situation are not frills, but basic education. For English monolingual students, too, learning to appreciate and communicate in other languages is a gift to be cherished. When we approach language diversity as a resource that is respected and fostered, all students benefit.

Nieto (2002), p. 96

The complex and diverse needs of a growing and changing population possessing a variety of values, backgrounds, and preparations have posed special challenges for educators, business leaders, and policymakers in the United States. Compounding the challenges are increasing global demands for a better educated, bilingual, and biliterate work force. In particular, the growing numbers of non-English speaking students have compelled practitioners and scholars to focus on the challenge of how to provide specific and expanded literacy, linguistic, and academic skills so that all students can fully participate in a variety of educational, social, linguistic, cultural, and economic contexts. Dual language education may offer a sound alternative that increases culturally and linguistically diverse students' academic and linguistic educational attainment and augments their social and economic potential. In turn, dual language education may be a viable approach to move a more polyglot society to provide bilingual education for all students.

Although dual language education is not a new concept, it has gained increasing popularity in the United States in the last decade as a desirable alternative to other bilingual education models (Cummins, 2000; Thomas & Collier, 1997). Educators and policymakers are beginning to recognize the need to improve the linguistic and academic outcomes of students who participate in language education in the United States. For English dominant students, traditional foreign language models have not promoted high levels of proficiency in the second language of study (Corson, 2001). For language minority students, educational programs that stress rapid transition to English, and that provide little or no native language development and use, have proven to be detrimental and ineffective for their academic and linguistic attainment (August & Hakuta, 1998). Furthermore, for English-language learners, monolingual English-oriented schooling has resulted in low levels of native language proficiency and inadequate literacy skills in the native language, which lead to the eventual loss of the mother tongue.

Dual language can provide unique teaching and learning opportunities to all its participants: students, parents, teachers, administrators, and communities.

Because the languages and cultures of all the participants are highly valued, every person involved in the school has something to offer. This model of bilingual education, when well implemented, can be a linguistic and cultural bridge for students, educators, parents, and the community, and it has the potential to embrace and promote linguistic and cultural pluralism inside and outside of the school.

For students, dual language education supports the meaningful and significant development of two languages and cultures as students engage in the acquisition of biliterate, academic, multicultural, and social competencies through dynamic and challenging curricula. The multicultural and bilingual educational experiences that encompass dual language instruction allow students to form a positive self-image as well as expanded understandings of and respect for other cultures and languages. For English language learners, dual language education presents an authentic environment in which to use and develop their native language, to be proud of their heritage, and to contribute to the learning of their native English-speaking peers. For majority language students, the opportunity to interact daily with native speakers of the target language in the common pursuit of acquiring a second language and developing academically becomes a door to a multiethnic, multilingual, and multifaceted world.

For teachers and staff, dual language education provides forums for meaningful collaboration and opportunities for gaining new insights, both culturally and linguistically, about all the members of the school and the community. Monolingual English-speaking teachers occasionally find themselves with English-language learners in their classrooms and are often at a loss in addressing the linguistic, affective, and academic needs of these students. By participating in a dual language program, such teachers gain firsthand knowledge about second language acquisition theory, pedagogy, and cultural awareness. By collaborating side by side with bilingual and English as a second language (ESL) teachers, as well as language minority parents and students, monolingual English teachers develop a deeper linguistic, cultural, and social appreciation for English-language learners' backgrounds and needs. For bilingual teachers, dual language offers valuable opportunities to work with general-program students, parents, and teachers. The resulting collaborations between bilingual and general-program teachers in the education of all children provide a much-needed bridge between the traditionally segregated bilingual/ESL teachers and programs and the rest of the school community.

Because dual language education highly values the languages and cultures of the communities from which students come, it affords optimal and ongoing opportunities for communication, understanding, and collaboration among its members. Parents are an integral part of dual language education, and they are encouraged to collaborate with the school in both traditional and nonconventional ways. As educators become more knowledgeable about and aware of the distinct cultural and social practices of their students and families, teachers begin to accommodate the diverse styles of parental involvement in the school. For parents and community, this open and flexible partnership leads to an increased sense of belonging in the school community and greater investment in their children's educational experiences. Dual language can also offer parents and families a wide range of resources for their own personal growth and for assisting in their children's academic, linguistic, and social development.

Among the most critical considerations that educators must examine in implementing dual language education are the theoretical, sociopolitical, and pedagogical frameworks of language acquisition, literacy development, and academic attainment for culturally and linguistically diverse students. Because a fundamental component of dual language education is the integration of majority and minority language children in the common pursuit of acquiring knowledge, developing proficiency in two languages, and building cross-cultural understandings, this model of bilingual education has the potential to offer enrichment education for all students (Cummins, 2001). Dual language education extends beyond first and second language acquisition to include social, cultural, and political dimensions, concepts sometimes overlooked in many schools serving culturally and linguistically diverse populations. Moreover, culturally responsive pedagogy that allows for the development of cross-cultural awareness and intergroup adeptness must be at the core of dual language education (Genesee & Gándara, 1999; Torres-Guzmán, 2002). As schools and communities strive to develop bilingualism and multiculturalism in their children and youth, enrichment language programs such as dual language education must be well conceptualized and defined, adequately funded, and vigorously supported. Creating and maintaining an effective and long-lasting dual language program requires a clear understating of the complexities of language education in general and of sound pedagogical instructional paradigms.

ABOUT THIS BOOK

This book is addressed to preservice and in-service teachers, administrators, and other professional educators who are or will be involved in the planning and operation of dual language education. The purpose of this book is to examine the pedagogical and organizational principles embodied in dual language instruction and to outline the specific conditions and features that are necessary for the effective implementation of dual language education programs. The book covers the multiple issues that must be considered when putting dual language instruction into practice, as well as the various complications and dilemmas that frequently arise while developing and implementing a dual language program. Vignettes of actual classroom and school practices and events that illustrate the discussions presented in the book accompany each chapter. In order to maintain confidentiality, all the names of the people represented in the vignettes have been changed.

Chapter 1 begins by presenting a broad definition of dual language education and delineates the essential elements that characterize effective dual language instruction, such as balanced language representation and integration of all students for instruction in the two languages. The discussion of the effectiveness of dual language education is corroborated by findings of three recent, large-scale research studies that examine the linguistic and academic achievement of students participating in dual language education in the United States. The results of these studies provide critical information about the conceptual frameworks of dual language education and the linguistic, academic, and cultural outcomes of participating students. To situate dual language education within the various models of second language programs, the chapter offers a brief overview of the major educational models in which language learners participate in the United States. The second language models discussed include submersion, immersion, English-structured immersion, English as a second language, transitional bilingual education, maintenance, and newcomer centers.

Chapter 2 examines the fundamental characteristics of dual language education, including program models, language issues, and organizational concerns. The chapter begins by delineating the differences between the two most prevalent dual language program models, total and partial immersion, and discusses issues relating to program selection. The recommended length of program implementation, parental involvement, and balanced language representation of students from both language groups is also presented. In this chapter, a great deal of attention is given to issues relating to language distribution and usage, such as the relevance of separating the two languages for instruction, the role of students' codeswitching, and decisions on the language of initial literacy and language of homework. The final section of this chapter focuses on classroom organization, with a discussion of the differences between self-contained and team-teaching classroom composition, and quality bilingual instruction.

Chapter 3 presents a synopsis of first and second language acquisition theories and research that provide the theoretical constructs for dual language pedagogy and practice. The discussion of second language acquisition recapitulates and challenges two of the most cited myths about acquiring English as a second language, the language deficiency myth and the English exposure myth, and provides more current perspectives on how a second language is more effectively developed. This chapter also examines theories of literacy development in the first and second language.

Chapter 4 recommends several steps to be taken when schools are in the planning stages of implementing a dual language program. The planning phase of implementation is particularly significant because the fundamental building blocks of a sound program are laid out during this period. Some of the recommendations include visiting existing dual language programs, consulting universities and educational centers, involving parents in the planning stages, and writing a strategic plan that includes creating a vision and mission statement for the program, that projects a timeline for implementation, that delineates the program goals and student outcomes, and that makes programmatic decisions about classroom organization, program model, and degree of program inclusion in the school. This chapter also presents other program considerations, such as admissions and placement procedures, administrative roles and support, and ideas for funding sources. The final section of the chapter discusses issues related to teachers and staff, including professional development, curriculum planning, the overall school environment, information dissemination, and ways to promote and support the program.

Chapter 5 considers the fundamental teaching and learning components of effective dual language instruction. The learning and teaching elements presented here are broad in scope and are intended to provide a general framework to guide instructional practices in the dual language classroom. The essential learning elements of dual language education include students' language and literacy development in the first and second language, learning content areas in both languages, and students' engagement in multicultural curriculum. The most critical teaching components introduced in this chapter consist of the home connection, cooperative learning, thematic approach, integrated and literature-based curriculum, sheltered language instruction, grouping techniques, and authentic assessment approaches.

Chapter 6 explores in more depth the instructional practices alluded to in Chapter 5. A discussion of cooperative learning is extended in this chapter to include grouping strategies, such as numbered-heads-together, jigsaw, and literature circles, as well as pairing strategies like partner reading, think-pair-share, and cross-age buddies. Other effective strategies that are particularly appropriate for the dual language classroom, such as anticipation guides, language experience approach, preview-review, total physical response, and graphic organizers, are also discussed. The last section examines varied instructional resources and ways to use them for dual language instruction. These include bilingual and multicultural children's literature, multimedia resources, and technology.

Chapter 7 presents numerous considerations related to the maintenance and revitalization of existing dual language programs and explores possible solutions to potential challenges and dilemmas. The discussion in the first part of the chapter highlights issues associated with administrative support, professional development, staffing matters, and program maintenance. The later section centers on troubleshooting and problem-solving points of concern, such as teacher ambivalence, parent skepticism, shortage of qualified teachers, and imbalanced language representation of students.

Each chapter concludes with Discussion Questions that open and extend diverse dialogs about issues presented in the chapter, as well as Field-Based Inquiries that provide ideas to conduct investigations in classrooms, schools, and communities related to the issues discussed in the book. Finally, each chapter includes a list of recommended references in the Suggestions for Further Reading. A Glossary is included to provide brief definitions of concepts and terminology used throughout the book.

The four appendices included at the end of the book provide a variety of resources for educators. Appendix A offers a selected list of children's fiction that is available in Spanish and English. The list includes bilingual fiction books (Spanish and English text within the same book); pattern and predictable language books; fiction series; books about Latino culture, the immigrant experience, diversity and multiculturalism, and urban issues; wordless picture books; and selected author sets. The appendix also provides a list of publishers that offer children's books in Spanish and English as well as other languages, and several children's literature Web sites. Appendix B includes an annotated list of recommended videos for professional development that feature dual language classrooms and schools, first and second language acquisition theory and practice, multicultural education, and best practices. Appendix C provides a list of professional organizations and research centers, as well as national conferences related to dual language and language education. Appendix D offers an annotated list of selected educational software programs in Spanish and English and contact information for their distributors.

The recommendations presented in this book give a comprehensive basis for planning, designing, organizing, implementing, evaluating, and maintaining effective dual language programs. The described theoretical and pedagogical frameworks provide the critical foundations necessary for effective and enduring implementation of dual language education.

ACKNOWLEDGMENTS

This book has come about as a result of my long involvement in participatory action research in dual language programs in public schools. My research interests originated from my own experiences and reflections in urban and semi-rural schools that struggled to implement additive bilingual programs for linguistically diverse students.

Being a product of dual language education myself in elementary school and high school in Latin America, I have experienced the linguistic, academic, and affective benefits and satisfaction of dual language education. I thank my parents for this. During my sixteen years of involvement with dual language education as a teacher, administrator, and researcher, I have been fortunate to have collaborated with some of the most outstanding and dedicated practitioners, parents, and children. Students, parents, and colleagues alike have shaped and contributed to my continuing understanding of dual language education and the field of education in general. I am especially grateful to two of my dual language team-teaching partners and friends, Caroline Carlson and Demetrya Collier. Their passion for teaching, their dedication to students and their families, and their reflective and profound knowledge of education still inspire me. I am also grateful to Renuka Mehra, a colleague and close friend who supported me in the struggle to advance dual language education in our school and from whom I learned much. Blanca Treviño, Director of the Dual Language Education Program in Chicago,

Marina Escamilla and Marta Moya-Leang, have also been instrumental in giving me the extraordinary opportunity to work with twenty-nine dual language programs and more than two hundred teachers in the Chicago Public Schools over the past six years. My heartfelt gratitude to Quinn Hanzel, who was generous enough to give me feedback on the manuscript and to encourage me throughout the writing process. Finally, I want to thank José, who not only encouraged and motivated me to write this book, but who has also been exceptionally patient and supportive. My experiences as a learner, teacher, and researcher in schools, in classrooms, and at the university continue to inform and shape my views and multiple understandings of dual language education. Lastly, I would like to thank the following reviewers for their input and criticism: Fabiola Ehlers-Zavala, Illinois State University; Linda Lippitt, Community Learning Collaborative; Judith H. Munter, University of Texas, El Paso; and Sharon Ulanoff, California State University, Los Angeles.

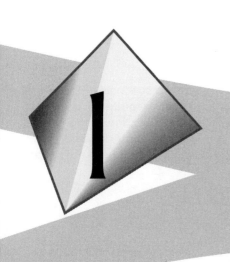

Dual Language and Bilingual Education

In its purest, most natural form, language diversity should be celebrated and nurtured. Without it, life would be less stimulating, human interaction more uniform and boring. Those who know only one language have access to a limited range of human contacts; those who know more than one language are able to enter into many different social groups.

Dicker (1996), p. viii

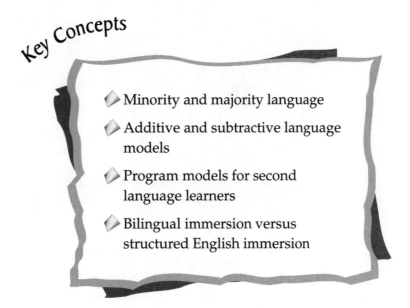

Key Concepts

- ◆ Minority and majority language
- ◆ Additive and subtractive language models
- ◆ Program models for second language learners
- ◆ Bilingual immersion versus structured English immersion

A critical understanding of the complexities, variations, and intended outcomes of language education in general is necessary for dual language educators, parents, and policymakers to make informed decisions about effective program implementation. This chapter begins by introducing a working definition of dual language education that situates it within an additive bilingual education framework. A brief overview of the major program models for language learners in the United States follows. Effective language models of instruction, such as dual language education, are based on empirical research and sound theoretical foundations. Thus, this chapter also presents a synopsis of the major findings of three recent, large-scale research studies that examine the academic achievement of students participating in dual language education in the United States. The multiple interpretations of implementation are explained and broad perspectives on key features that characterize dual language programs are articulated in the last part of this chapter.

A WORKING DEFINITION OF DUAL LANGUAGE EDUCATION

As with any other complex concept, dual language education does not have one clear-cut definition. Definitions range from broad to very precise and explicit. Much like other models of bilingual education, dual language is also accorded many aliases, including **developmental bilingual education**, **bilingual immersion**, **double immersion**, **bilingual enrichment,** and **two-way immersion** (Baker, 2001). For the purpose of this book, the term **dual language education** is defined as a long-term additive bilingual and bicultural program model that consistently uses two languages for instruction, learning, and communication, with a balanced number of students from two language groups who are integrated for instruction for all or at least half of the school day in the pursuit of bilingual, biliterate, academic, and cross-cultural competencies.

This broad description provides the basis for an expanded definition. In dual language education, two languages (usually a majority language and a minority language) are used for bilingual, biliterate, academic, cultural, and social development (Christian, Montone, Lindholm & Carranza, 1997; Lindholm-Leary, 2001). The program is usually offered for a period of six to eight years, typically from preK to sixth grade or beyond (Mora, Wink & Wink, 2001). Literacy may be acquired in the first or second language, and subject matter is learned in both languages. The learning environment aims to promote positive attitudes toward each language and culture and foster full bilingual and biliterate proficiencies in both languages (Lindholm, 1991; Montague, 1997). Students from both language groups should be equally represented (although this is not always the case), ideally 50 percent of the students from each language in a classroom that integrates them for all or most of their academic instruction. In this book, **language majority students** refers to speakers of English, since in the context of the United States English is the language used by the majority of the population, and **language minority students** refers to speakers whose first language is not English and who use their native language as the primary vehicle of communication. The terms *majority* and *minority* are in no way intended to imply that one language is superior or inferior to any other language; rather, they are used in reference to the number of individuals using each language in the context of the United States.

Dual language education is an **additive bilingual education** model. This term refers to an educational context that promotes the continual development of the native language and maintenance of the home culture while adding a second language and culture (Cummins, 2000). In the additive form of bilingual education, the child's home language and culture are not replaced by the second language and culture; rather, they are further developed in conjunction with the acquisition of the second language and culture (Baker, 2001). For example, in additive Native American bilingual programs in the United States, children receive instruction in the tribal language while extending their knowledge about Native American culture, and at the same time develop English and learn other aspects of North American culture (McCarty & Watahomigie, 1998).

In contrast to dual language education and other additive bilingual programs, most education models for second language learners in the United States, (transitional bilingual education, structured English immersion, newcomer centers, or ESL programs) are subtractive. In **subtractive bilingual education,** the home language and culture are replaced by the English language and the mainstream U.S. culture (Cummins, 2000). The most widely implemented additive and subtractive education models for second language learners in the United States will be discussed more in depth in the following section.

BILINGUAL EDUCATION AND SECOND LANGUAGE PROGRAM MODELS

In the evolution of dual language education in the United States, misconceptions and confusion have at times been cause for concern for bilingual and mainstream educators and administrators. Negative perceptions of dual language education have been created due to lack of information and an unclear understanding of what dual language is, what it is not, and how it relates to bilingual education in general. Additional misconceptions have been created by the media's misrepresentation of subtractive immersion education for minority language learners. A result has been the recent passage of legislation in states like California and Arizona replacing bilingual education with short-term structured English immersion programs. The passage in 1998 of California's Proposition 227, English Language Education for Children in Public Schools Initiative, spearheaded by affluent software entrepreneur Ron Unz, aimed to disband and outlaw bilingual education and institute compulsory one-year structured English immersion programs for English language learners (Crawford, 2001). Even though the implementation of the bill varies across districts, instruction of English language learners has been overwhelmingly in English (Baker, 2001). In 2000 Arizona passed a similar initiative, Proposition 223, which also virtually eliminated bilingual education for culturally and linguistically diverse students. Even though both measures allow parents to request bilingual education services for their children, these requests are often complex and entwined with complications. For example, for English language learners to receive bilingual services in California, at least twenty parents must sign a waiver, and they must reapply each year. Because school districts tend to adopt their own interpretations of the law, parents often are either not given choices or are given vague information about their right to request waivers (García & Curry-Rodríguez, 2000).

Unfounded and sweeping claims about the ineffectiveness of bilingual education coupled with the media's predisposition against it have allowed for the dissemination of inaccuracies and fabrications (Crawford, 2001). The inadequate implementation of many bilingual programs has further cultivated the notion that bilingual education is a failure. The low performance of most bilingual education programs is closely correlated to the lack of adequate funds, scarcity of qualified educators, large classes, and absence of proven teaching methodology (Dicker, 2000). Solidly designed bilingual programs that address these fundamental factors have proven to be highly effective for linguistically diverse students (August & Hakuta, 1997). Another common misconception about dual language education comes from mainstream monolingual English teachers, many of whom believe that their jobs are in jeopardy because they are not proficient in a second language. Quite to the contrary, in 50–50 programs, monolingual majority language teachers who come from diverse ethnic and cultural backgrounds can contribute greatly to the overall teaching and learning experiences of parents, students, and the educators themselves. African American, European-descendant, Asian, Muslim, and Jewish teachers, to name a few, add to the pluralism and diversity that is essential to dual language education. In addition, monolingual English teachers not only provide a model for the language, but also are in the exceptional position of becoming second language learners themselves and of developing solid understandings of second language acquisition and cultural diversity.

The second reaction often comes from bilingual educators who mistakenly perceive dual language to be in competition with other bilingual education models, such as transitional programs. Some bilingual teachers believe that by implementing dual language education, the bilingual education program in their schools will be at risk of being discontinued. In fact, by implementing dual language, schools are still offering bilingual education to students, only in a different and more effective form (Thomas & Collier, 1997, 2002) that is open to all students: English language learners, native English speakers, and even linguistically diverse English proficient students who are no longer in bilingual education but wish to continue developing in their native language and culture.

In an effort to clarify the potential false impressions concerning dual language and bilingual education, the following section delineates the different program models of instruction for second language learners in the United States. Given that the terms and characteristics that define each model vary widely across schools and classrooms, it is important to note that there is significant overlap, blurring, and blending of program types for second language students. Researchers and educators differ in their conceptions and definitions of these models (Brisk & Harrington, 2000). For example, Baker (2001) refers to structured English immersion as a form of submersion; DiCerbo (2000) considers late-exit transitional bilingual education to be a developmental model; and Brisk (1998) regards bilingual education and dual language as different programs (one serves minority language children and the other is aimed at majority language students). Nevertheless, the descriptions of the models presented in the next section provide general characteristics of the types of educational programs that are available to second language learners in the United States.

Program Models for Second Language Learners

In the United States, educational models for non-native English speakers range from additive programs that promote bilingualism and include the native language for an extended period of time (**dual language, maintenance,** and **heritage language bilingual programs**) to subtractive programs that exclude the native language altogether and aim for monolingualism and programs that include the native language for a short period of time but also have monolingualism as the intended goal (**transitional bilingual education**). Educational programs for non-native English speakers that offer limited or no first language instruction consist of **structured English immersion** (limited or no native language support), **English as a second language** programs (limited or no native language instruction), and **newcomer programs** (limited or no native language support). Programs that use the native language for some or most academic instruction are under the umbrella of bilingual education, which include transitional, maintenance, heritage language, and dual language models (see Figure 1.1).

Bilingual education is not a monolithic endeavor; rather, it is a multidimensional concept used to refer to numerous types of programs and designs. Bilingual education encompasses a diverse number of models with divergent goals, differences in length of implementation, variations in amount of use of each language, and distinctions in programmatic composition (Crawford, 1999). Mackey (1978) categorized ninety variations of bilingual education. To add to the com-

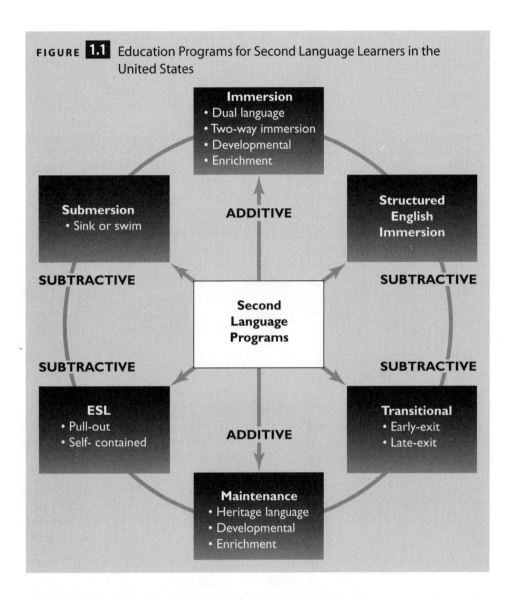

FIGURE 1.1 Education Programs for Second Language Learners in the United States

plexity and range of bilingual education designs, many programs go by numerous pseudonyms. Nevertheless, all programs in which second language learners participate fall under two critical paradigms: they are either additive (such as maintenance, heritage language, and dual language) or subtractive (such as transitional and structured English immersion). Programs that aim to develop full bilingualism, biliteracy, and biculturalism by adding the second language and maintaining and developing the first language are considered additive bilingual education models. In contrast, the primary purpose in subtractive bilingual education is to become monolingual in the second language by abandoning the native language. Table 1.1 describes the most widely implemented language education program models for language learners in the United States and categorizes them as either additive or subtractive.

Subtractive Second Language Models

SUBMERSION. Although **submersion,** also known as **sink or swim,** is not in fact a program at all, it is often included when describing the different types of

■ **TABLE 1.1** | **Educational Models for Second Language Learners in the United States**

Language/s	Names	Population	Linguistic Outcome	Curriculum and Number of Years
Native Language and English	■ **Immersion** Dual language Two-way immersion Enrichment Two-way bilingual	English language learners (who speak the same language) and native English speakers	***Additive:*** bilingualism and biliteracy in L1 and English	Content in L1/L2 Long term (6–12 years)
	■ **Maintenance** Developmental Enrichment Heritage language	English language learners (who speak the same language)	***Additive:*** bilingualism and biliteracy in L1 and English	Content in L1/L2, ESL Long term (6–12 years)
	■ **Transitional** ■ Early-exit	English language learners (who speak the same language)	***Subtractive:*** monolingualism in English	Content in L1, rapid transition to L2, ESL Short term (1–3 years)
	■ **Transitional** ■ Late-exit	English language learners (who speak the same language)	***Subtractive:*** monolingualism in English	Content in L1 with transition to L2, ESL Long term (4–6 years)
English	■ **Structured English immersion**	English language learners (who speak the same language or speak different languages)	***Subtractive:*** monolingualism in English	ESL, sometimes limited L1 support Short term (1–3 years)
	■ **ESL**	English language learners (who speak the same language or speak different languages)	***Subtractive:*** monolingualism in English	Pull-out or in class Short term (1–3 years)
	■ **Newcomer centers**	English language learners (who speak the same language or speak different languages)	***Subtractive:*** monolingualism in English	ESL, Sheltered English Short term (1–2 years)
	■ **Submersion** Sink or swim	English language learners (who speak the same language or speak different languages) placed in mainstream English classrooms	***Subtractive:*** monolingualism in English	No ESL or L1 support

programs in which culturally and linguistically diverse students participate. Submersion is regularly cited because many English language learners frequently end up in this type of sink-or-swim situation, with no specialized assistance in either the native language or in the form of English as a second language (Ovando & Collier, 1998). In submersion, language minority students are taught exclusively in English alongside fluent English speakers. Because teachers are seldom prepared or trained to accommodate the needs of second language learners or to effectively modify the curriculum and instructional practices, most students in submersion conditions do not receive comprehensible input and fall behind academically (Freeman & Freeman, 1998). In Díaz-Rico and Weed's words (2002, p. 169): "As a result, the strongest of these language minority students may survive or even succeed academically (they 'swim'), but the majority do not have the cognitive or academic foundation in the primary language at the time of education in English and thus do not obtain the level of success educators might wish (they 'sink')."

STRUCTURED ENGLISH IMMERSION. The United States implements two types of immersion programs: a subtractive model, known as structured English immersion, and an additive model, known as two-way immersion or dual language education, which will be further discussed later in this chapter. The most widespread and popular program in the United States is structured English immersion, designed only for English language learners. In this subtractive program, English language learners receive English instruction with limited or no first language support and minimal ESL assistance, usually in the form of pull-out language instruction (August & Hakuta, 1997). Language minority students are immersed in English and are expected to learn it and the academic content at the same pace and level as their native English speaking peers, who do not have the added burden of learning a second language that is the only mode of instruction (Cummins, 1992; Lessow-Hurley, 2000).

ENGLISH AS A SECOND LANGUAGE. ESL is a major component of all bilingual education models, as well as of newcomer centers and structured English immersion programs. At times, ESL may be a stand-alone program, usually provided in school communities in which students come from multiple language backgrounds or that have no bilingual programs or personnel. According to Thomas and Collier (1997), ESL programs are implemented across the United States in several forms and with varying degrees of effectiveness. The two most common forms of ESL are traditional and content-based, delivered either as a pull-out service or conducted within the student's regular classroom, individually or in a group. In the pull-out version, English language learners are removed from their regular classrooms to receive ESL instruction for certain periods of the day or week. In high schools, English language learners usually have separate ESL class periods. Whether ESL is implemented as a pull-out or inclusionary practice, in the most effective programs ESL teachers coordinate instruction, and the academic objectives are covered in the student's regular classroom (Ovando & Collier, 1998).

In traditional ESL, English is taught as a subject matter, and the focus is entirely on linguistic systems: phonology, syntax, morphology, semantics, and pragmatics. Considerable emphasis is given to grammar, vocabulary, and error correction, usually through drill and practice. Traditional modes of language instruction that focus on the language itself have proven to be ineffective for certain groups of second language learners (Corson, 2001). For instance, adults who are educated in their native languages and have experienced similar types of traditional teaching styles may be more inclined to take advantage of language-oriented methods and be successful second language learners. Also, educated adults tend to focus solely on learning the language, whereas preK–12 students have the added burden and responsibility of acquiring content and literacy competencies. For most learners with limited prior exposure to formal education, whether children or adults, grammar-oriented methods are not conducive to natural and meaningful language acquisition (Ovando & Collier, 1998).

A more desirable and effective method for English language instruction is content-based ESL, in which students learn all or part of the content curriculum through the second language. Rather than learning the language as discrete skills, as in the case of traditional ESL, content-based ESL aims to develop the second language as it is being acquired and used in the context of learning the academic curriculum (Faltis, 1997). Language is taught as students are engaged in learning science, math, social studies, and other subjects. This form of ESL instruction subscribes to highly effective language acquisition teaching practices, such as **English Language Development** (ELD) which is aimed at learners at the beginning stages of second language development, and Sheltered English Instruction, Specially Designed Academic Instruction in English (SDAIE) and the Cognitive Academic Language Learning Approach (CALLA) (Chamot & O'Malley, 1994), which are both intended for second language learners who are at the intermediate fluency level. Content-based second language instruction works exceptionally well for all second language learners in dual language programs. These instructional approaches to second language development are discussed in detail in Chapters 5 and 6.

NEWCOMER CENTERS.   These programs provide academic, linguistic, and social support to recently immigrated students. They are typically located in middle or high school settings and are designed to address the needs of recent arrivals who have limited or no native literacy skills or who lack formal education in their native countries (Castro Feinberg, 2002). Newcomer centers were created to address special needs of English language learners that regular bilingual or ESL programs are not adequately equipped to manage. A key feature of most newcomer centers is the provision of an emotionally safe learning environment that supports rapid second language learning, adaptation to the host culture, and development of a positive self-image (Díaz-Rico & Weed, 2002). Thus, the major emphasis is on the integration of academic and social support to help students adjust to the new culture, school customs, and academic curriculum (Short, 2002). Although English development is the priority, the home language may be used for instruction. This is a short-term program, typically lasting six months to two years, and is implemented either at a school site or as a separate center. After participating in this intensive language and acculturation program, students enroll in or transfer to regular or bilingual classrooms, with continued second language support in the form of ESL instruction. Some programs have additional goals, such as developing students' native language skills and acclimating students and their parents to the community.

TRANSITIONAL BILINGUAL EDUCATION, EARLY-EXIT AND LATE-EXIT. This subtractive bilingual education model temporarily supports students' academic development as they acquire English through ESL by providing native language instruction in literacy and content areas for a period of one to eight years (Crawford, 1999). The purpose of initially using the primary language is to build a solid literacy and academic foundation as students acquire English. The major goal of transitional bilingual education is to acquire sufficient English proficiency to function at grade level in the mainstream English classroom. Typically, instruction is initially provided in the native language for all the content areas as well as literacy, along with ESL lessons. Gradually, the amount of English for content curriculum is increased until students are transitioned into all English instruction.

Transitional bilingual education consists of two program types: early-exit and late-exit.

In **early-exit bilingual education,** which is the transitional bilingual education model most widely implemented in the United States (Baker, 2001; Crawford, 1999), English language learners receive native language instruction in literacy and the content areas while they are acquiring English. In this model, second language learners are mainstreamed, or exited, into the general education program after being in the transitional bilingual program for one to three years, once they have achieved proficiency in English. The principal objective in early-exit is to facilitate students' academic progress through the language they understand, while they acquire sufficient proficiency in the second language to function academically in English. In contrast, students in **late-exit bilingual education** continue to receive instruction in the native language for a few more years even after having achieved proficiency in English. Although the primary goal in late-exit is to continue to develop students' literacy and oral language skills in the native language as well as in English for a longer period of time, it is still considered to be a subtractive model of instruction because students are eventually exited into the mainstream English program.

Additive Second Language Models

MAINTENANCE BILINGUAL EDUCATION.   This additive model of bilingual education may also be known as developmental, enrichment, or heritage language education. In this model, English language learners maintain and develop their native languages as they acquire English, usually through eighth grade or beyond. Students initially receive most instruction in their native language as English is added, through ESL, in increasing amounts each year. As they progress through the grades, students engage in meaningful academic content learning in English and continue to participate in challenging learning experiences in their first language. By fourth or fifth grade, students receive instruction equally in both languages.

The primary aim of maintenance bilingual education is for students to develop bilingual and biliterate proficiencies and to achieve academically at grade level. Maintenance bilingual programs are culturally responsive because they value and build on students' home cultural and linguistic knowledge (Krashen, Tse & McQuillan, 1998). One critical difference between maintenance and dual language education is the student linguistic composition. In contrast to maintenance bilingual education in which all students are English language learners, dual language education integrates English dominant students and English language learners.

BILINGUAL IMMERSION.   This additive form of immersion, also known as two-way immersion or dual language education, integrates English native speakers with speakers of another language in the common pursuit of continuing to develop their native language while acquiring a second language. Because all students are acquiring and developing a second language, this immersion model, when implemented effectively, utilizes best practices that aim to expose students to comprehensible input and lower the learners' affective filter (Krashen, 1982). Bilingual immersion in the United States was adapted from the Canadian educational experimental program that began in 1965 in St. Lambert, Montreal, where English speaking children received curriculum instruction in French (Lambert & Tucker, 1972). In immersion bilingual education in Canada, academic and language instruction is primarily conducted in the minority language in the initial grades, gradually increasing the amount of instruction in the majority language until the two languages are used. The aim is to develop additive bilingualism, biliteracy, and academic competencies in two languages (Genesee, 1987). In the United States, there has been a history of misunderstanding, particularly from policymakers, regarding the additive or subtractive approaches to immersion programs (Cummins, 2000). That is, English-only programs for English language learners have been misconstrued as immersion education (Díaz-Rico & Weed, 2002). These structured English immersion programs gained popularity in the United States because of the success of French immersion programs in Canada (Lessow-Hurley, 2000). Many policymakers and opponents of bilingual education continue to misunderstand the fundamental differences between immersion programs in Canada and the United States and the way these differences drastically impact student outcomes. Table 1.2 delineates the fundamental differences between the two forms of immersion.

Immersion programs in Canada are designed for English speaking and French speaking children to acquire the second language and to develop their na-

◼ TABLE 1.2	Canadian Immersion versus U.S. Structured English Immersion	
Canadian Model . . .	**U.S. Model . . .**
The goal is *bilingualism* and *biliteracy* in English and French	The goal is *monolingualism* in English
Teachers are *bilingual* in French and English	Teachers are *monolingual* in English
Teachers have *specialized training* in second language acquisition theory and pedagogy	Teachers have *no specialized training* to address English language learners' needs
The minority language, French, holds *equal or greater status* to the majority language, English	The minority language—Spanish, Korean, etc.—holds a much *lower status* than the majority language, English
The curriculum is increasingly conducted in *both languages*	The curriculum is mostly in the second language, *English*
All the students are learning a second language	*Only* language minority students are learning a second language
Majority language students receive *some instruction in their native language*	Minority language students usually receive *no instruction in the native language*
The second language is taught *through content* and meaningful interaction	The second language is taught *as a subject,* devoid of context
Parents *chose* to have their children in the program	Parents have *no choice* in the placement of their children

tive language as they become bilingual and biliterate in English and French (Cummins, 1992; Genesse, 1987). In contrast, in the United States structured English immersion programs are designed for language minority children (Latinos, Asians, Africans, and other minority groups) to learn the majority language (English) and become monolingual and monoliterate in English. Therein lies one of the major flaws of structured English immersion programs for minority children. These critical discrepancies prove to be highly problematic when attempting to equate the two models. The positive and negative impacts on students are directly linked to how each model is implemented and to the ideological principles to which each model conforms. Consider some of the disparities: the goal in Canadian immersion is for students to become fully bilingual and biliterate, and the teachers are bilingual and knowledgeable about second language acquisition theory and pedagogy; there is some initial native language instruction for Anglophone students, and English instruction increases over several grade levels to eventually reach a balance of French and English as the two mediums of instruction; and parents choose to place their children in the program. Conversely, structured English immersion in the United States has as its primary goal the production of monolingual English-proficient students; teachers are monolingual and have little, if any, specialized training in second language acquisition theory and pedagogy; there is little to no native language instruction, and the sole medium of instruction is English; and parents are required to place their children in the program (Cummins, 2000).

In her discussion of the inequities in education for language minority students, Brisk (1998) proposes a "compensatory vs. quality schooling" paradigm. Within this view of education, structured English immersion in the United States is a compensatory program that seeks to teach English to language minority students as quickly as possible. In an effort to accomplish this goal, structured English immersion aims to eliminate students' native language and culture. Thus, structured English immersion strips children of their linguistic and cultural capital, subjugating them to assimilation and loss of what otherwise are considered to be desirable assets: literate and oral proficiencies of a second language and intimate knowledge of another culture. Numerous studies (August & Hakuta, 1997; Ramírez, 1992; Thomas & Collier, 1997, 2002) have demonstrated that students who participate in programs that use the native language for instruction for more than three years show better academic performance, achieve greater mastery of English, and have lower dropout rates.

The above synopsis of the distinctions between Canadian and U.S. immersion models is important to revisit because of the recent backlash against bilingual education and the great emphasis on structured English immersion programs for language minority children in the United States (Cummins, 2000). Legislation that imposes structured English immersion for English language learners, such as that passed in California and Arizona and similar looming propositions in states such as in Colorado and Utah, have created a great deal of confusion about immersion programs and typically result in unrealistic expectations for English language learners.

A CLOSER LOOK AT DUAL LANGUAGE EDUCATION

Language education has been, and will continue to be, a highly politicized and contentious field, particularly when it involves culturally and linguistically diverse students (Crawford, 2001). Additive bilingual education programs like dual language are intricately connected to the language rights of minority groups in the United States and their struggles to maintain and develop native languages and cultures (Corson, 2001). Dual language educators ought not ignore the sociopolitical and sociolinguistic implications for both language minority and majority students. Dual language educators then become promoters of multilingualism and multiculturalism, advocates for language minority children, and agents of culturally and linguistically responsive education.

Interestingly, some of the educators and policymakers who scorn bilingual education are supporters of dual language education. One such educator is Charles Glenn, an academic and administrator , who vehemently opposes bilingual education but strongly endorses dual language programs:

> The best setting for educating a linguistic minority pupil—and one of the best for educating any pupil—is a school in which two languages are used without apology and where becoming proficient in both is considered a significant intellectual and cultural achievement. (Glenn & LaLyre, 1991, p. 43)

Cummins (2001) aptly suggests that this dichotomy constitutes a "doublethink" mentality. That is, there exists incongruent and contradictory support for both structured English immersion (an English instructional program for English language learners that offers limited to no support in the native language and has monolingualism as its primary objective) and dual language education (bilingual instruction in English and the native language aimed at developing bilingualism, biliteracy, and biculturalism). How can educators support English immersion for language minority students, which provides almost exclusive English exposure and very little, if any, native language instruction, and at the same time advocate for dual language immersion, which initially involves considerably less English and much native language instruction? Cummins proposes that the common ground shared by these divergent perspectives may provide a new vision: enriched education for all students, perhaps in the form of dual language education.

Dual Language Education and Bilingualism

According to Mackey (1978), bilingual education has existed for five thousand or more years. Trade, politics, land appropriation, and reconstruction of geographical boundaries created fertile ground for bilinguals and multilinguals to flourish in the ancient world. More recently, the advent of the information and communication age, increasing international travel, and growing migration have augmented the bilingual population across the globe. A study recently conducted by the United Nations found that 66 percent of the world's children are now bilingual or multilingual, a remarkable increase over the last century (Goble, 2001). This boost in multilingualism is largely due to the fact that more people around the world are choosing to educate their children in a second language, particularly in English, Chinese, Spanish, Arabic, or Russian (Skutnabb-Kangas, 2000).

Unquestionably, English has become the global *lingua franca* (preferred language), not only because it is perceived as a language of status, but also because it is widely used for international commerce and the Internet. Unfortunately, the global thrust to acquire English has promoted monolingualism among English native speakers and often has resulted in negative attitudes toward acquiring other languages (Crawford, 2001). The antagonistic view of bilingualism in the United States is clearly reflected in the general apathy toward foreign language learning in schools and universities, the relentless efforts to eliminate bilingual education for language minority populations, and the obsessive push to impose official English language laws (Dicker, 2000).

Enter dual language or two-way immersion education. Contrary to popular belief, dual language education is not a new concept; Sweden, Switzerland, China, and Canada, among numerous other countries, have successfully practiced and encouraged this form of bilingual and, in some cases, multilingual education for decades. Prior to the nineteenth century, German, French, and indigenous languages, to name a few, were used daily in the United States in the public and private sectors, including in schools (Crawford, 2001). More recently, the success of bilingual education programs established in Florida after the Cuban revolution inspired the implementation of dual language programs across the nation. Coral Way Elementary, a dual language English-Spanish school established in 1963 by Cuban exiles in Dade County, Florida, restored this additive model of bilingual education in the United States (Baker, 2000).

Since the early 1990s, this form of bilingual education has received ever-increasing attention by U.S. media, policymakers, and educators as an ideal model of a true bilingual, biliterate, and bicultural education—that is, an education model that incorporates two language groups (speakers of the majority language and speakers of a minority language) in the pursuit of academic, linguistic, social, and cultural development. This education model is driven by the fundamental goal of developing bilingual, biliterate, and bicultural individuals (Lindholm-Leary, 2001). In 2000 a substantial amount of Title VII (now Title III) funding was earmarked by the federal government for schools to implement new dual language programs and/or extend existing programs. Richard W. Riley, U.S. Secretary of Education during the Clinton administration, proposed increasing the number of dual language programs by one thousand over five years. Title VII was based on the Bilingual Education Act of 1968 designed to assist language minority students by federally funding bilingual education programs. It has been reformulated under George W. Bush's administration into Title III, which eliminates the stipulation that the federal government give preference to requests for funding for bilingual education rather than for English-only programs (Castro Feinberg, 2002).

According to the *Directory of Two-Way Bilingual Immersion Programs in the US* (http://www.cal.org/twi/directory), there are currently about 266 dual language programs in twenty-three states (including the District of Columbia), a significant increase from the fewer than forty programs listed in 1990. The majority of the programs are implemented in grades preK–6. Approximately one-fifth of the dual language programs are found in middle schools and high schools. Of the programs listed, 244 are Spanish-English, 6 are French-English, 5 are Chinese-English, 4 are Korean-English, and 2 are Navajo-English (Center for Applied Linguistics, 2002). Because of the tremendous increase in dual language programs in recent years and the countless variations of model implementation, the *Directory of Two-Way Bilingual Immersion Programs in the US* has limited the inclusion of programs to those that meet three fundamental criteria: student integration, bilingual instruction for all participants, and balanced student representation of the two languages. In addition, dual language programs are undoubtedly underrepresented in this directory, given that it is a voluntary listing and that many schools with dual language programs may not be aware of its existence and/or have not yet entered their programs.

Points of Clarification

Dual language education does not necessarily have to include a majority and a minority language. Dual language programs may be implemented in two majority languages or two minority languages. Dual language programs that use two majority languages, such as Dutch-German in some parts of Europe or Malay-Tamil in Singapore, are commonly found in societies in which much of the population is already bilingual or multilingual (Baker, 2001; Skutnabb-Kangas, 2000). Other programs may use two minority languages, such as Yaqui-Spanish in the southwestern United States or other secondary languages in highly multilingual regions like China and India. In this book, the discussion of dual language education is founded on North American models with a principal focus on U.S programs, which mainly consist of a minority and a majority language.

Spanish and English are not the only language combinations in dual language programs. Nevertheless, Spanish is undoubtedly the language most commonly used in the United States after English, both by native speakers and by others who have acquired it as a second language (Cummins, 2000). Spanish speakers make up 76 percent of all English language learners in the US, followed by Vietnamese (2.3 percent), Hmong (2.2 percent), Haitian Creole (1.1 percent), Korean (1.1 percent), and Cantonese (1.0 percent). All other language groups represent less than 1 percent of the English language learner population (for regularly updated information on the linguistic composition of English language learners in the United States, see the National Clearinghouse for Language Acquisition site at http://www.ncela.gwu.edu/askncela/05toplangs.htm). The majority of bilingual and dual language programs in the United States are offered in Spanish and English (Center for Applied Linguistics, 2002). Although attention may, on occasion, be focused on Spanish-English dual language programs, the discussions here are for the most part applicable to programs that use other languages. Schools that use languages other than Spanish do, however, experience certain constraints that are not as apparent for Spanish language programs, such as a scarcity of certified bilingual teachers and shortages of instructional materials in the minority language.

Dual Language Education Goals

At the core of dual language education are linguistic, academic, and sociocultural dimensions (Christian, 1994; Lindholm, 1990). Regardless of program design, dual language education emphasizes four student goals that constitute the guiding principles for program and curriculum implementation (see Figure 1.2): first language development, second language development, academic attainment, and multicultural competencies. Through interactive and integrated curricula, dual language students develop social and academic linguistic competencies in two languages in the four language domains: listening, speaking, reading, and writing. Because effective dual language programs are also closely aligned to national and state learning standards, all students are expected to achieve academically at or above grade level in all content areas in both languages. Finally, a critical objective of dual language education is for the student to develop positive cross-cultural perspectives, intersocial aptitudes, and a healthy self-concept (Cazabon, Nicoladis, & Lambert, 1998; Christian, 1994; Lessow-Hurley, 2000; Lindholm-Leary, 2001). Thus, the aim of an effective dual language education program extends beyond producing bilingual and biliterate students. Advanced intersocial and cross-cultural competencies constitute vital objectives of dual language programs. Occasionally, schools that implement dual language education overlook these two critical goals. In an attempt to fit an ever-expanding curriculum into what seems a shrinking school day, bicultural awareness and multicultural knowledge are sometimes left out of students' learning experiences.

Effectiveness of Dual Language Education

The effectiveness of dual language education has been well documented outside the United States, especially in Canada (Lambert & Tucker, 1972; Swain & Lapkin,

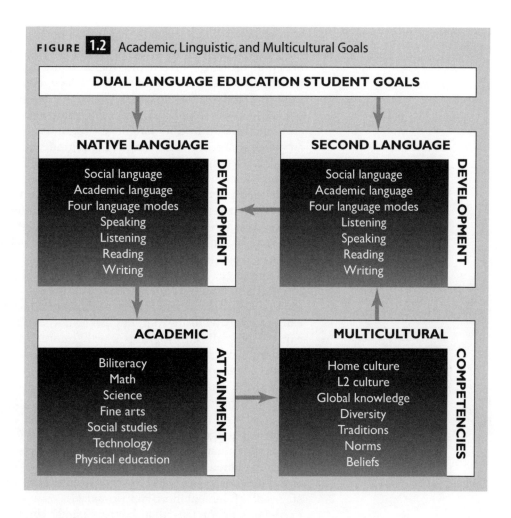

FIGURE 1.2 Academic, Linguistic, and Multicultural Goals

DUAL LANGUAGE EDUCATION STUDENT GOALS

NATIVE LANGUAGE DEVELOPMENT
Social language
Academic language
Four language modes
Speaking
Listening
Reading
Writing

SECOND LANGUAGE DEVELOPMENT
Social language
Academic language
Four language modes
Listening
Speaking
Reading
Writing

ACADEMIC ATTAINMENT
Biliteracy
Math
Science
Fine arts
Social studies
Technology
Physical education

MULTICULTURAL COMPETENCIES
Home culture
L2 culture
Global knowledge
Diversity
Traditions
Norms
Beliefs

1982; 1991). In the United States, there has been a recent increase in empirical research conducted on the effectiveness of dual language education (Cazabon, Lambert & Hall, 1993; Cazabon, Nicoladis & Lambert, 1998; Lindholm, 1991; Lindholm-Leary, 2001; Thomas & Collier, 1997, 2002). The following section presents the most current and compelling empirical research on the effectiveness of dual language education on academic and language achievement for language minority and majority students.

In their most recent study on program models for linguistically and culturally diverse students in the United States, Thomas and Collier (2002) analyzed English language learners' academic achievement in grades K–12 from 1996 to 2001, using national standardized tests in English to measure academic achievement in five urban and rural districts. They focused on academic outcomes in eight program models in which minority language students participate: 90–10 total immersion dual language; 50–50 partial immersion dual language; 90–10 developmental bilingual education; 50–50 developmental bilingual education; 90–10 transitional bilingual education; 50–50 transitional bilingual education; content-based ESL; and submersion. They analyzed 210,054 student records representing eighty primary languages, although in three of the five districts the focus was on the largest linguistic group—Spanish speakers.

Thomas and Collier found that English language learners who participated in dual language education outperformed comparable monolingually schooled students in academic achievement after four to seven years in the program. Students who received dual language instruction for at least five years reached the 50th percentile on the reading standardized tests by fifth or sixth grade and maintained this level of performance in subsequent grades. The authors propose that, in order for students to achieve grade level competencies, they must receive at least four years of schooling in the native language and at least four years of schooling in the second language. The study also examined native English speakers' achievement in dual language programs. The results indicate that majority language students in dual language programs maintained their English, acquired a second language, and achieved well above the 50th percentile in all subject areas on norm-referenced tests in English (Thomas & Collier, 2002).

In their previous cross-sectional and longitudinal study conducted from 1982 to 1996, Thomas and Collier (1997) examined more than 700,000 student records in five large U.S. school systems to analyze the effect of school programs and instructional variables on the long-term academic achievement of English language learners. They evaluated six program models for language minority children: dual language; late-exit with content-based ESL; early-exit with content-based ESL; early-exit with traditional ESL; pull-out content-based ESL; and pull-out traditional ESL. They found that by sixth grade, students in dual language and late-exit programs were ahead in English achievement compared to students in early-exit or ESL pull-out programs. Furthermore, achievement in English language standardized tests for students in dual language and late-exit programs was close to those of native English speakers (around the 50th percentile). Students in early-exit and ESL pull-out programs scored around the 30th percentile on the same tests. By 11th grade, students in dual language programs scored above the average level for native English speakers on standardized tests in English compared to English language learners in the other programs (see Figure 1.3).

In another significant longitudinal and cross-sectional study, Lindholm-Leary (2001) examined the academic achievement of 4,900 students over a period of four to eight years in twenty U.S. schools with dual language programs at different stages of implementation. Her primary focus was on total immersion (90–10) and partial immersion (50–50) in English-Spanish dual language programs. Lindholm-Leary analyzed language and academic achievement in several areas and through

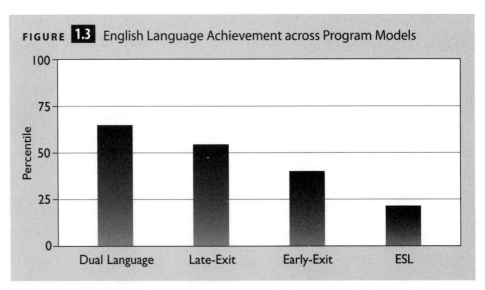

FIGURE 1.3 English Language Achievement across Program Models

ELL student achievement in English language standardized tests in grade 11 according to program model (Thomas & Collier, 1997).

varied evaluative instruments: students' oral language proficiency and bilingual attainment through teacher ratings and language proficiency tests; students' reading and language achievement based on traditional standardized reading tests and teacher-developed rubrics; and students' levels of achievement in content areas as indicated by standardized tests.

Regarding oral language and bilingual attainment, Lindholm-Leary found that native English speakers developed high levels of proficiency in their first language regardless of whether they participated in total (90–10) or partial (50–50) dual language immersion programs. In addition, dual language students from both language groups developed high levels of second language proficiency in both total and partial immersion models, though their proficiency was higher in total immersion programs. Thus, the results show that both dual language models (90–10 and 50–50) promote proficiency in two languages, although students developed higher levels of bilingualism in total immersion programs. Native English speakers did not vary in their first language proficiency according to their participation in total or partial immersion programs. English speaking students who received as little as 10 percent or 20 percent of their instruction in English scored as well as English-dominant students who received their instruction in English 50 percent of the time. These findings were true for African Americans, Latinos, and students of European descent, and did not vary according to their socioeconomic status. Spanish speakers evidenced greater benefit from total immersion than from partial immersion, a differential larger than the difference for English speakers, supporting the notion of native language development for language minority students (August & Hakuta, 1998; Cummins, 1989). English speakers in total immersion scored higher in Spanish proficiency than those in partial immersion programs. For Spanish speaking students, the program model was not a factor in English development. Hence, Spanish-speaking students who received considerably less English instruction in total immersion than Spanish speakers who received 50 percent of instruction in English in partial immersion scored about the same in English tests. Thus, receiving less English instruction in 90–10 programs did not negatively affect Spanish speakers.

In literacy and academic attainment, Lindholm-Leary (2001) found that English and Spanish speaking students made significant improvements in reading and academic achievement in both the native and second language across grade levels, and scored on a par with their peers using standardized norms for English and Spanish speakers, although results varied somewhat according to program type, grade level, and language background. The results showed that higher levels of bilingual proficiency are associated with higher levels of reading achievement, corresponding with other research findings that point to higher levels of bilingual proficiency leading to increased academic and cognitive functioning (Hakuta, 1986; Peal & Lambert, 1962). Spanish and English dominant students in dual language programs outperformed their peers across California in English reading and academic achievement tests. With regard to content, Lindholm-Leary's study (2001) shows that students in dual language education programs function at grade level or above in two languages in the content areas and score on par with their peers across California.

These and other research studies on bilingual immersion education provide a critical platform for the development and understanding of dual language programs in the United States. Research-based educational programs, such as dual language education, provide directions with respect to what educators and parents can expect from different program models. More importantly, research findings such as those presented above, which point to the effectiveness of well-implemented dual language programs, offer the necessary empirical evidence to contest misguided and misinformed perspectives and practices.

SUMMARY

Dual language education, an additive form of bilingual education that provides enriched education both for language minority and majority students, has gained recognition in the last ten years as a desirable alternative to subtractive programs for language minority children. Empirical research studies, like the ones conducted by Thomas and Collier (1997, 2002) and Lindholm-Leary (2001), have provided strong evidence of its effectiveness both for English language learners and native English speakers.

Program models for second language learners differ greatly in their implementation, ideological stance, first and second language goals, and degrees of cultural affirmation or assimilation. In an effort to dispel misconceptions about dual language education and how it relates to other second language education models, the distinctions outlined here provide a base for comparison and understanding of the fundamental dimension of each program model. Knowledge about different second language education designs is necessary for dual language educators who are involved in programmatic decision making and for the dissemination of accurate and current information. Because dual language education extends beyond language learning, those who are directly involved in this form of bilingual education become advocates not only for linguistic and cultural pluralism for all, but also for the language rights of cultural and linguistic diverse groups. Cummins (2001) contends that "the most powerful ways of incorporating students' language and culture into the curriculum are through dual language (two-way) or developmental (late-exit) bilingual programs that aim to promote bilingualism and biliteracy" (p. 214).

DISCUSSION QUESTIONS

1. Why do you think dual language education does not have a precise, clear-cut definition? What are some issues or elements in dual language education that may vary in implementation?

2. What are the fundamental principles that underlie dual language education? Create a list of critical concepts that encompass the philosophical, ideological, theoretical, and sociopolitical positions and frameworks of dual language education.

3. How would you explain and describe dual language education to someone who has no background in bilingual education or in education in general? Include the program goals, basic organization characteristics, language compositions, and so on.

4. What are the fundamental differences between the Canadian form of immersion and structured English immersion in the United States? In your opinion, which model is more effective for English language learners, and why?

FIELD-BASED INQUIRY

1. Ask several dual language teachers and administrators to define dual language in their own words. Ask them to consider the fundamental elements, philosophical and ideological foundations, sociopolitical dimensions, and pedagogical and organizational structures. Compare the different definitions given to you by the dual language educators you interviewed. What are the underlying elements that are common across the educators' definitions? What are some differences in their perceptions of dual language education?

2. Visit a structured English immersion classroom and a bilingual maintenance classroom. Observe and document the social and pedagogical interaction between teachers and students, the patterns of language choice and use between teachers and students and among the students themselves, and the cultural compatibilities between the curriculum

and students' background knowledge. Analyze the differences and similarities between the two classrooms. Examine students' observed behaviors in relation to the inclusion or exclusion of their native language and culture.

FURTHER READING

Castro Feinberg, R. (2002). *Bilingual education. A reference handbook*. Santa Barbara, CA: ABC CLIO.

Crawford, J. (1999). *Bilingual education: History, politics, theory and practice.* Los Angeles, CA: Bilingual Education Services.

Cummins, J. (2000). *Language, power and pedagogy. Bilingual children in the crossfire*. Clevedon, England: Multilingual Matters.

Day, E. M., & Shapson, S. M. (1996). *Studies in immersion education.* Clevedon, England: Multilingual Matters.

Johnson, R. K., & Swain, M. (1997). *Immersion education: International perspectives.* New York: Cambridge University Press.

Torres-Guzmán, M. E. (2002). *Dual language programs: Key features and results*. Directions in Language and Education, 14. National Clearinghouse for Bilingual Education.

Dual Language Program Models and Features

It is high time we begin to treat language skills as the asset they are, particularly in this global economy. Anything that encourages a person to know more than one language is positive—and should be treated as such. Our nation can only grow stronger if all our children grow up learning two languages.

Richard W. Riley (2000), Former U.S. Secretary of Education

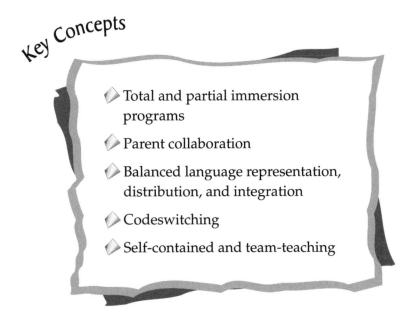

Key Concepts

- Total and partial immersion programs
- Parent collaboration
- Balanced language representation, distribution, and integration
- Codeswitching
- Self-contained and team-teaching

The potential for dual language programs to promote bilingualism, biliteracy, and biculturalism for all students greatly depends on the educational foundations on which they are built and the commitment on which they are sustained. Mora, Wink, and Wink (2001) propose that the first step in the implementation of an effective dual language program is the "selection of a contextually-appropriate model and a clear articulation of how its principles are applied to meet the needs of language minority and language majority students" (p. 427). They further argue that dual language educators must continually reflect on the types of program organizations and functions that are at odds with the program's intended goals. For educators to identify and address conflicting or incompatible practices in program implementation, they must first have a clear understanding of the theoretical, pedagogical, and programmatic tenets of effective dual language education. The first section of this chapter examines the two most widely implemented dual language program designs—total and partial immersion—and presents a discussion of the factors that schools should consider in the selection of a model. The remainder of the chapter is devoted to program features and characteristics that include parental involvement, programmatic considerations, instructional practices, and language distribution issues.

DUAL LANGUAGE PROGRAM MODELS

The actual implementation of dual language education varies greatly from school to school. Student demographics, parental expectations and support, teacher beliefs and qualifications, and administrative leadership all contribute to shape the design and direction of a dual language program. In whatever form the program is put into practice, one of two models is usually implemented in schools: **total immersion** or **partial immersion.** The primary distinction between these two models is the amount of time allocated to each language for instruction at each grade level (see Figure 2.1). In the total immersion model, the amount of instruction in the minority language is initially greater than in the majority language, usually 80 percent to 90 percent of the time in the primary grades, with English instruction increasing by each grade level until students receive equal amounts of majority and minority language instruction by the intermediate grades. In the partial immersion model, on the other hand, the minority and majority languages are used equally for instruction in all grade levels. In addition, total immersion programs require that most teachers be proficient in two languages because the majority of the instruction is conducted in the non-English language, whereas in the partial immersion model, monolingual English teachers can team-teach with bilingual teaching partners. Other programmatic similarities (such as heterogeneous grouping of students and language of content instruction) and differences (such as literacy of instruction and ratio of time allocated to each language) are presented in Table 2.1. According to Howard and Sugarman (2001), 42 percent of dual language schools listed in the *Directory of Two-Way Bilingual Immersion Programs in the US* implement total immersion models, while 33 percent of the schools implement a partial immersion model. The other schools listed in the directory implement different variations of these two program types. The following section provides further discussion of each model and presents issues to be considered when selecting a program model.

Total Immersion

Total immersion, also known as the minority-language dominant model (Howard & Sugarman, 2001) consists of two program types: 90–10 and 80–20 dual language models. In each, the initial amount of minority language and majority language exposure corresponds to the amount of time dedicated for instruction in each language. That is, instruction is conducted in the minority language (e.g., Spanish, Japanese, Polish) 90 percent or 80 percent of the time and in the majority language (English) 10 percent or 20 percent of the time, usually from preK to first or second grade. In second or third grade, instruction in English is increased to 20 percent or

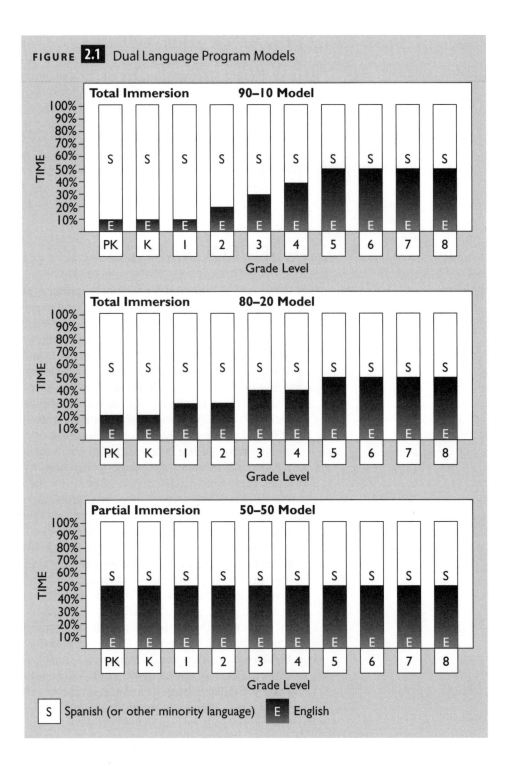

FIGURE **2.1** Dual Language Program Models

30 percent while instruction in the minority language is decreased to 80 percent or 70 percent. By the time students reach fourth or fifth grade, there is a balance of instructional time in each language. Thus, total immersion immerses both language minority and language majority students in the minority language in the initial years of the program. From the onset of students' participation, however, all students receive English instruction for a portion of the day. For English-dominant children, this English instruction is offered for literacy and/or language development, and for minority language children, English instruction is usually offered in the form of ESL (Cloud, Genesee & Hamayan, 2000).

■ **TABLE 2.1** | **Dual Language Education Models and Components**

		Total Immersion 90–10 or 80–20	Partial Immersion 50–50
Language		The minority language is used the majority of the time in the early grades, increasing English to reach an equal balance by grade 5 or 6.	Both languages are used in equal amounts of time at all grade levels.
Literacy		Formal literacy instruction may be in the minority language for all students, or in the students' native language.	Formal literacy instruction is typically in the students' native language.
Content		Instruction of content areas is in the minority language the majority of the time in the early grades, increasing instruction in English to reach an equal balance by grade 5 or 6.	Instruction of content areas is in both languages at all grade levels.
Grouping		Students from both language groups are integrated for all or most of the day.	Students from both language groups are integrated for all or most of the day.
		Students may be separated by language for literacy or second language instruction for short periods during the day or week.	Students may be separated by language for literacy or second language instruction for short periods during the day or week.
Setup		Classrooms may be set up in self-contained or team-teaching arrangements. Most teachers are bilingual proficient.	Classrooms may be set up in self-contained or team-teaching arrangements. At least half the teachers are bilingual proficient.

In total immersion programs, all academic content areas (math, science, social studies, art) are initially taught in the minority language. In second or third grade, there is a gradual shift to English instruction for some of the content areas, for example, math may begin to be taught in English, while science and social studies continue to be conducted in the minority language. In the next year, both math and social studies may be taught in English, and science continues to be taught in the minority language. By fifth or sixth grade, all content areas are either taught in both languages, alternating by day, week, or month, or each content area is assigned a language of instruction (for example, math in English and science in the minority language). Initial literacy instruction is usually conducted in the minority language for all students in the 90–10 model. That is, majority and minority language students all learn to read and write in the minority language. By third grade, students receive more formalized literacy instruction in English, even though students are exposed to English literacy and print from the beginning of the program (Lindholm-Leary, 2001). Sometimes, in 80–20 models, literacy instruction is conducted in the students' native language. That is, minority language students learn to read and write in their native language, and English-dominant students learn to read and write in English. Issues in determining the language of instruction for initial literacy development in total immersion programs will be further discussed later in this chapter.

Partial Immersion

Partial immersion, also known as 50–50 or balanced program model, provides instruction in both languages in equal amounts of time from preK on. In other words, instruction is conducted in the minority language 50 percent of the time and in English the other 50 percent of the time. In most 50–50 programs, literacy instruction is initially offered in the students' native language. Researchers in the field of dual language education recommend that in 50–50 models, literacy instruction be conducted in the native language for English-dominant students (Lindholm-Leary, 2001). Conducting literacy instruction in the second language for language majority students in a 50–50 program becomes overwhelmingly arduous for two primary reasons. First, majority language students have not had sufficient exposure to the minority language and thus have not developed a strong enough language base in kindergarten to begin second language literacy instruction in first grade. Second, majority language students usually do not have minority language exposure at home to support literacy development in the second language.

In partial immersion programs, content instruction is commonly taught in both languages by alternating between each language by time or teacher. Often, in partial immersion models that have a team-teaching organization, students alternate days between the English and the minority language teacher to receive content instruction in both languages. In self-contained classrooms, the bilingual teacher alternates instruction in each language by day. The essential elements of team-teaching and self-contained classroom organizations will be further elaborated later in this chapter.

Total or Partial Immersion?

Whether to implement a partial or total immersion model becomes a critical decision that must be carefully weighed by a school prior to launching a dual language program. Although research findings on dual language education have generally pointed to total immersion as more effective than partial immersion in developing higher levels of minority language proficiencies (Lindholm-Leary, 2001; Thomas & Collier, 1997, 2002), this does not mean that all schools can or should implement total immersion models. Lindholm-Leary (2001) argues that selecting a dual language model involves knowledge about the linguistic and educational background of the community, understanding the expectations of students' language proficiencies, and the availability of qualified teachers and appropriate instructional resources. Choice of program design is often dependent on school and community circumstances and attitudes.

One critical factor that seems to influence the decision to implement a partial or a total immersion program is the second language skills of the existing teaching staff, as well as the likelihood of hiring new bilingual teachers in the school. The total immersion model requires most, if not all, teachers in the program to be bilingual, leading to implications for the existing teaching staff and prospective new hires. Another significant factor in design selection is student mobility. High levels of student transfers, where students come into and leave the school and leave, or practice circular mobility (regularly transfer in and out of the same school) negatively affect students' abilities to sustain and develop their second language skills. This is particularly problematic for English-dominant students in total immersion programs because most content instruction, and often literacy instruction, is conducted in the minority language. School demographics (the linguistic makeup of both teachers and students), the philosophical and political positions regarding bilingualism and biculturalism, and teacher and parent expectations for students' linguistic proficiencies all bear in the decision to implement a total or a partial immersion model (see Box 2.1).

 # PROGRAM FUNDAMENTALS

Based on extensive research in the field, leading dual language researchers and educators have identified a number of key components that comprise highly successful dual language programs in the United States and abroad (Christian, Montone, Lindholm & Carranza, 1997; Day & Shapson, 1996; Lindholm-Leary, 2001; Thomas & Collier, 1997). Figure 2.2 presents a compilation of program features that have been identified by researchers and educators as the most salient aspects of effective dual language programs: length of participation, parent collaboration, balanced language representation, student integration, language

---

BOX 2.1

How One School Decided on Total Immersion

After much discussion and deliberation, members of this suburban community's preK–6 school made the decision to implement a Spanish–English dual language program in their school. Parents, teachers, support staff, and administrators considered the academic, linguistic, and cultural needs of the students, the balanced linguistic background of the community, and the qualifications of the teaching and support staff. They decided to implement the program gradually, starting in preK and K, and made the decision to offer the program to all students rather than a strand within the school. The next step was to determine whether to implement an 80–20 total immersion or a 50–50 partial immersion model.

Parents and the majority of teachers expressed concern about implementing an 80–20 model because they felt that students would fall behind academically and not develop strong literacy skills in English. Some teachers also had reservations about the effect of student mobility on program effectiveness. Although teachers and parents had already visited two nearby schools that were implementing the 50–50 program model, they had not observed any schools that implemented an 80–20 design. A few teachers who had recently attended a regional dual language conference and had gathered information

on both models felt that the school had the right "ingredients" to implement an 80–20 model. The school had a near-balanced student representation of the two languages; more than two-thirds of the teachers were bilingual proficient; and most had bilingual endorsements. In addition, the school had already been implementing a bilingual and a FLES (foreign language in the elementary school) program in Spanish. Because of these two programs, the school had accumulated many bilingual and Spanish materials. In addition, parents were highly supportive of Spanish language development for their children.

The teachers who supported the total immersion model began to collect and share information about the pros and cons of each model, invited a dual language specialist to talk to parents and staff, and arranged for a day-long field trip to visit a school implementing an 80–20 model in an adjacent state. All this proved to be successful in convincing parents, teachers, and the principal that the school could effectively implement a total immersion program model. The teachers created a letter of commitment for parents to sign to address the problem of student mobility. The teachers and the principals also made a year-long plan for teacher professional development and parent workshops to assist parents and teachers in better understanding second language acquisition and dual language education.

FIGURE **2.2** Fundamentals of Successful Dual Language Programs

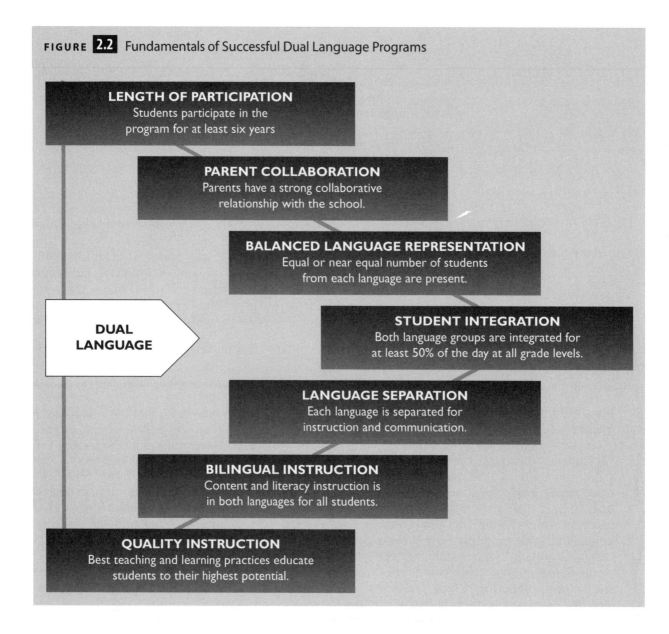

considerations, and bilingual quality instruction. The next section examines these essential characteristic of effective dual language programs in greater detail.

Length of Program Participation

For dual language students to function academically and attain oral and literate proficiency in two languages, they should participate for a minimum of between six and eight years. Researchers concur that most second language learners take five to seven years to reach academic competencies in English on a par with their native English-speaking peers (Cummins, 1981; Hakuta, Butler, & Witt, 2000; Thomas & Collier, 1997; Wong, Fillmore, & Snow, 2000). Even though conversational second language skills are achieved more rapidly, usually from six months to two years, the academic second language needed to function successfully in schools involves more time. Cummins (2000) maintains that the differences in length of time required to learn conversational language (also known as **basic interpersonal communicative skills** or **BICS**) and academic language (also known as **cognitive academic language proficiency** or **CALP**) can be explained by considering the language demands of each dimension and their situational contexts. Conversational second language is greatly facilitated by contextual cues (gestures, intonation, situational context), is often motivated by social and personal interests (playing, socializing, interacting with others), has relatively few cognitive demands, and is not generally used for academic tasks. On the other hand, academic language requires high levels of cognitive involvement, is more abstract, has fewer contextual cues, and is usually outside the familiar realm of students' worlds, sometimes even beyond their interests. Academic language is much more cognitively demanding than conversational language because it requires students to use linguistic and cognitive functions associated with such higher order thinking tasks as analyzing, evaluating, hypothesizing, and predicting (Cummins, 1984, 2000). The distinction that Cummins makes between academic and conversational language is critical for parents and educators to understand, because the acquisition of children's second language conversational skills may lead to false interpretations about students' academic second language competencies.

Some schools that implement dual language programs do not take into account the time that is required to attain high levels of academic proficiency, oral and literate, in a second language. Schools that implement dual language as an enrichment program for primary grades only, usually from kindergarten to third grade, halt students' development of the second language when they are just beginning to engage in increasingly sophisticated literacy and language curricular experiences in the second language. Designing a dual language program that takes students into the upper elementary grades greatly enhances their opportunities to develop high academic and literacy proficiencies in the second language, and better prepares them to continue into advanced language classes in high school and beyond. Thus, researchers and educators stress the importance of providing dual language education programs for at least six to eight years.

Parent Collaboration

For dual language programs to work at their highest potential, parent involvement must be viewed by both families and schools as one of the most fundamental components of implementation. Beyond having a good conception of the program's basic goals, organizational structures, and pedagogical practices, parents must have a clear understanding about their own critical roles in supporting their children's linguistic, academic, and sociocultural developments. However, educators must be cautious about traditional definitions of parent involvement and the assumptions that are implicit for students and families from linguistically and culturally diverse backgrounds (Nieto, 2000). Mainstream views of parent involvement commonly include such practices as attending school functions, volunteering, supporting children's linguistic and academic development by assisting with homework and by reading and providing other enriching opportunities for learning. Parents from diverse backgrounds are sometimes either not familiar or not comfortable with these conventional forms of parental involvement. Thus, schools must take into account the varied ways in which parents can contribute to their children's education.

Research findings have pointed to the vital role parents exert on children's language acquisition and the positive attitudes and manners in which parents integrate language reinforcement in everyday activities (Delgado-Gaitán, 1991). However, these same studies portray significant differences between parents' interaction with their children and teachers' interaction with their students. Tharp and Gallimore (1988) suggest that there are social and cultural differences that create a mismatch between the learning environments of the home and the school.

This results in a mismatch between the school's traditional expectations of parents and parents' interpretations or perceptions of what "parent involvement" really means (Valdés, 1996). The school–home mismatch (Cummins, 2000) is significantly reduced when the school and the community collaborate to accommodate *all* the existing language, literacy, and cultural practices found in the community. That is, schools should consult parents to find out about the different linguistic and literacy practices that are used in the community so that these can be used in the classroom to support learners' academic and linguistic development. Parents, students, and teachers must collaborate to formulate appropriate instructional strategies, discover and use relevant instructional materials, and develop sound practices for support at home and school. This collaborative notion views the *community* as a vast resource of knowledge (Moll, Tapia, & Whitmore, 1993).

In addition to drawing from students' cultural and linguistic capital and accommodating nonconventional forms of parental involvement, educators and parents must also establish commitment agreements in regard to students' language, academic, and cultural development. Parents and families should understand that the acquisition of a second language is a long-term process that requires children stay in the program for an extended period of time. Thus, parents in dual language programs must commit to maintaining stable student enrollments to ensure the best possible academic, cultural, and language outcomes for their children.

Schools are also responsible for providing information and resources that can facilitate parents' support of their children's educational progress in dual language programs. Often, parents who are monolingual or dominant in one language become concerned that they are incapable of helping their children in the second language. Educators must stress to parents the importance of continuing support for their children in the language of the home, and provide assistance for supporting the second language through such activities as second language parent classes, after-school homework sessions, reading clubs in the second language, and computer language programs.

A Balanced Language Population

The most effective dual language programs have a balance of language minority and language majority students (Christian, 1994; Lindholm, 1990). The Center for Applied Linguistics (2002) recommends a language balance that approximates near-equal proportions, with each language group making up between one-third and two-thirds of the total student population. Because one of the essential premises of dual language education is the social, academic, and cultural interaction between students from the two languages, an imbalanced representation of the two linguistic groups seriously weakens the program's effectiveness.

A substantial imbalance in linguistic representation creates serious problems for dual language programs. The high levels of second language proficiencies attained by both language groups, particularly by English-dominant learners in the minority language, are largely attributed to the interaction between students from the two languages. Students themselves become authentic and concrete language and cultural models for their peers (Lindholm-Leary, 2001). Because students have a real and immediate purpose for communicating in the second language, both socially and academically, the language acquisition process is more comprehensible, motivating, and interesting and less arduous than traditional foreign or second language learning contexts. But when one language group dominates the classroom learning space, this opportunity is diminished, since students no longer have the pressing need to communicate in the other language. More alarming is that the less represented language is suppressed, and its speakers may become disengaged and alienated (Baker, 2001).

Establishing and maintaining proportionate numbers of students from the two languages is for many schools the most problematic issue relating to dual language programs (Amrein & Peña, 2000). Neighborhood schools that receive their student enrollment from their immediate communities are bound to their specific linguistic and cultural demographics. Student attrition also affects this language balance. Program desertion is particularly evident and problematic in dual language programs that are implemented as a strand within a school with only one classroom per grade level. In some one-strand dual language schools, an initial class that may start with twenty-five children in kindergarten may end up with only ten or fifteen students by the time they get to fourth or fifth grade. For dual language education, accepting new students, particularly English-dominant students, into the program after second or third grade is not recommended (Cloud, Genesee & Hamayan, 2000). Because the curriculum becomes more demanding and less contextualized in third grade and beyond, monolingual English speaking students who enter the program at these levels tend to have more difficulty with comprehending academic concepts in the second language.

LANGUAGE CONSIDERATIONS

Language Distribution

As discussed previously, one of the three key elements in dual language education is the integration of *all* students for instruction (Christian, Montone, Lindholm & Carranza, 1997). Depending on the dual language model, majority and minority language students are together either the entire day or at least half of the school day at all grade levels. That is, students from both languages are together in mixed-language groups for subject matter instruction and other academic and social activities. In 90–10 and 80–20 models, this means that students from both language groups are integrated for all or most of the day or week for content and sometimes literacy instruction in the minority language. In 50–50 models, students may also be integrated for almost all of the day or week; they are normally grouped homogenously by language for literacy instruction in the native language for at least one hour a day. During this time, students from each language group are not integrated.

Because social interaction between students from both linguistic groups provides an optimal forum for social and academic language development, as well as opportunities for cultural transactions (Cummins, 2000; Baker, 2001), students should also be integrated during transition times, play, or rest periods. Thus, the recommendation is for students from both language groups to be integrated in the class roster, especially in team-teaching arrangements. Integrating the class rosters so that students from both language groups are officially listed in the teacher's record book ensures that students are not segregated by language according to the assigned language of the teacher. Although the purpose of integrating the students from both language groups is to provide optimum opportunities for them to interact during transition times as well as instructional time, this is not always the case. In some dual language programs that use team-teaching with a bilingual teacher and a monolingual majority language teacher, students are sometimes segregated by language and placed on the class roster of the primary language teacher. For example, the Korean-dominant students are on the class roster of the Korean bilingual teacher, and the English-dominant students are on the class roster of the English monolingual teacher. Although students are then integrated for content, language, and literacy instruction throughout the week, they still miss out on valuable time to hear and use the second language in social contexts and for meaningful purposes. Consequently, students should be integrated in the class roster to optimize every minute of the school day for potential linguistic, social, and cultural development.

Arrival and dismissal times, particularly in the early grades and during cold winters, sometimes can take up to fifteen minutes of class time. Rich linguistic, social, and cultural transactions happen while students, with the teachers' guidance, take off or put on heavy winter gear, collect or distribute homework, make welcoming or departing announcements, gather lunch money, and take attendance. If students are integrated in the class roster they can also take advantage of these linguistic and cultural exchanges during other curricular activities and experiences, such as field trips, assemblies, and science fairs.

Accounting for the actual percentage of time that students spend in each language is another important aspect of language distribution that needs special attention. Both in total immersion and partial immersion programs, educators should verify that students are actually exposed to the amount of the two languages prescribed by each model. For example, in a 50–50 program, all students are estimated to spend 50 percent of the time in the minority language and 50 percent of the time in the majority language either daily or weekly. How is this ensured? A language distribution count provides a basic system to check the minutes that students from both language groups spend in each language, including instructional, transitional, and play or rest times. Classroom teachers monitor whether the time spent in each language corresponds to established times according to the dual language model (total or partial immersion) or the grade level (language distribution varies in total immersion models according to grade). Coordinators can help teachers determine the weekly time distribution based on teachers' weekly schedules, which are normally the baseline schedule for the entire year.

Many schools provide special classes, such as computers, music, or library classes offered by resource or specialized teachers. The language in which these classes are conducted must also be included in the language time count. Table 2.2 is a simple grid for counting the minutes of the week that students spend in each language. For instance, a primary 90–10 total immersion dual language class that integrates all students 100 percent of the time, with a seven-hour school day five days a week, and with a daily 45-minute period of majority language instruction is close to the intended 90 percent minority language time exposure and 10 percent majority language time exposure during a week. On the other hand, if students spend an additional five 45-minute periods a week in music and art classes in the majority language, the amount of time spent in the minority language is reduced to 77 percent and the amount of time spent in the majority language is increased to 23 percent. Consequently, the program is no longer implementing a 90–10 model but, rather, an 80–20 model.

Counting instructional minutes may appear to be restrictive and artificial, reminiscent of back-to-basics and transmission-oriented education. However, the sole purpose of counting the amount of time spent in each language is to verify that the actual language allocation correlates to the model's stated language distribution. On occasion, frustrated parents and teachers protest when students, especially majority language learners in 50–50 programs, are not making sufficient progress in the second language. On closer inspection, and after counting the actual minutes students spend in each language, teachers and parents find that many language majority students are simply not receiving enough exposure to the second language.

■ TABLE 2.2	Language Distribution Form		
Dual Language Model 90–10 80–20 50–50 (circle one) Grade Level ____	_____ Language Dominant Students	English Language Dominant Students	
TIME IN _____ (specify language)	number of minutes per week	number of minutes per week	
TIME IN ENGLISH	number of minutes per week	number of minutes per week	

Separation of the Two Languages

Cummins (2000) cautions that the notion of rigid separation of the two languages is not as necessary or as desired as previously believed, and that allowing students to explore the two languages in more natural contexts may be more beneficial. Traditionally, however, separation of languages is the preferred option for most bilingual and dual language education programs. In dual language programs, the two languages are usually separated by time, space, person, or subject (see Table 2.3). In self-contained dual language classrooms, especially in the early grades, the languages are usually separated by time, either by using one language in the morning and the other in the afternoon, or by alternating the use of each language every other day. In team-teaching situations, the languages are usually separated by teacher and classroom, and students alternate between the two teachers every other day.

Baker (2001) delineates three major reasons for maintaining the two languages separately. First, formal time allocations with established purposes for utilizing the minority language are necessary mechanisms to bestow on the minority language a high linguistic status and to ensure its survival. Second, the one parent, one language circumstance, wherein a mother and a father each speaks a different language to a child, has been shown to be highly effective in developing child bilingualism. Because children are exposed to two distinct language systems and mediums of communication, they can simultaneously develop stronger linguistic bases. This natural separation of the two languages is replicated in effective bilingual programs. Finally, Baker contends that the development of unstable **codeswitching,** in which the two languages are used simultaneously with limited syntactical consistency, may indicate a move toward the majority language. In addition, in dual language education the tendency for students and teachers to lean toward the language that most participants speak may hamper efforts to develop the language that is less commonly used. Although the two languages are maintained separately and the teacher does not codemix, adults should accept and value students' participation and approximations in either language. Because codeswitching may be a natural progression of language acquisition, or because the students use both linguistic systems at home for communication, codeswitching should not be corrected; rather, the teacher can model the utterance in the second language of the day.

■ TABLE 2.3 | Separation of the Two Languages

Person	One teacher uses one language, and another teacher uses the other language.
	Parents, teacher assistants, or volunteers can be designated to use one or the other language.
Time	Alternate mornings and afternoons in each language.
	Alternate days in each language.
	Alternate weeks in each language.
Place	One classroom uses one language, and another classroom uses the other language.
	Specialty classes, such as library, computer, or science labs, can be designated to use either language.
	Other spaces, such as lunchroom and office, can be designated to use either language.
Subject	Certain content areas may be designated for instruction in either language (for example, math and science in one language and social studies and art in the other language).
Theme	Certain themes, such as cultural or author studies, may lend themselves to being conducted in one language (for example, a theme on Mexico in Spanish and a theme on Shakespeare in English).

Codeswitching in the Classroom

Codeswitching is a common linguistic behavior of bilinguals or developing bilinguals that is frequently misunderstood and often frowned upon by educators and parents (Huerta-Macías & Quintero, 1992). In dual language education, the concept of codeswitching becomes a critical aspect of language acquisition that has to be understood in the context of bilingual development. Codeswitching, the alternate use of two languages interchangeably or simultaneously, is a natural linguistic phenomenon that occurs among bilinguals and developing bilinguals (Valdés Fallis, 1976). This behavior is a normal cross-linguistic outgrowth of becoming or having become bilingual, which implies that the speaker has some degree of competencies in the two languages (Durán, 1994). Codeswitching includes mixing of the two languages (*this niña is very bonita*—this girl is very pretty), transferring from one language to another (*mi troca está parqueada*—my truck is parked [in standard Spanish it would be *mi camioneta esta estacionada*]), and borrowing from each language (*The embargo had long-lasting effects*).

Teachers and parents often view codeswitching as a random mixing of two languages due to interference or confusion between the two. However, research indicates that codeswitching is a rule-governed mechanism used by bilinguals to express a variety of communicative objectives, such as placing emphasis in speech, creating bonds with speakers of the two languages, or establishing cultural identity (McLaughlin, 1995). Box 2.2 illustrates how codeswitching occurs in a dual language classroom in which all students, who are at varying levels of

Codeswitching in a Dual Language Kindergarten

BOX 2.2

An African American English-dominant student requesting information and clarification from the Spanish teacher.

Student A: **Maestra, where do I put the libro?** [*Teacher, where do I put the book?*]
Teacher: Ponlo allá, en la canasta. [*Put it over there, in the basket.*]
Student A: **Canasta? What's that?** [*Basket? What's that?*]
Teacher: Si, aqui en la canasta. [*Yes, here in the basket.*]
Student A: **Oh, the basket . . . canasta . . . okay.** [*Oh, the basket . . . the basket . . . okay.*]
Student B: What did she say?
Student A: To put it in the basket . . . **canasta**. [*To put it in the basket . . . basket.*]

A Latino Spanish-dominant student interacting with the self-contained teacher on English day.

Teacher: After we finish the centers we'll go to the computer lab.
Student: **Vamos a ir a las computers again?** [*Are we going to the computers again?*]
Teacher: Yes, Mr. M. told us we could finish our projects today.
Student: **¡Que suave! Computers again! Vamos.** [*How cool! Computers again! Let's go.*]

Two Latino bilingual students conversing about the homework.

Student A: **¿Hiciste tu homework?** [*Did you do your homework?*]
Student B: **No, I forgot. ¿Y tu?** [*No, I forgot. And you?*]
Student A: **Sí, yo sí. La teacher te va a regañar, pero a mi no.** [*Yes, I did. The teacher is going to scold you, but not me.*]
Student B: **Sí te va a regañar, because you did it wrong.** [*She is going to scold you, because you did it wrong.*]
Student A: **Nooo . . . I didn't . . . yo sí lo hice bien.** [shows the homework] [*Nooo . . . I didn't . . . I did do it right.*]

competency in the majority or minority language, use them interchangeably. According to Huerta-Macías and Quintero (1992), children who are acquiring two languages simultaneously do attempt to separate them when they are in situations that require it. They also contend that children's codeswitching to Spanish diminishes as they progress through grade levels of schooling, but their switching to English remains the same across grades. This shift to the dominant language by bilingual children indicates that not only is there a need for more exposure to the minority language but also for a change to a more positive attitude toward languages of lesser status (McCollum, 1999). As bilinguals grow into adulthood and become proficient in the two languages, they once more begin to codeswitch by making use of both language codes to communicate. In dual language education, codeswitching should be viewed as a natural progression of second language acquisition, where developing bilingual children first make use of both language systems to fill linguistic or conceptual gaps in their communication. Later, as children become balanced bilinguals and achieve competencies in both languages, it represents children's increasing metalinguistic and pragmatic sophistication.

Language of Initial Literacy

The discussion surrounding the language of initial literacy instruction for students in immersion programs has become an issue of contention and debate. In dual language programs that implement partial immersion models (50–50), all students learn to read and write in their native language. That is, English-dominant students learn to read and write in English, and minority language students learn to read and write in their native language. However, in total immersion models (90–10 and 80–20), the language of initial literacy instruction is typically in the minority language for all students. For example, in a Navajo–English total immersion dual language program, Navajo- and English-dominant students all learn to read and write in Navajo first. Gradually, throughout the primary grades, English literacy instruction is introduced, and eventually all students become biliterate (able to read and write in both languages). Dual language educators and parents, however, are sometimes apprehensive about English-dominant children developing literacy in the minority language first. This is of particular concern to parents and educators in regard to majority language children who are still developing essential literacy and language skills in their primary language, English. On the other hand, studies of dual language education have revealed that majority language learners can successfully learn to read and write in the second language before they have developed literacy in their native language (Cloud, Genesee & Hamayan, 2000). Research studies conducted in Canada and the United States have also shown that teaching literacy through the second language to majority language students does not interfere with their acquisition of literacy in their first language or their development of the two languages. This holds true even for low-income African American students in French immersion programs (Lindholm-Leary, 2001; Thomas & Collier, 2002). Nonetheless, concerns over the initial language of literacy instruction for majority language students—who are still developing language skills in their native language and who may not have strong language and literacy support at home—need to be carefully considered.

One point upon which scholars and educators in the fields of language and literacy agree is that learning to read and write only happens once (Ferdman & Weber, 1994; Krashen, 1996). Developing literacy in a second language does not involve starting from ground zero. Rather, once a learner has developed an understanding of print concepts, the alphabetic principle, text structures, and how to use graphophonic, syntactic, and semantic cues to derive or create meaning from text in the primary language, the learner transfers this knowledge to the process of reading in the second language (Brisk & Harrington, 2000; Cummins, 2001). Lessow-Hurley (2000) contends that, while reading in a new language, we apply literacy skills that we already know. Even when the two languages have different writing systems, general literacy concepts such as inferencing, predicting, and familiarity with text structures are easily transferred from one language to another (Escamilla, 1993; Krashen, 1996).

Research findings in immersion education (Lindholm-Leary, 2001) and first and second language literacy development (Hakuta, 1986; Hornberger, 1990; Krashen, 1996; Swain & Lapkin, 1991) concur with the notion that strong literacy development in the native language facilitates overall academic achievement and proficiency in the second language, especially for minority language students.

Moreover, academic and linguistic skills developed in the first language transfer to the second language (Cummins, 2001). Extensive research also points to the importance for minority language students to develop literacy skills in the language they command and understand better, their native language (Goodman, Goodman & Flores, 1979; Hakuta, 1990; Krashen, 1982). Thus, the literature in the field supports initial literacy instruction for language minority students in their native language, a practice that is followed in dual language education in the United States. But for majority language students in dual language education, the issue is not as apparent. Because dual language education programs that implement total immersion models follow the recommendation that all students receive initial literacy instruction in the minority language (Cloud, Genesee & Hamayan, 2000), concerns have arisen about majority language students who lack adequate native language skills. Researchers and educators recognize that learning to read and write in a second language becomes problematic when children are still developing their native language and have insufficient literacy-related experiences at home (Krashen, 1996; Lindholm-Leary, 2001). Thus, when determining the language of initial literacy instruction, schools must carefully consider such factors as students' language and literacy experiences, background knowledge of literacy and linguistic concepts, and parental literacy support. For majority language students who come to school with a strong native language and literacy foundation and who participate in total immersion programs, initial literacy instruction is recommended in the minority language; however, for majority language students who come to school with a weak language and literacy base and thus need more time at school to develop their native language, and who are in either total or partial immersion programs, the recommendation is that they acquire initial literacy in their native language.

What about providing simultaneous initial literacy instruction in the two languages? Teaching children to read and write in two languages at the same time is not a recommended practice in dual language education in the United States. A substantial amount of time is already dedicated to language and literacy development in one language in the early grades. To add literacy instruction in another language results in diluted literacy instruction in both languages due to time constraints, overload of similar and divergent literacy concepts in each language for the students, and less time for content area learning. Cloud, Genesee and Hamayan (2000) also caution against teaching literacy in both languages simultaneously. They emphasize that children who are taught to read in two languages at the same time are at risk of not developing reading fluency and comprehension, and not internalizing the letter-sound code well enough in either language. While learning literacy in two languages simultaneously occurs successfully in other countries, the recommendation for dual language programs in the United States is to follow a sequential order of literacy instruction: first develop a strong literacy and language base in one language, then introduce literacy instruction in the other language.

Language of Homework

Home projects and study assignments sometimes become problematic for teachers, students, and parents due to insufficient second language competency. Assigning homework in just one language for all students may result in confusion and frustration, particularly on the part of parents who are monolingual in the other language and are trying to assist their children at home. This dilemma frequently arises in dual language programs and more often in total immersion models. In 90–10 or 80–20 models, majority language students learn most of the content areas in the minority language, sometimes making it difficult for them to complete homework assignments in their second language. Assignments should account for parents' and students' levels of language proficiency and students' ability to do independent homework. In Box 2.3, a seventh-grade dual language bilingual teacher describes his experiences with this sometimes thorny issue. In response to student and parent concerns, the dual language teachers in this school created a homework handbook that delineates the guidelines and expectations for home assignments.

There are several options to be considered regarding homework. First, written instructions for homework can be bilingual in the minority and majority languages. Then, choice of language for completing home assignments may be left up to each student. For example, in a third-grade class all students receive an assignment that involves interviewing a family member. The written directions for the project are given in both languages, but the actual interview and written report may be done and submitted in either language, depending on student preference. Second, homework may be designed to be carried out independently at home, with no need for parental assistance. Such assignments can take the form of routine projects, such as daily dialog journals, free voluntary reading, or direct

BOX 2.3

The Homework Dilemma

When he taught as a Spanish-English bilingual seventh-grade teacher for eight years, José seldom had any problems communicating his homework expectations or assignments to his students or their parents. This is probably because all his students and their families spoke Spanish, and most of their homework was in that language. Work that was to be done at home consisted of reading books, doing writing assignments, solving math problems, and conducting social studies and science projects in Spanish. But several years ago, when José became a dual language teacher, he experienced a remarkable increase in homework anxiety coming from students and parents in both languages.

From parents he heard: "How can I help my child do the homework when I don't speak the language?" "I don't understand what my child is supposed to do!" "You can't expect my child to do the homework in a language she doesn't know!" And from students he heard: "What am I supposed to do? And in what language?"

After meeting with the other dual language teachers in his school, José realized that they all had similar problems when it came to homework. They decided to develop a brief homework handbook with guidelines for parents and students. In the handbook they explained the importance of homework, ways parents and other family members can be involved in homework activities, and the differences between independent and assisted homework projects. For instance, the reading part of the homework (to read silently or with someone at home for twenty minutes each night) would continue to be done in the students' native language or the language of their choice. When students elected to do home reading in their second language, the teachers decided they would make sure that students selected books that were appropriate for their reading and language levels and with which they were familiar. For all other assignments, the teachers agreed to send the instructions for homework in both languages, so that parents and students understood what was expected. The teachers also agreed that they would go over homework assignments in class. For the most part, José and his colleagues want students to complete homework in the language in which they are most comfortable, usually their native language. Depending on the nature of the assignment, José may ask students to do their homework in the second language. When this happens, José makes sure that students can do it independently and that they have a clear understanding of what they are to do.

José thinks that developing a homework handbook based on teacher, student, and parent feedback was useful because it forced teachers to think about this issue carefully and to be very clear about the procedures and expectations for homework in their classrooms.

follow-ups to class activities. Instructions for independent homework assignments must be very clearly explained and teachers must make sure that all students understand the expected outcomes.

Many districts now require students to read or be read to at home for a certain number of minutes each evening as part of the homework load. Extensive research in literacy supports this notion of reading at home every day as a way to increase students' familiarity with a variety of text structures and their understandings of different functions of literacy, and to expose them to unfamiliar vocabulary (Delgado-Gaitán, 1991; Epstein, 1987; Krashen, 1993; Wells, 1986). When students are engaged in reading at home, especially in free voluntary reading—in which students select their own literary materials—they should also have a choice of language. Independent readers who have been in the program for a time and are ready to read in the second language will usually do so on their own, particularly when the reading topics and selections come from the students' themselves (Krashen, 1996).

LANGUAGE GROUPING

Classroom Organization and Grouping

Dual language education can have several types of classroom arrangements, the two most common being team-teaching and self-contained classrooms. Programs commonly are either self-contained, team-taught, or a combination of both. In the following section, the self-contained and team-teaching classroom organization are described.

SELF-CONTAINED. In this type of classroom organization, there is one teacher who is proficient in the two languages and who conducts all or most of the instruction in both languages with a mixed-language group of students. The classroom has instructional materials and print in both languages, which may be color-coded for preliterate students in the primary grades. In 50–50 models, books, posters, bulletins, and other classroom print should equally represent both languages. In 90–10 or 80–20 models, more minority language print and other instructional materials may be represented in the early grades, eventually reaching an equal amount by fifth or sixth grade.

Self-contained teachers organize students in numerous grouping combinations that include both heterogeneous and homogenous language groups. Figure 2.3 illustrates how a bilingual English–Spanish self-contained teacher can organize instruction by language. For content area instruction, students from both languages are combined in cooperative learning groups and the teacher alternates between each language by time, day, or subject matter. If students receive native language literacy instruction, while the teacher works with one language group the other language group works independently on group or individual literacy projects. The same holds for ESL or SSL (Spanish as a second language) instruction. There are generally three student grouping arrangements in self-contained settings: the mixed-language group, the native language group, and the second language group. The mixed-language group includes students from both languages who are on the teacher's classroom roster and who participate in academic learning and engage in social interaction for at least two-thirds of the day or week. The native language group consists of students grouped homogenously by language, usually for literacy learning and instruction in their native language for one to two hours a day. The second language group consists of students

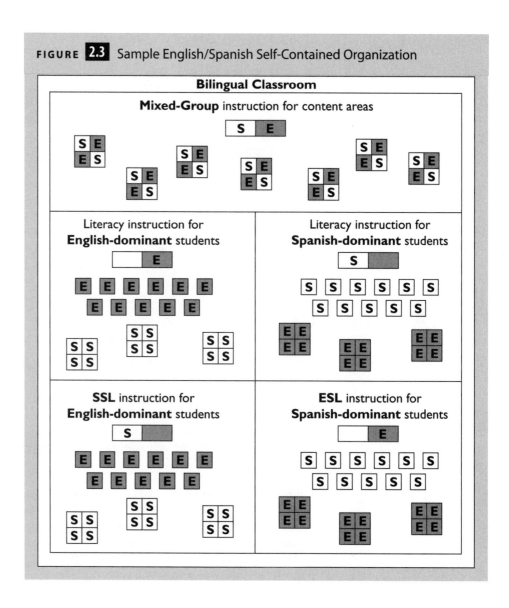

FIGURE 2.3 Sample English/Spanish Self-Contained Organization

grouped homogenously by language for second language development instruction for a few periods a week (see Figure 2.4). In self-contained classrooms with bilingual teachers, it is sometimes difficult to keep the two languages separate and to encourage students to use the language of instruction.

Scheduling in self-contained classrooms requires skillful organization and excellent time management. Table 2.4 illustrates how a first-grade teacher may organize a weekly schedule in a Spanish–English 50–50 dual language program. In this sample schedule, the teacher alternates between Spanish and English every other day. On Fridays, the two languages can either be allocated between morning and afternoon or alternated by week, so that every other Friday the minority or majority language is used. That is, if Spanish is the language of instruction on Friday this week, next Friday English will be the language of instruction, and so on. For language arts, the teacher groups the students by language and provides instruction separately to each group in its native language. For ESL and SSL, the students are again grouped by language and receive instruction in their second language. For the rest of the instructional time, the students from both language groups are integrated.

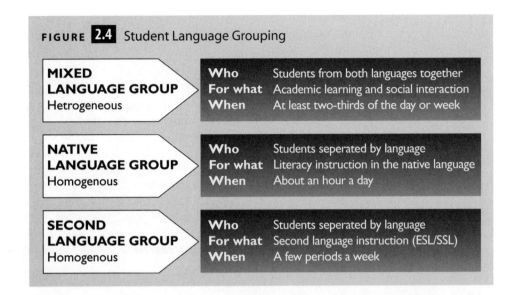

FIGURE 2.4 Student Language Grouping

MIXED LANGUAGE GROUP Hetrogeneous		
Who	Students from both languages together
For what	Academic learning and social interaction
When	At least two-thirds of the day or week

NATIVE LANGUAGE GROUP Homogenous		
Who	Students seperated by language
For what	Literacy instruction in the native language
When	About an hour a day

SECOND LANGUAGE GROUP Homogenous		
Who	Students seperated by language
For what	Second language instruction (ESL/SSL)
When	A few periods a week

TEAM-TEACHING. In contrast to self-contained classrooms, the team-teaching classroom arrangement consists of a partnership between two teachers who either instruct in two separate classrooms or together within one classroom. Either both teachers are bilingual, each assigned to one language, or one teacher is bilingual and the other is monolingual in the majority language. In a team-teaching situation, where two teachers collaborate within one classroom and with one group of students, the instructional materials in the two languages are distributed and displayed in the classroom as in self-contained settings. In a team-teaching situation with two separate classrooms with two groups of students, however, the instructional materials are allocated to each classroom according to the language of the teacher.

In team-teaching, the grouping organization is similar to self-contained classrooms, but in cases of two separate rooms, students travel between the two settings for instruction. For most schools, having two teachers within one classroom is not economically feasible; thus, most team-teaching compositions have two teachers in two separate classrooms. Figure 2.5 shows a team-teaching situation in two classrooms with a Spanish teacher and an English teacher. Students are grouped in integrated (mixed-group) clusters for instruction and social interaction for most of the day. Students are also grouped by language either for native language literacy development or second language instruction. The mixed-language groups alternate between the two teachers for content area, literacy, and language instruction. Since the two languages are naturally kept separate by room and teacher, students generally alternate languages between the two rooms by day or time.

Each teacher can have up to four different groups of students in team-teaching setups: the homeroom group (students who are in the teacher's classroom roster should be a mixed-language group), the partner-room group (students who are on the partner's classroom roster should be a mixed-language group), the native language group (students from both classrooms are grouped homogenously by language, usually for literacy learning and to receive instruction in their native language), and the second language group (students from both classrooms are grouped homogenously by language for second language development instruction).

In addition to good time management and organization, team-teaching arrangements also require collaborative teamwork and well-coordinated planning.

TABLE 2.4 | **Sample First-Grade Class Schedule: Self-Contained, 50–50 Model, Spanish–English Classroom**

Time	Monday	Tuesday	Wednesday	Thursday	Friday
8:30–9:00	**Opening Activities:** attendance, calendar, lunch count, homework, announcements **Literacy:** journal writing, shared, partner, independent reading				
	Spanish	*English*	*Spanish*	*English*	*Spanish and English*
9:00–9:45	**Spanish Language Arts:** shared reading and writing, guided reading, reading and writing workshop *Spanish-dominant students receive instruction from the teacher while English-dominant students do literacy projects in groups, pairs, or independently*				
9:45–10:30	**English Language Arts:** shared reading and writing, guided reading, reading and writing workshop *English-dominant students receive instruction from the teacher while Spanish-dominant students do literacy projects in groups, pairs, or independently*				
10:30–11:30	**Math:** integrated and thematic-based math instruction				
	Spanish	*English*	*Spanish*	*English*	*Spanish and English*
11:30–12:00	LUNCH: lunch count, directions				
	Spanish	*English*	*Spanish*	*English*	*Spanish and English*
12:00–1:00	**Science or Social Studies:** (alternate each month or depending on the focus of the theme)				
	Spanish	*English*	*Spanish*	*English*	*Spanish and English*
1:00–1:30	**ESL**	**SSL**	**ESL**	**SSL**	**Health**
	Language development related to theme or topics of study through literacy, music, drama … *While the teacher instructs one group (ESL or SSL), the other group does follow-up projects in the second language in groups, pairs, or independently*				*Spanish and English*
1:30–2:15	**Special Classes or Preps:** art, music, P.E., computers, library				*Spanish or English*
2:15–2:30	**Literacy:** Journal writing, partner or independent reading **Closing Activities:** homework, announcements, clean up				
	Spanish	*English*	*Spanish*	*English*	*Spanish and English*

Table 2.5 shows how two first-grade teachers may organize a weekly schedule in a Spanish–English 50–50 dual language program. In this sample schedule, the teachers' homeroom and partner room (heterogeneous language groups) alternate between the two classrooms for subject matter teaching and learning. For language arts, students are grouped by language and receive literacy instruction in the native language from one of the teachers. For ESL and SSL, the students are grouped again by language and receive second language instruction from one of the teachers.

QUALITY BILINGUAL INSTRUCTION

Because the aim of dual language education is not simply to learn a foreign language, but also to use the written and oral forms of the second language for

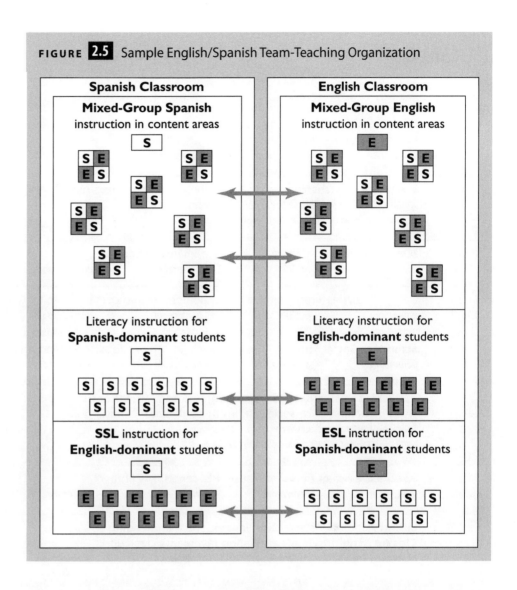

FIGURE 2.5 Sample English/Spanish Team-Teaching Organization

academic purposes, instruction in both languages for all students is essential. Effective bilingual instruction engages, challenges, and supports students' academic, bilingual, biliterate, and multicultural development (Brisk, 1998). Research on best practices for second language learners have pointed to the importance of *active engagement* through the inclusion of topics that are relevant and interesting to students, integrating students' experiences and cultural capital (students' knowledge and understandings of their sociocultural backgrounds) in the classroom, allowing students to make decisions about the curriculum, and making negotiation and co-construction of knowledge possible (Freeman & Freeman, 1997; McCollum, 1999; Moll, Tapia & Whitmore, 1993; Nieto, 2000; Trueba, 1991; Wells, 1986).

Vygotsky's (1978) **zone of proximal development** (ZPD) asserts that children's attempts to acquire knowledge are mediated by formal and informal interactions with members of the society at large. This assisted performance is what the child can do with the help of adults and the environment. These interactions are embedded in social and cultural systems in which cultural tools (such as language, music, and writing) are used. One of the teacher's functions, then, is to create learning contexts in the classroom where the social tools and processes are used to interact with others. The ideal teacher creates an environment in which students are engaged in collaborative activities that combine their interest and

■ TABLE 2.5 | **Sample First-Grade Class Schedule: Team-Teaching, 50-50 Model, Spanish Classroom and English Classroom**

Time	Monday	Tuesday	Wednesday	Thursday	Friday
8:30– 9:00	**Opening Activities:** attendance, calendar, lunch count, homework, announcements **Literacy:** journal writing, shared, partner, independent reading				
	homeroom	*partner room*	*homeroom*	*partner room*	*homeroom and partner room*
9:00– 10:30	**Language Arts:** shared reading and writing, guided reading, reading and writing workshop *Spanish-dominant students in the Spanish classroom* *English-dominant students in the English classroom*				
10:30– 11:30	**Math:** integrated and thematic-based math instruction				
	homeroom	*partner room*	*homeroom*	*partner room*	*homeroom and partner room*
11:30– 12:00	LUNCH (teachers alternate taking their homeroom and partner room to lunch each day)				
	homeroom	*partner room*	*homeroom*	*partner room*	*homeroom and partner room*
12:00– 1:00	**Science or Social Studies:** (alternate each month or alternate depending on the focus of the theme)				
	homeroom	*partner room*	*homeroom*	*partner room*	*homeroom and partner room*
1:00– 1:30	**ESL & SSL:** oral language development related to theme or topics of study in math, science, social studies through literacy, music, drama … *Spanish-dominant students in the English classroom* *English-dominant students in the Spanish classroom*			**Health** *homeroom and partner room*	
1:30– 2:15	**Special Classes or Preps:** art, music, P.E., computers, library				
	homeroom	*homeroom*	*homeroom*	*homeroom*	*homeroom*
2:15– 2:30	**Literacy:** journal writing, partner or independent reading **Closing Activities:** homework, announcements, clean up				
	homeroom	*partner room*	*homeroom*	*partner room*	*homeroom and partner room*

experiences with the four language domains: speaking, listening, reading, and writing (Pérez & Torres-Guzmán, 2002). In this constructivist view of education, the learner uses ways of thinking, cultural tools, texts, and symbols in the active process of constructing knowledge and meaning (Bruner, 1996). For dual language education, this tenet is particularly significant because students are using the second language for meaningful and authentic learning and communicative purposes. Acquiring the second language in the context of dual language education is a positive consequence of academic and social engagement.

Creating the conditions that are conducive for optimum learning incorporates a strong sense of community through group cohesiveness and responsibility. Most importantly, creating an authentic learning environment within the classroom places the teacher as a participant of that learning community. Beyond the learning environment created by the teacher is the role the teacher adopts. Traditional roles dictate that the teacher initiate interactions and evaluate students the majority of the time, while students passively respond. Harman and Edelsky (1989) suggest more effective approaches in which the teacher and student roles are flexible and open, so that both students and teachers are learning as well as teaching. Thus, the roles of the students and the teachers constantly shift and alternate. By building a climate of trust in which learners interact without fear of threat, ridicule, or failure, the teacher's role becomes that of an interested person who has the resources to assist students' development of language, literacy, and knowledge. Rather than assume the role of the conventional teacher who relies on teaching manuals and employs direct, didactic teaching strategies, transactional teachers guide and motivate students to become critical thinkers and independent problem solvers (Soltero, 1997). Constructivist teaching and learning practices are further discussed in Chapters 5 and 6.

SUMMARY

Dual language education is not simply an instructional program conducted in two languages that can be easily implemented by following a prescribed set of criteria. The decision to implement a dual language program involves a deep understanding of the philosophical views of community and school regarding bilingualism and multiculturalism. When these two fundamental aspects of dual language education are perceived to be highly desirable and worth long-term investment of resources and commitment by the school and the community, this additive bilingual program is more likely to be successful. Dual language education must be developed and shaped by the members of each individual school and by considering the specific characteristics of that particular learning community. At its best, dual language education becomes a collaborative education effort between communities that have been traditionally at odds with each other, both within and outside of the school walls.

Dual language programs vary considerably in how they are implemented. Included in these variations are differences in program models, language distribution, integration of students, initial language of literacy instruction, and program goals. Key elements are language issues, such as how the two languages are distributed and separated, and which is the language of initial literacy instruction and homework. Other decisions include the types of grouping organizations of students and the classroom or teacher arrangements. Although dual language education is implemented in many forms, depending on factors relating to pedagogy, funding, and demographics, there are several key elements that must be present in any effective dual language program: six to eight years of program implementation, parent involvement, balanced representation of each language, integration of students from both language groups, and quality bilingual instruction. (Christian, Montone, Lindholm & Carranza, 1997; Lindholm-Leary, 2001; Thomas & Collier, 1997, 2002; Torres-Guzmán, 2002).

DISCUSSION QUESTIONS

1. Why is it so critical for dual language education to integrate students from both language groups for most of the teaching and learning time? How does separating by language for most of the instructional and social time in dual language programs affect students' academic, linguistic, and sociocultural progress?

2. Consider the arguments for and against separation of the two languages during instruction. Where do you stand on this issue, and why?

3. As a teacher, how would you react to students' codeswitching? Would you allow, restrict, or accommodate codeswitching in the classroom discourse? Why? How?

4. If research suggests that it is better for minority language students to learn to read and write in the language that they know best, their native language, how do you explain having majority language students learning to read and write in the second language first?

5. What are your perceptions about teaching in self-contained versus team-teaching settings? What are the advantages and shortcomings of each? In which setting would you prefer to teach, and why?

FIELD-BASED  INQUIRY

1. Observe several dual language classrooms that implement self-contained and team-teaching arrangements. What are the major differences and similarities that you encounter? How is the time allocated and managed in each setting? How are the instructional materials selected and displayed? What might be the strengths and weaknesses of each arrangement? How would you change or adapt each setting?

2. Interview two students who have been in the dual language program less than one year, and then interview two students who have been in the program for at least three or four years. Ask the students about their general perceptions of dual language education and their feelings about learning a second language and culture. Ask them what they find most challenging about being in the program and what they find most rewarding. Compare their responses, and find common themes.

FURTHER  READING

Christian, D., Montone, C., Lindholm, K., & Carranza, I. (1997). *Profiles in two-way immersion education.* Washington DC: Center for Applied Linguistics.

Freeman, R. (1998). *Bilingual education and social change.* Philadelphia, PA: Multilingual Matters.

Jacobson, R., & Faltis, C. (1990). *Language distribution issues in bilingual schooling.* Philadelphia, PA: Multi-lingual Matters.

Lessow-Hurley, J. (2000). *The foundations of dual language instruction.* New York: Longman.

Lindholm-Leary, K. (2001). *Dual language education.* Philadelphia, PA: Multilingual Matters.

Mora, J. K., Wink, J., & Wink, D. (2001). Dueling models of dual language instruction: A critical review of the literature and program implementation guide. *Bilingual Research Journal, 25* (4): 417–442.

Theoretical Constructs

Language is essential to the process of dialogue, to the development of meaning, and to the production of knowledge. From the context of its emancipatory potential, language must be understood as a dialectical phenomenon that links its very existence and meaning to the lived experiences of the language community and constitutes a major cornerstone for the development of voice.

Darder (1997), p. 333

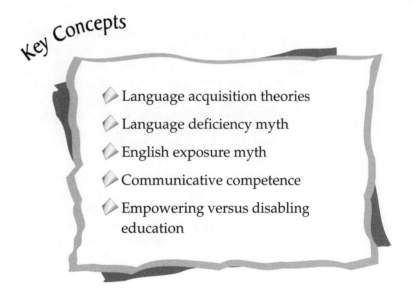

Key Concepts

- Language acquisition theories
- Language deficiency myth
- English exposure myth
- Communicative competence
- Empowering versus disabling education

D ual language education requires more than an understanding of its mechanics and procedures that go beyond model components and organization. Although having a solid grasp of these elements is critical, understanding the theoretical foundations relating to dual language education is central to its effective implementation and desired student outcomes (Torres-Guzmán, 2002). Without a clear sense of the theories and research findings relating to first and second language acquisition, culturally responsive and multicultural education, and constructivist pedagogy, the implementation of dual language education is seriously impaired. Because dual language education is not a prepackaged program that comes with a manual detailing how to implement it, educators must possess adequate background knowledge of language acquisition and constructivist pedagogy to make appropriate programmatic and instructional decisions. This chapter presents, in brief, the most relevant theoretical constructs relating to dual language education: language acquisition, literacy development, and sociocultural responsiveness.

LANGUAGE ACQUISITION

The connection between language and culture has been viewed as a fundamental influence in the process of acquiring knowledge and developing cognition (Halliday, 1975). The difficulties that some linguistically diverse groups experience in adopting a new culture and language have been attributed to cultural conflict in relation to language use (Trueba, 1991). To arrive at a better understanding of the interplays between language, culture, and schooling in the context of dual language education, the following section reviews current theories on language development and first and second language acquisition paradigms.

First Language Acquisition

Understanding the development of a child's second language involves a meticulous analysis of the language development process in general as well as the relationships between first and second language acquisition. Despite their cultural or linguistic backgrounds, all children master basic syntactic, semantic, and phonological structures of their language before they enter school. How does this occur? Different theoretical positions exist regarding the answer to this question. The three most prominent theoretical frameworks include behaviorist, nativist, and interactionist perspectives.

BEHAVIORIST PERSPECTIVE.   People have often assumed that children develop language by imitating what they hear from adults; this was once the popular view of language development. According to the behaviorist point of view, language learning is determined by stimuli from the environment; children reproduce language, or approximations of what they hear, which is then reinforced by rewards and attention. Skinner's (1968) theory of linguistic behavior was an extension of his general theory of learning by conditioning. Children are believed to develop language through reinforcement and, therefore, are considered passive recipients of environmental stimuli (Brown, 2000). However, this theoretical framework does not account for children's utterances unheard in adult speech, such as *two mouses* or *taked*. Although children do not hear adults produce these types of utterances, they are common generalizations found in young children's early speech. For behaviorists, second language learners acquire language through imitation, repetition, and reinforcement of syntax and morphology.

NATIVIST PERSPECTIVE.   Nativists maintain that children are born with an innate capacity to acquire language. According to this position, humans are genetically predisposed to acquire and transmit language. Chomsky (1957) contends that the human brain has a built-in mechanism called the **language acquisition device (LAD)** that infers the rules of language when triggered by the stimulation of spoken language. Once the language acquisition device is activated, children discover the regularities of language and begin to internalize the rules of grammar (Brown, 2000). This happens despite external reinforcement or training. Thus,

Chomsky maintains that language is acquired and not learned. In other words, language is embedded in our brains and automatically comes to the surface when we are exposed to the spoken word. However, nativists fall short in accounting for understanding the behaviors that correspond to language use: that is, understanding the contexts in which language occurs that go beyond the internalization of appropriate grammatical rules.

INTERACTIONIST PERSPECTIVE. Interaction theorists combine behaviorists' beliefs that language is learned through conditioning and nativists' beliefs that humans are born with the innate ability to acquire language. Thus, according to this paradigm, language is a product of both genetic and environmental factors as humans are born with the ability to produce and learn language by using their genetic capacity and by interacting with their environment and other humans. The interactive model not only emphasizes children's comprehension and production of language, but also the context and intent (McLaughlin, 1984).

Interactionist theory of language development is based on three major interrelated principles. First, children are regarded as constructive learners and active meaning makers (Wells, 1986) who decipher and make sense of their world based on their prior knowledge. Unfamiliar words or sentence patterns alert children to make connections between what they already know and the new language they hear. Second, language can be interpreted and understood only when it is being related to the context in which it is being used. That is, language is used for various purposes, resulting in meanings being expressed in countless ways through different language patterns. Children learn how the indirect distinctions of meaning are expressed—direct and indirect requests, different types of questions, expressions of attitudes—by using different selections and sequences of words and structures (Lightbown & Spada, 2000). Third, knowledge is created, categorized, and modified through social interactions and personal experiences. Thus, knowledge represents a process of negotiating meanings and becomes a function of language development. Furthermore, the functional interpretation of children's meanings indicates a sociolinguistic and cultural framework in which the learning of language takes place through interaction and collaboration of the children and other human beings (Halliday, 1994).

The term **communicative competence,** coined by Dell Hymes (1971), refers to the ability to use language effectively in social situations to convey meaning. Contrary to Chomsky's view of the underlying grammatical competence assumed common to all native speakers, Hymes's concern with meaning focuses on the social interactions between speaker and listener. Savignon (1983) provides a set of characteristics that reflect the integration between communication and culture involved in communicative competence. First, *competence* and *performance* are theoretically different; competence is the presumed underlying ability, while performance is the overt manifestation of that ability (Brown, 2000). Through performance, competence can be developed, maintained, and evaluated. Second, communicative competence is considered to be a dynamic process in which meaning is negotiated between two or more persons who share the same or a similar symbolic system. It is an interpersonal, rather than an intrapersonal, characteristic. Third, communicative competence involves both written and spoken language. Fourth, communicative competence takes place in a variety of situations and is dependent on prior knowledge and on a basic understanding of context. It is said to be context specific.

The development of communicative abilities occurs when the learner is able to interpret or create discourse in context by using linguistic cues (Savignon, 1983). Thus, the emphasis shifts from the isolated drill and practice of linguistic skills to the natural reinforcement of these competencies through a purposeful speech or written act. Children's linguistic abilities are reinforced while they engage in meaningful communicative interactions between themselves and others. For dual language education, the notion that language develops through meaningful and authentic linguistic interactions becomes a fundamental premise for teaching and learning practices.

CHARACTERISTICS OF LANGUAGE DEVELOPMENT

Research suggests that most children experience similar patterns of language acquisition very early in life. Halliday (1978) found that a one-day-old baby would stop crying to attend to his mother's voice. He maintains that this reaction, found within a social construct, is the first step toward language development. Infant cries also contain elements of speech, such as intonation, pattern, and pitch. Skutnabb-Kangas (1981) cites studies of English and Chinese newborn babies conducted by Condor and Sanders in 1974. The studies show that children react rhythmically to speech by imitating the rhythm of the speech in their own movements. Assumptions have been made that the intonation and rhythm of the first language are imprinted so early in life that detecting the mother tongue is even possible after it has been substituted by another language.

Very young children react and listen actively to human voices by the turn of their heads, babble, or facial expressions. Babbling allows children to explore speech production and control (Lessow-Hurley, 2000). During the first year of life, children begin to acquire the grammatical and pragmatic knowledge that governs language. This acquisition comes from the children's membership in a language community. Concrete objects acquire certain properties and relations when a child begins to learn language. The child then attaches meanings to things, and later words begin to be differentiated. For instance, *mama* may at first refer to any adult, or *doggie* to any animal. The child later begins to understand the differences between conceptual meanings and differentiates which label refers to which concept.

In learning to speak, children develop their own increasingly complex rules for structuring language. Children are not formally taught language in a mechanical way, bit by bit; rather, they learn language by interacting with the environment in a natural way (Halliday, 1978). Although we do not teach children how to speak, we do facilitate their language development in several ways. First, by exposing children to a language-rich environment, adult language is modeled in naturalistic, real-life contexts that are used to explain, describe, and command. Second, adults have appropriate expectations and responses regarding children's language development. Children are expected to be successful and eventually speak like adults. The main focus of the caregiver is on the child's meaning rather than the form, and, generally, the caretaker gives immediate feedback to the child. Adults respond to an infant's first attempts at speaking with joy and pride, accepting the approximation of the language use (Holdaway, 1979). Later, adults support the child's language development by modeling and surrounding the infant with an abundance of diverse language experiences. The acquisition of language rules in children takes place unconsciously and without direct instruction. For parents or other caregivers, meaning rather than form is the primary focus of the child's acquisition of a first language. Despite the many distinct language experiences children have, an underlying commonality exists: they are all real communicative events.

For language minority children, the development of the mother tongue is particularly important, given that it is through the native language that children acquire cultural knowledge and values, shape their social and cultural identity, and develop cognitive skills for learning (Wong Fillmore, 1991). Language is a contextualized interactive process in which learners use their cognitive and linguistic knowledge to communicate for meaningful purposes in social contexts (Heath, 1983; Wells, 1986). The ways in which language is used varies greatly across cultures, communities, and settings. This variation in the pattern of language use can have a powerful impact, either positive or negative, on literacy teaching and learning (Wong Fillmore & Snow, 2000).

In her seminal study of language and literacy practices in two culturally diverse communities, Heath (1983) found that the specific discourse patterns of each community were directly shaped by their cultural and social experiences. Heath examined how children learned and developed language and literacy in Roadville, a white working-class community, and Trackton, an African American working-class community. In Roadville, white rural families engaged their children in literacy by viewing text as a set of discrete skills and facts, discouraging children from interpreting text creatively or imaginatively, and answering factual questions about the text. In Trackton, African American children were encouraged to have multiple interpretations of the text, use fantasy and imagination, and engage in oral retelling of stories. Heath found that although these two communities supported the language and literacy development of their children, neither matched the literacy and discursive behaviors of the school and teachers. When teachers were exposed to the multiple forms of oral and written literacy practices of the Trackton community, they were able to reformulate their teaching instruction to accommodate and use children's language and literacy modalities (Heath, 1983).

SECOND LANGUAGE ACQUISITION

Our understanding of the complex processes involved in native language acquisition provides a basis for the development of numerous theoretical frameworks. Current research in second language acquisition has, in turn, contributed to our understanding of the processes and conditions of language learning in general. Theoretical developments concur with the notion that proficiency in a second language may be acquired under similar circumstances as the first language (Cummins, 2001). That is, second language proficiency may be acquired and developed more effectively under more natural and meaningful conditions. Effective instruction for linguistic minority children should be conducted within a progressive and flexible structure in which the teachers and the students have a certain degree of control of the instructional practices and activities.

Language Deficiency Myth

Many negative myths about bilingualism have advocated the notion that children's use of two languages causes cognitive, social, and emotional damage (Cummins, 1984). The language deficiency myth describes language minority children as nonverbal, alingual, and semilingual, often with learning disabilities and speech impediments. Research studies conducted in the fields of linguistics and education have refuted the language deficiency myth (Cummins, 2000; Hakuta, 1986; Hornberger, 1994). Based on the need to clarify conflicting theoretical issues like these, research on bilingualism and cognitive processes has shifted to a focus on metalinguistic abilities. This refers to the ability to think about language in a flexible and abstract manner, such as making judgments about the grammar of sentences, understanding innuendos, and perceiving play-on-words in jokes. Although both monolingual and bilingual children develop metalinguistic abilities, bilingualism induces children to better control their mental processes (Hakuta, 1990). Metalinguistic abilities have been linked with the development of early reading skills in monolingual children. Therefore, it follows that, all other variables being equal, bilingual children have an advantage over monolingual children in the acquisition of literacy.

Research has shown that children who live in supportive and nurturing bilingual environments do not develop linguistic handicaps. García (1985) reports on studies that documented the development of bilingualism in Mexican American children and compared the results with the development of monolingual English-speaking children. The comparisons on measures of vocabulary, phonological, and syntactic development suggest that bilingual children do not differ from monolingual children. Bilingualism in itself does not seem to interfere with the development of either language. Bilingual acquisition involves a process that builds upon a fundamental base needed for the development of both languages. A lack of empirical evidence refutes the notion that there is a competition between the two languages over mental process. On the contrary, the evidence suggests that there indeed is a cognitive advantage to bilingualism (August & Hakuta, 1998). Why, then, are certain linguistic minorities consistently struggling to achieve in our schools? Part of the reason is that success in the educational system for minority children goes beyond language. That is, culture and ethnicity, within sociopolitical and sociohistorical constructs, are the critical ingredients in the development of culturally responsive and transformative pedagogy for minority students (Ferdman & Weber, 1994; Ruiz, 1997).

English Exposure Myth

Other myths of bilingualism have perpetuated the instrumentation of inappropriate educational programs for language minority students. The English exposure myth maintains that language minority children must be exposed to great amounts of English to become proficient in that language. Moreover, instruction in the native language has been considered a hindrance for the acquisition of English. Research evidence rejects this myth. Language minority children who receive instruction in the native language develop the second language more efficiently than children who are immersed in the second language (August & Hakuta, 1998; Wong Fillmore & Valadéz, 1986).

However, researchers have been cautious when proposing this tenet, claiming that the negative or positive effects of first or second language instruction depend considerably on the context in which it takes place (Cummins, 2000). That is, the context of the language use, rather than the language itself, is the deciding factor in whether initial instruction in the first language or the second language is more conducive to overall academic success. Hornberger (1994) proposes that contextual factors, such as the child's cognitive and linguistic development in the first language, parental support, and the status of each language within and outside the school, are the strongest determinants in the outcome of initial first or second language instruction.

Despite research evidence showing that native language instruction promotes second language acquisition, state policies increasingly sponsor the **structured English immersion** program model as an alternative to bilingual education (Crawford, 1999). This method often offers a simplified and diluted version of the academic content in English as the medium of instruction. Proponents of this approach cite the success of Canadian immersion models. Researchers have warned that immersion programs in the majority language are not effective for language minority children (Crawford, 1999; Cummins, 2001). In contrast to the Canadian model, immersion programs in the United States have distinct social and political factors that severely cripple their effectiveness for culturally and linguistically diverse students: the students' first language bears a substantially subjugated position compared to English; students tend to be from impoverished socioeconomic classes, parents have little say and few opportunities for significant involvement; teachers are monolingual English speakers; and the primary objective is to become monolingual in English.

Current Perspectives

In the United States, English is perceived to be a fundamental tool for achieving in school and becoming a successful member of society. The loss of the home language and culture is often seen as necessary for the appropriate development of English. Hence, linguistic minorities not only experience a loss of personal identity and emotional bonds with the community, but also experience rejection from the mainstream society. Ada (1995, p. 237) asserts that

> Despite its widespread acceptance, the subtractive model of bilingualism, in which mastery of the second language is achieved at the expense of proficiency in the first, need not be the framework on which bilingual education rests. Additive bilingualism, in which a second language is acquired while maintaining and continuing to develop the first, is a healthy and viable alternative to subtractive bilingualism.

Bartolomé (1994) points to contradictory disparities in the status of languages in the United States "while we discourage the maintenance of linguistic minority students' native language throughout their education, we require English-speaking students to study a foreign language as a prerequisite for college" (p. 207). Trueba (1989) contends that educators must create a culturally appropriate learning environment (p. 69) that is in harmony with the values and beliefs of the home culture to maximize the cognitive development in language minority children. Cognitive skills are best acquired through the primary language and then transferred to the second language. The use of the home language helps children develop critical thinking abilities and cognitive skills. This cognitive structuring is shaped not only by linguistic knowledge but also by cultural knowledge and the context in which that knowledge is obtained (Trueba, 1991).

Cummins (1989) proposes three principles relevant to bilingual development and language teaching. First, the additive bilingual enrichment principle contends that "the development of additive bilingual and biliteracy skills entails no negative consequences for children's academic, linguistic or intellectual development . . . the evidence points in the direction of subtle metalinguistic and intellectual benefits for bilingual children" (p. 21). Numerous studies have indicated that bilingual children demonstrate a greater awareness of linguistic meanings and seem to be more flexible in their thinking than monolingual children (Cummins, 2000). Bilingual children must decipher much more linguistic input through the effort of gaining command of two languages than monolingual children, who are exposed to only one language system.

Second, the interdependence principle is based upon the premise that there is an underlying cognitive and academic proficiency common across all languages regardless of their distinct surface features (see Figure 3.1). Cummins maintains that first and second language academic skills are interdependent. His claim is based on the empirical evidence that there is no relationship between the amount of instructional time spent in the second language and academic achievement.

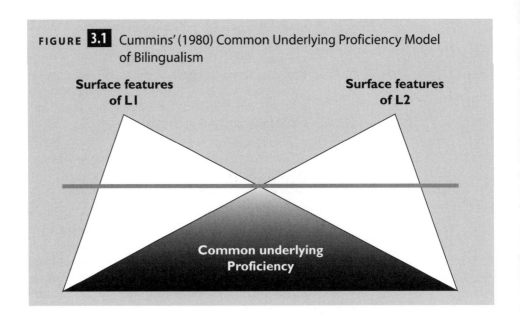

FIGURE 3.1 Cummins' (1980) Common Underlying Proficiency Model of Bilingualism

According to Cummins, the **common underlying proficiency** makes possible the transfer of literacy-related skills between languages. He found that transfer is more likely from the minority to the majority language due to the greater exposure to literacy in the majority language and the social pressures to learn it.

Third, the interactive pedagogy principle subscribes to Krashen's (1981) assertion that language is acquired involuntarily and effortlessly only when it is comprehensible. The key factor in Krashen's theoretical model is **comprehensible input**—messages in the second language that make sense when modified and facilitated by visual aids and context. He contends that we acquire grammatical structures in their natural order when sufficient amounts of high-quality input are present. Rules are then generalized from verbal stimuli according to innate principles of grammar. The principle of comprehensible input is based on the idea that the main function of language is meaningful communication. The importance of meaningful language use at all stages in the acquisition of second language skills has become recognized as a critical and determining factor for the successful development of a second language and the maintenance of the first language. The interactive pedagogy principle provides significant insights for educators because of its relevance to literacy and first language development. As noted earlier in this discussion, children negotiate meaning by focusing on understanding what is being communicated and by using language for a variety of meaningful purposes. Research and theories on language development have advanced our understanding of the processes involved in the acquisition of a second language. The complex issues of second language acquisition must be viewed in the context of sociocultural and communicative frameworks (Pérez, 1998).

BILINGUAL AND SOCIOCULTURAL PERSPECTIVES

During the past thirty years, educators and policymakers have implemented a series of costly reforms in an effort to reverse the pattern of educational failure among minority students. Cummins (1995) contends that a major reason these reforms have proved unsuccessful is that the relationships between students and teachers, and between school systems and the communities they serve, remain the same. He suggests that, beyond the legislative and policy reforms, educators need to redefine their roles with respect to minority students and communities.

Cummins (2000) argues that the underachievement of some groups can be directly attributed to the specific kinds of interactions between teachers and students and their families. He further contends that these interactions are negotiated through the roles that educators assume in relation to four dimensions of school organization and the degree to which each is carried out. First, the culture and language of students should be incorporated into the school agenda and curriculum in meaningful and permanent ways. Second, schools must advocate for community involvement as a critical element in the education of culturally and linguistically diverse students. Third, students must be intrinsically motivated to actively use language for generating their own knowledge. Finally, educators must be involved in assessing academic outcomes that promote and support minority students.

Educators can be at various points along a continuum, one end of which promotes empowerment and the other end of which fosters disabling attributes. Cummins (2001) proposes an empowering versus disabling framework for the academic outcomes of students. That is, students who are empowered by their educational experiences develop a secure cultural identity, appropriate interactive structures, and a knowledge base that allows them to succeed academically. Empowered students are better equipped to tackle academic challenges because they are engaged in an environment that nurtures their confidence and motivates them to achieve in school. Conversely, students who are disabled by their school experiences do not develop an adequate cognitive and academic base or a solid social and emotional infrastructure. The educators' role has begun to shift from teachers who hold unintentional or intentional disabling attitudes and misconceptions based on subtractive ideologies to teachers who advocate intercultural and linguistic empowerment of minority students through an additive perspective (Cummins, 2001). Incorporating students' language and culture into the school curriculum reinforces learners' native language and cultural identity. This approach results in a stronger cognitive and academic foundation for language minority students. Consequently, the minority culture and language are viewed as advantages that enrich the lives and opportunities of the minority group and broaden the awareness and understanding of the majority group (Tse, 2001).

The development of academic proficiency is largely dependent on context-embedded instruction. Teachers facilitate academic growth by providing opportunities that validate students' backgrounds and encourage the sharing and expanding of students' prior experiences. This approach is effective because learners take on active roles by engaging in real communicative events about their lives while learning about others' experiences. Learning is also facilitated because students take ownership of the processes involved in acquiring language and literacy in the context of their own experiences. As a counter example to Cummins' position, Britton (1992) provides a fitting portrait of the effects of the power relationships between transmission-oriented teachers and their students regarding discursive practices: "It is an act of faith for a small child to address an adult he does not know; to do so across the silence of thirty other children can only magnify the difficulty; add to that the fear of rejection of what he offers and the picture is complete" (p. 181). Consider the additional burden for children who do not have full proficiency of the second language or an understanding of the dominant culture.

This type of traditional school talk is particularly limiting to children whose homes do not include "meaningful discourse" in reference to schooling (Heath, 1983). Teachers generally blame the home or culture for failing to provide children with adequate language development and thinking skills. However, Gallimore and Tharp (1990) point out the irony that schools themselves have consistently used the interactional patterns so often attributed to disadvantaged homes. Adjusting the talk of the classroom in a manner that allows learners to share more of themselves and their background knowledge requires educators to be willing to be informed and "re-formed" by learner input (Bean, 1997). That is, seeking personal and cultural information about the learners' worlds helps the teacher acquire and understand the schema that students bring to the academic task.

LITERACY DEVELOPMENT

Theories regarding the acquisition of literacy in a second language have changed with evolving views on language development and related instructional practices. Traditionally, oral language was separated from the written mode of language in the process of teaching and learning a second language. Linguists and foreign language educators placed an intense emphasis on speech and grammar, which resulted in a rigid sequence of teaching the four domains of language: first listening and speaking, then reading and writing. This orientation to language learning was also evident in certain teaching methods, such as Krashen and Terrell's natural approach, which was based on first language acquisition theories and stressed oral language development before literacy (Ramírez, 1994). According to Krashen and Terrell (1983), reading is not a necessary skill to the implementation of the natural approach in attaining adequate levels of oral language competence. However, they proposed that reading serve as a source of comprehensible input. In recent years, the focus of second language literacy learning has shifted from being segmented into discrete components to being connected as interrelated dimensions within a range of contexts (Thonis, 1994). As noted earlier, Cummins and other prominent researchers have documented the positive effects of native language literacy on the development of literacy in a second language (Cummins, 2001; Edelsky, 1986). Furthermore, readers and writers who are proficient in their first language can become proficient in a second language because they transfer universal literacy strategies from one language to the other. These universal literacy concepts do not need to be relearned in the second language.

Developing Literacy in Two Languages

Goodman and Goodman (1990) argue that although "second-language learning is facilitated by the 'advanced knowledge' of the first language" (p. 230), the processes of learning the mother tongue and a second language are similar. This view has led educators toward instructional practices that allow the learner to interact with the second language under natural, meaningful, and decontextualized conditions. Similarly, González, Moll, and others (1993) maintain that social and cultural conditions are central to the socialization of authentic literacy practices. That is, students use both languages as tools for inquiry, communication, and thinking. According to Cummins (2000), social and pragmatic dimensions are situated within students' self-perceptions and attitudes inside their cultural and social realms. That is, those students who are literate in their first language will consider themselves already literate, and thus will tackle the challenge of second language literacy with cognitive strategies previously acquired.

Literacy features that involve syntactic, semantic, pragmatic, morphological, and phonological characteristics as well as orthographic and graphophonic aspects are regarded as universal (see Figure 3.2). Semantic and syntactic characteristics become part of students' repertoire when acquiring literacy in the first language. Not only is meaning already assumed to be attached to the printed

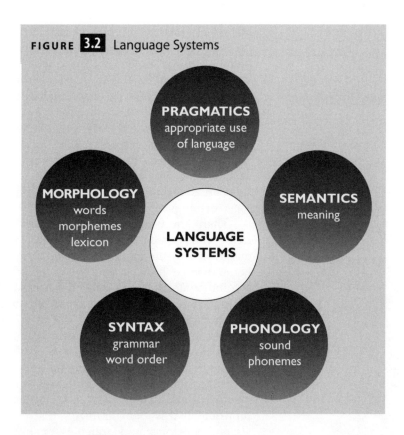

FIGURE 3.2 Language Systems

PRAGMATICS
appropriate use
of language

MORPHOLOGY
words
morphemes
lexicon

SEMANTICS
meaning

LANGUAGE
SYSTEMS

SYNTAX
grammar
word order

PHONOLOGY
sound
phonemes

material, but prior knowledge of concepts in the first language is also transferred to the reading and writing of concepts in the second language. Although students may not yet know the specific grammar of the second language, they do know that language is governed by syntactic and grammatical rules. Finally, students familiar with the orthographic and graphophonic systems of their first language can transpose the notion that writing is symbolic and expresses meaning (Pérez, 1998).

Escamilla (1993) points out that not all aspects of literacy are universal, such as the schema of cultural ideas and knowledge of discourse forms. She suggests that students learning literacy in a second language must also develop multi-literacies to incorporate the variations of literacy structures that exist in each language. These multiliteracies encompass the ability of readers and writers to use their schematic knowledge to make connections and relate to the text. This skill of interacting meaningfully with the text goes beyond the ability to decode (read) or encode (write) the words. That is, a student reading in the second language must have sufficient prior cultural knowledge to understand subtleties or culture-specific connotations in the text. Multiliteracies also account for text structures and discourse differences across languages. For instance, English story grammar is linear, but in Asian and Native American languages the structure is circular. Similarly, in Spanish and Russian the story grammar allows for considerable di-gression, and in Hebrew and Arabic the story composition is repetitive in nature (Escamilla, 1993; Pérez, 1998). Moreover, Escamilla refers to several types of lan-guage forms that are essential for understanding English texts, such as idioms (*nitty gritty*), tag verbs (*set up*), and modals (*would, should*). These examples show how structure and logic vary across languages and become integral components of understanding text beyond simple decoding of words.

When second language literacy development is assessed based on these as-sumptions, it becomes evident that the comprehension of text and the content of literacy are learned through socially constructed interactions with the world and the text (Freire & Macedo, 1987). Giroux (1989) stresses that critical pedagogy of literacy must be rooted in a framework that allows students to speak so that their voices become integral components of the curriculum. He adds that teachers must develop pedagogies that encourage students to affirm and formulate their personal narratives by exercising their own voices. Repetition and practice of facts and skills disconnected from readers' own experiences have been documented to be ineffective and detrimental for children, in particular for language minority students. This assertion implies that practitioners need to look beyond prepackaged reading programs that reduce literacy to simplistic decoding skills, and consider an adaptive pedagogy approach that incorporates children's cultural and social experiences (Delgado-Gaitán, 1993; Ramírez, 1994).

Tharp and Gallimore (1988) suggest that social and cultural differences often create a mismatch between the learning environments of the home and the school, manifested in the mainstream expectations of parent involvement. The school-home mismatch disappears when the school and the community collaborate to accommodate all genres as well as to introduce new ones. Heath (1983) suggests asking families to elaborate upon the genres that are used in the community. Heath claims that to expand the ways to develop language and literacy, the schools must attain a certain level of community awareness.

In order to break down the barriers that the education system has fostered for so many years toward minority culture and language, schools must begin to involve the community as an important component and resource in decision making on curriculum. Parents, students, and teachers must collaborate to formulate appropriate instructional strategies, discover and use relevant instructional materials, and develop sound strategies for support in the home and the school. The collaborative notion views the community as a vast resource of knowledge (Moll, Tapia & Whitmore, 1993). Educators become responsible for encouraging parents to participate in their children's education. Moll and Díaz (1987) discuss the reorganization of instruction based on information gathered through community resources (language and culture). They contend that the use of this information is a key factor in changing children's academic performance, and they propose that connections between the school and community will promote educational change.

SUMMARY

The preceding review has examined a range of topics in which language, literacy, bilingualism, and pedagogy come together. Thus, despite their scope and diversity, a common thread is woven throughout each section of the chapter—the impact of theories and pedagogical practices on bilingual and biliterate development. The primary aim of this analysis is to present broad theoretical perspectives on the acquisition of language and the development of literacy in relation to bilingual learners. In recent years, researchers and educators have pursued a better understanding of how language and literacy development theories and teaching practices are linked with broader sociopolitical forces. The complex relationships between bilingualism, literacy, and educational attainment have propelled educators and researchers to have a stronger grasp of language development theories, emergent literacy perspectives, and sociocultural views that are linked to diverse student populations.

Research has advanced our understanding of language development and transformed our definition of literacy. This has resulted in new insights about the significance of creating classroom communities of literate thinkers. A strong theoretical framework of early literacy development, language acquisition, and bilingual and sociolinguistic paradigms provides the foundation for the development of appropriate classroom instructional strategies, particularly in dual language instruction. The pedagogical and theoretical implications for language minority students are profound. The decisions that teachers make daily inside the classroom both shape and are shaped by the social order outside the classroom. Although pedagogical choices about methodology, content, curriculum development, and classroom pro- cesses appear to be guided by impartial professional considerations, they are inherently ideological and have significant implications for all students' educational success or failure, and in particular for the success or failure of culturally and linguistically diverse children.

DISCUSSION QUESTIONS

1. Which theory of language development best fits your beliefs about how children acquire their first language? What are some of the implications for teaching and learning practices for each of the theories of language acquisition presented in this chapter (behaviorist, nativist, and interactionist)?

2. What are the fundamental premises expounded by Hymes' notion of communicative competence? How do these aspects of developing communicative competence relate to the acquisition of a second language in the context of dual language education?

3. Some parents of English language learners believe in ideas that support the language deficiency myth and the English exposure myth. As a teacher, how would you address parents' misconceptions about bilingualism and second language acquisition? What arguments would you use to present your case in challenging these myths?

4. Based on your understandings of the theories of language and literacy development, what issues would you take into account when deciding on the language of initial literacy instruction for an English native speaker in dual language education?

FIELD-BASED INQUIRY

1. Select two children of similar age who belong to two different cultural or ethnic groups. Observe them at home as they engage in language and literacy practices with other family members or caregivers. What are some of the patterns of language and literacy use in the home? How are the children supported in their development of linguistic and literacy development? How are the home language and literacy interactions related to the linguistic and literacy practices of school? What similarities and differences did you observe? How can teachers and schools tap into children's linguistic and cultural capital?

2. Make a few visits to a culturally and linguistically diverse community that is different from yours. Observe the linguistic and literacy practices of the community in public spaces, such as restaurants, banks, self-service laundries, community agencies, and churches, synagogues, or mosques. Note the amount and type of print environment, as well as the languages used. Speak to the librarian at the local or nearest library about library attendance by the public, funding for books, library programs for children, and languages represented in the library collection. Consider how and to what extent literacy is used in the community, how the language of the community is represented in the print environment, and what the status of the language of the community is in relation to standard English.

3. Interview the parent of a culturally and linguistic diverse student about the family's discursive practices in the home. Ask how family members communicate with each other, what language patterns adults use with children, how children interact with each other linguistically, and what the conventions and traditions for communication are within the community. Also inquire about the literacy practices, both oral and written, of the family. What literacy routines are followed? How are oral literacies incorporated in their lives? What types of texts are present in the home, and how are they used?

FURTHER READING

Freeman, D. E., & Freeman, Y. S. (1997). *Teaching reading and writing in Spanish in the bilingual classroom.* Portsmouth, NH: Heinemann.

Freeman, D. E., & Freeman, Y. S. (2000). *Teaching reading in multilingual classrooms.* Portsmouth, NH: Heinemann.

Krashen, S. (1993). *The power of reading.* Englewood, CO: Libraries Unlimited.

Lightbown, P. M., & Spada, N. (2000). *How languages are learned.* Oxford, England: Oxford University Press.

Mcleod, B. (1994). *Language and learning: Educating linguistically diverse students.* New York: State University of New York Press.

Tinajero, J. V., & Ada, A. F. (1993). *The power of two languages: Literacy and biliteracy for Spanish-speaking students.* New York: Macmillan/McGraw-Hill.

Planning Considerations

A child's learning ability, employment potential, and cultural interests are enriched by achieving competencies in a language beyond his/her own, in a classroom where children from various cultures learn and share together. . . . We believe that the racial and ethnic diversity of the Oyster student body are the bases through which we will enrich and further promote the goals of building a culturally pluralistic society.

Oyster Bilingual School Philosophy Statement in Freeman (1998), p. 108

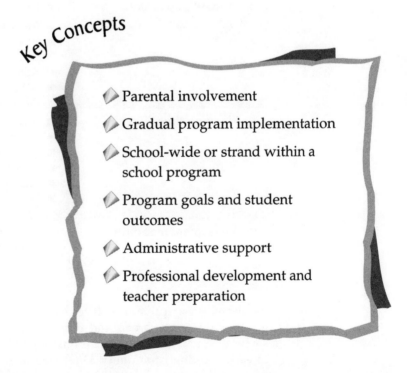

Key Concepts

- Parental involvement
- Gradual program implementation
- School-wide or strand within a school program
- Program goals and student outcomes
- Administrative support
- Professional development and teacher preparation

This chapter delineates the multiple considerations that may arise during the planning stages prior to implementing a dual language program. Not all the recommended steps need to be addressed or even followed in the order presented here. Nonetheless, attending to the recommendations in this planning strategy (Table 4.1) may facilitate the decision-making process and reduce unexpected situations and problematic issues. The recommendations are by

■ **TABLE 4.1**	**Organization Planning Steps**
1. Information	■ Review theory and research literature ■ Visit existing programs ■ Consult knowledgeable agencies
2. Written plan	■ Vision/mission/philosophy statement ■ Timeline of implementation ■ Goals and outcomes ■ Program description
3. Program models	■ Partial immersion or total immersion ■ Language of initial literacy instruction
4. Organization	■ Team-teaching or self-contained ■ Class size
5. Parents and community	■ Information dissemination ■ Parent and community meetings ■ Promoting the program
6. Student population	■ Language, culture, mobility rate
7. Staff	■ Preparation ■ Recruiting qualified teachers ■ Administration ■ Other school staff
8. Planning time	■ Scheduling ■ Curriculum planning ■ Instructional materials selection ■ Home language survey ■ Classroom language count ■ Teacher input
9. Assessment measures	■ Program evaluation ■ Student progress evaluation

no means prescriptive in nature. As discussed in previous chapters, dual language education is broad and multifaceted. Programmatic choices and philosophical formulations must be intimately connected to the unique characteristics of each learning community. Dual language education is not and cannot be a packaged program; therefore, this should not be considered a manual for implementation. Rather, the recommendations found in this book are to be used as a buffet of ideas set out for consideration depending on a school's characteristics, needs, desires, and preferences.

To illustrate some of the stages involved in planning and implementing dual language education, Box 4.1 describes one urban school's journey from conception and preparation to application and implementation. Although the school in the vignette follows many of the planning and implementation steps recommended in this book, some are absent, such as creating admission policies and procedures and designing evaluative measures. Numerous factors account for

One School's Journey into Dual Language Education

For several years, parents, teachers, and administrators in this urban preK–8 neighborhood school had been discussing ways to improve its bilingual education program. Early in the school year, the principal and a group of teachers attended a district meeting on a number of proposed new initiatives for second or foreign language programs, among them dual language education. The principal and teachers thought that this program could be implemented in their school, given that they had a good balanced representation of Spanish- and English-dominant students, qualified teachers, and a strong whole language teaching and learning framework.

The local school council (LSC), consisting of six parents, two teachers, and a community representative, were presented with information through invited district speakers and discussions by the principal and teachers. The LSC's positive reaction about implementing a dual language program set in motion several meetings and discussion groups with parents and school staff. The principal selected a group of parents and teachers to participate in the district's dual language information sessions and attend other in-services and conferences related to dual language education. About mid-year, with the LSC's approval, the school staff voted in favor of implementing the program starting with Kindergarten and first grade. The principal selected a dual language coordinator and allocated funds for materials, teacher stipends for planning, and staff develop-

ment. The coordinator, principal, parents, and teachers attended in-services and continued to participate in district meetings as well as visiting established dual language programs in the area. Based on the information gathered, K–1 teachers began meeting after school and in the summer to create the program vision and mission, decide on the program model and classroom organization, plan the curriculum, and order instructional materials.

After the first year of planning, the dual language program began in all K–1 classrooms. Meanwhile, the coordinator organized monthly parent dual language meetings, teachers' biweekly discussion and planning meetings, and staff development. The coordinator also monitored student enrollment and language balance in all classrooms. By the end of the year, dual language students performed in both languages in their first end-of-the-year dual language celebration. K–1 teachers met to organize student placement for the next grade and pass students' portfolios to the next year's teachers. The coordinator, teachers, and principal met to discuss the success and challenges of the past year and to reformulate any policies or procedures that proved problematic.

During the spring, the second grade teachers met frequently with K–1 teachers, attended dual language professional development, and visited other dual language schools. Second grade teachers also met after school and in the summer to plan and order instructional materials. Throughout the planning and initial implementation phases, the entire school community was informed of the program's progress through staff meetings, memos, and newsletters.

omissions in the planning and initial implementation phases, but the most common is lack of information and inadequate understanding of the complexities of creating and carrying out a dual language program. Such was the case in this particular school. Table 4.2 summarizes the critical steps that the administration engaged in as they prepared and carried out their dual language program from the planning year to the first and second years of implementation.

Even before preliminary information about dual language education is gathered and the planning phase is conceptualized, school administrators, teachers, and parents might examine and discuss factors that could influence the implementation of the program. Issues such as balanced language representation among the student body, student mobility rates, levels of parental involvement, teacher preparation, and access to teacher professional development should be considered. The success or failure of a program may depend, in part, on the decisions made prior to launching it. A good starting point is to investigate and gather information on dual language bilingual education and related types of bilingual or foreign language programs.

■ **TABLE 4.2** | **One School's Journey into Dual Language Education**

YEAR 1 Plan	<ul><li>Principal, teachers, and parents attend program information sessions.</li><li>Parent council and school staff are informed and consulted.</li><li>Parent council and school staff vote in favor of starting the program.</li><li>Select a dual language coordinator who attends meetings and in-services with parents and teachers.</li><li>Funds are allocated for materials, teacher stipends, and staff development.</li><li>Principal, coordinator, and teachers attend staff development.</li><li>K–1 teachers meet after school and in the summer to create the program vision/mission, plan the curriculum, and order instructional materials.</li></ul>
YEAR 2 Implement	<ul><li>All K–1 classrooms start the dual language program.</li><li>Teachers assess students' academic and L2 proficiencies.</li><li>Parents attend monthly dual language meetings.</li><li>Teachers attend biweekly discussion and planning meetings.</li><li>Coordinator, teachers, and parents continue to attend staff development.</li><li>Coordinator organizes and monitors student enrollment.</li><li>Second-grade teachers begin attending dual language staff development.</li><li>Students present the first end-of-the-year dual language celebration.</li><li>Teachers meet to organize student placement for the next grade and pass students' portfolios to second-grade teachers.</li><li>K–1 teachers meet with second-grade teachers to discuss program.</li><li>Second-grade teachers meet after school and in the summer to plan and order instructional materials.</li><li>Teachers, coordinator, principal meet to evaluate program's progress.</li></ul>
YEAR 3 Implement	<ul><li>Second-grade classrooms start dual language program.</li><li>Teachers assess students' academic and L2 proficiencies.</li><li>Parents continue to attend monthly dual language meetings.</li><li>Teachers continue to participate in biweekly planning meetings.</li><li>Selected teachers attend national dual language conference.</li><li>Coordinator, teachers, and parents continue to attend staff development.</li><li>Coordinator organizes and monitors student enrollment.</li><li>Third-grade teachers begin attending dual language staff development.</li><li>Students present the second annual dual language celebration.</li><li>Teachers, coordinator, principal meet to evaluate program's progress.</li><li>A dual language task force is created to work on evaluative methods to assess the program.</li></ul>

GATHERING INFORMATION

Reviewing Current Theory and Research Literature

Exploring and reviewing current research findings on the effectiveness of developmental and enrichment bilingual education, such as heritage language and dual language programs, provides supporting evidence and necessary background knowledge for decision making. Multiple sources of information on dual language education are available in print and on line, such as books and journal articles that provide current research results and data and Internet sites that offer a wide range of instructional resources and general information (see Appendix B for an extensive listing of current videos, Appendix C for professional organizations and research centers, and the Suggestions for Further Reading at the end of each chapter).

Visit Dual Language Programs

Although every school has its own specific needs and characteristics, visiting both established and newly implemented programs can provide valuable insights on implementation, planning, and execution. The *Directory of Two-Way Bilingual Immersion Programs in the US* offers a comprehensive listing of dual language programs across states (see Appendix C for Web addresses.) Although many of the nation's partial and total immersion programs are listed in the directory, not all dual language programs are included. This is partly because not all dual language programs respond to the directory's request for information.

ESTABLISHED PROGRAMS.   Effective programs that have been in existence for some time are useful sources of information. Visiting an established dual language school can offer a good sense of how that program works, how the school adjusts to the needs of different program components, and how the program has evolved during implementation. Observing the actual day-to-day classroom practices of experienced dual language teachers is very beneficial as well. Many doubts and confusions can be resolved during this kind of preliminary observation and search.

NEW PROGRAMS.   Newly implemented programs can also provide fresh ideas and viewpoints about the struggles and successes of embarking on this effort. For instance, recently implemented dual education programs can shed light on how to consult and inform parents and the community, what to do about teacher ambivalence, and how to go about selecting and ordering appropriate materials. In addition, the planning and preparation phase prior to enacting dual language education can shed light on issues such as funding, teacher training, and organizational procedures. These issues are much more difficult to recall when a school has been involved in the program for some time. In contrast, schools that have recently started dual language education are likely to still be adapting and fine-tuning the program.

Consult Knowledgeable Agencies

Local and national universities that conduct research on bilingual education are added sources of information and research data that can support the effectiveness of dual language education. Universities and research centers can also play important roles as potential research collaborators in documenting a school's process and progress. Contact local university departments of education and inquire about professors or graduate students who conduct research on dual language education and related fields. Other sources of information are educational agencies and research centers that specialize in dual language and other enrichment bilingual education programs. The Center for Applied Linguistics, the Illinois Resource Center, the American Council of Immersion Education in Minnesota, and other centers are outstanding resources with up-to-date research on dual language education and second language acquisition theory and practice.

A thorough review of available information and current research is designed to provide background knowledge on the variations of additive bilingual education, what the research says about immersion education, and the optimal conditions required for effective dual language programs. Consulting agencies that specialize in dual language and enrichment bilingual education and visiting existing dual language programs provide vital information and knowledge on program essentials. Based on the information gathered from this search, the next step is to determine the program model, criteria, vision and mission, and goals that best suit the school's student and teacher population and its academic, linguistic, and cultural agendas. Selecting the most suitable program for a school requires careful consideration of the components that are most compatible with the school's existing organization, demographics, and philosophy, without deviating too far from the essential fundamentals of dual language education.

Parent and Community Involvement in the Planning Stages

Parents and community members can offer multiple and important contributions in shaping and building a dual language program. Seeking the opinions and views of parents is an essential step in the creation of a program that best fits the needs and aspirations of that entire learning community (Cazabon, Lambert & Hall, 1993). For parents to develop informed opinions and provide constructive input about dual language education in general and the school's program in particular, they need to be part of decision making from the very beginning (Sugarman & Howard, 2001). Parents and other interested community members can be asked to participate in dual language school visitations, seminars, and information sessions and school-based discussion and planning meetings. When parents and community members participate in school visits, professional development, and discussion groups, they will become better acquainted with the theoretical and pedagogical foundations of second language development and the benefits of dual language education (Soltero, 2002).

Through class or school newsletters, parent meetings, and telephone contacts, parents can be invited to be part of a planning committee and to attend informational sessions. During these gatherings, parents can convey their views through oral discussions or by completing surveys or questionnaires. This information can then be compiled and used in the planning and preparation of the program. It is helpful to continue soliciting and including parent viewpoints when reevaluating and restructuring the program.

WRITING A STRATEGIC PLAN

Many schools in the initial phases of implementing a dual language program fail to develop a written strategic plan. The planning phase affords an ideal point in time to develop the vision and mission statement, detail the projected timeline, delineate the goals and student outcomes, and describe the model, among other program features.

Vision, Mission, and Philosophy Statements

Formulating the program's vision and mission statements helps in conceptualizing its rationale and guiding principles and delineating how these will be accomplished. The philosophy statement helps define the inherent beliefs and values that constitute the program and that are embraced and upheld by the school community. The quotation that opens this chapter is from the philosophy statement created by members of the Oyster Bilingual School in Washington, D.C. This dual language school has had a two-way immersion program since 1971 and is the subject of an in-depth analysis of multicultural intergroup dynamics and bilingual discursive practices (Freeman, 1998). As illustrated by the excerpt, the school or program philosophy statement reflects the core beliefs of its participants, both in the larger social scheme and within the school and learning context. Generating the vision, mission, and philosophy statements may be among the most challenging undertakings of the initial implementation phase of a dual language program. The difficulty may lie in trying to create a genuine and accurate representation of a school's ethos without sounding formulaic, artificial, or overly ambitious.

Projected Timeline of Implementation

The inception of most dual language programs is conducted gradually, starting in preK or kindergarten and adding one grade level each year (see Table 4.3). This is the recommended method, given that starting a program in all grades at once may present difficulties for students in higher grades who do not have sufficient command of the second language (Lindholm-Leary, 2001; Montague, 1997; Sugarman & Howard, 2001). If dual language is initially implemented in all grade levels at once, older students will experience difficulty with literacy and academic areas when these are conducted in the second language of instruction. For English-dominant students who have insufficient command of the second language to perform academic tasks and who have no second language support at home, this is particularly problematic.

In preK through first grade, students acquire the second language gradually while being exposed to comprehensible input and context-embedded experiences. Although there has been an increasing emphasis on skills-based teaching in the early grades, the curricula still tend to subscribe to learner-centered, language-

■ TABLE 4.3	Sample Timeline of Program Implementation						
Year	**Progression of Grade Level Addition**						
1	PK & K						
2	PK & K	grade 1					
3	PK & K	grade 1	grade 2				
4	PK & K	grade 1	grade 2	grade 3			
5	PK & K	grade 1	grade 2	grade 3	grade 4		
6	PK & K	grade 1	grade 2	grade 3	grade 4	grade 5	
7	PK & K	grade 1	grade 2	grade 3	grade 4	grade 5	grade 6
8	PK & K	grade 1	grade 2	grade 3	grade 4	grade 5	grade 6	grade 7

rich, developmental teaching practices and learning experiences (Woods, Boyle & Hubbard, 1999). Thus, the optimal time to begin a dual language program is usually preK and kindergarten, and sometimes first grade (Lindholm-Leary, 2001). As the students who participate in dual language progress through the elementary years, one grade is added each year, to eventually reach middle school or beyond. The most advantageous and effective dual language programs are offered for at least six years (Christian, Montone, Lindholm & Carranza, 1997; Cloud, Genesee & Hamayan, 2000; Lessow-Hurley, 2000; Lindholm-Leary, 2001).

Programmatic Goals and Student Outcomes

Assessment and evaluation of program status and student development are critical for determining which goals and outcomes are being met and which are in need of more careful attention. The assessment components and procedures should be longitudinal and based on the specific goals and student objectives delineated in the program handbook. Programs that have defined explicit goals are better able to measure whether those objectives have been realized. The intent of the program should be clearly delineated and realistically conceived, as should the academic, linguistic, and sociocultural expectations. That is, the programmatic goals and student outcomes should take into account the school's existing language demographics, program model, parental support, and teacher preparation, among other factors.

PROGRAMMATIC GOALS. Dual language education varies widely in model implementation, school demographics, and philosophical positions. Consequently, the goals of a program normally reflect those individual and specific characteristics. The following list presents examples of dual language programmatic goals.

1. Students from both languages are integrated for at least 50 percent of the day.
2. Students stay in the program for at least six years.
3. A coordinator provides administrative and curricular support.
4. Funding (provide an amount) is allocated for the program each year.
5. The school library increases (provide a percentage) the number of bilingual and multicultural books each year.
6. Educators attend professional development in-services or conferences related to dual language education at least four times a year.
7. Teachers meet at least twice a week for planning and discussion.
8. Dual language parent meetings are convened once a month.

Explicit program goals, such as the ones outlined here, provide a more precise focus for implementation and evaluation criteria. Many dual language programs have no program evaluation procedure in place. Periodic reviews are a critical tool to reflect on the progress, successes, and challenges of the program. Such evaluations also provide checks and balances to ensure that the programmatic goals are being met (Did the school designate a program coordinator? Did the teachers attend professional development seminars?). The recommendation is that teachers themselves, in collaboration with parents and students, assess the extent to which program goals are being met. Other program goals may be added or changed each year, depending on needs or the yearly school goals. This process provides the forum for educators, parents, and students to examine and build on what has been accomplished and to reformulate areas that are problematic or not yet developed.

Program evaluation can take the form of a checklist accompanied by semester or yearly reports, which do not need to be lengthy or involved, but should include past accomplishments, future revisions, and improvement needs. Sometimes, evaluations are based on features outlined in the school improvement plan and take the form of a rubric. Figure 4.1 is a sample showing what a program evaluation may look like, what criteria it may include, and how it may be assessed. In this example, the criteria to be evaluated come directly from the program's goals and objectives. Rating methods can vary according to the needs and preferences of each school. The example provides a basic user-friendly rating system that

---

FIGURE 4.1 Yearly Program Evaluation

Has Each Programmatic Goal Been Implemented?

1—YES   2—SOMEWHAT   3—NO

Students

1	2	3	Students from both languages are integrated for at least 50% of the day.
1	2	3	Students stay in the program for at least four to six years.
1	2	3	Data are gathered on students' academic and language development and progress.
1	2	3	Support for struggling students is offered in the L1 and/or L2.
1	2	3	Additional support in L2 is provided to new students third grade and above.
1	2	3	Showcase students' academic and linguistic successes in the form of performances or exhibits.

Teachers

1	2	3	Dual language teachers participate in monthly meetings.
1	2	3	Teachers attend weekly dual language grade level meetings.
1	2	3	Teachers and other staff attend dual language and related staff developments.
1	2	3	Teachers new to the program are mentored and given additional staff development opportunities.

Curriculum

1	2	3	The dual language program is compatible with the school's existing programs.
1	2	3	The curriculum is learner-centered, literature-based, hands-on, culturally relevant, and integrated.
1	2	3	Teaching and learning is based on cooperative learning, thematic teaching, project approach, sheltered instruction, and hands-on approaches.
1	2	3	Teaching and learning focuses on language and literacy development, content area knowledge, critical thinking, and problem solving.
1	2	3	Authentic and performance-based assessment tools and techniques are used to evaluate students' linguistic and academic progress.

Parents and Community

1	2	3	Communication with parents regarding their children's progress is consistent.
1	2	3	Parents and community are invited to share their cultural and linguistic expertise with the school.
1	2	3	Parents attend monthly dual language meetings and receive a monthly dual language newsletter.
1	2	3	Parents participate in training to support children's learning and progress in the two languages at home.

Administration

1	2	3	A dual language coordinator provides administrative and curricular support.
1	2	3	Sufficient funding is allocated for the program.
1	2	3	The school library substantially increases the bilingual/multicultural collection.
1	2	3	Administrators attend professional development/professional conferences.
1	2	3	Time is allotted for teachers to dialog within the school and with colleagues in other dual language schools.

reflects the extent to which the program has implemented its goals and objectives each year. Although this evaluative form can be completed individually, it is much more valuable when each goal is discussed in a group and consensus is reached about the program's successful and problematic areas.

After teachers, administrators, and parents (and sometimes the students themselves) have evaluated each programmatic component, members of the dual language community should engage in reflective analysis of goals that have been partially implemented or not implemented at all, and how these will be addressed. Table 4.4 shows how problematic areas in program implementation can be identified, explained, and resolved. Understanding the source of problems or obstacles facilitates the discovery of potential solutions and actions to be taken. Evaluative processes such as these provide direct and continual analysis and reflection on the program's progress and needs. Data collection over a period of several years is recommended in order to more accurately determine program effectiveness and student achievement (Sugarman & Howard, 2001). Assessment tools that measure students' academic and linguistic achievement must also be part of program evaluation.

STUDENT OUTCOMES.   All dual language programs share the same three broad student learning goals: academic attainment, bilingual and biliterate proficiency, and cross-cultural competence. In addition to these goals, programs can also include more specific student objectives. Linguistic student outcomes are sometimes challenging because they tend to be too general. One such broad and common objective is "all students will become fully bilingual and biliterate." In some cases, students do not meet this linguistic and academic goal not because they do not possess the capacity, but because of extenuating factors such as length of time in the program, motivation to acquire the second language (sometimes related to compulsory or voluntary participation in the program), and program model (Baker, 2001). Dominant-language students who have no second language contact outside school, but who participate in total immersion (90–10 or 80–20) programs, will more likely attain higher levels of bilingualism and biliteracy than students in partial immersion (50–50) models (Lindholm-Leary, 2001; Thomas & Collier, 2002). Student linguistic outcomes ought to be considered in light of these factors.

The learning goals, objectives, or outcomes of any dual language program should be aligned with the district, state, and national academic standards. For example, district or state learning standards delineate what all students should know and be able to do academically. These are the same academic goals for dual language education, the only difference being the expectation that they will be achieved in two languages rather than one. In Box 4.2, a teacher describes the ways she and her dual language colleagues conceptualized and incorporated the district standards with the dual language learning goals and outcomes.

Student assessment in most schools is made up of mandated district and/or state standardized tests along with school and/or classroom assessments such as performance-based evaluation, authentic assessment, and teacher-generated tests. The increasing emphasis on standardized testing in most public schools places an undue burden on many students, particularly those from culturally and linguistically diverse backgrounds (Lessow-Hurley, 2000; Nieto, 2000). Because dual language programs, like most other exemplary forms of education, are developmental and constructivist in nature, standardized testing is often not as valid and reliable a measurement tool as it is perceived to be. However, high stakes such as student retention, loss of school funding, and threats to teacher or principal employment may create an inhospitable and difficult environment for dual language education. Most dual language programs cannot opt to be exempt from, or delay,

■ TABLE 4.4 | Problem-Solutions Sample Form

Specify each programmatic goal that has not been fully implemented or has not been implemented at all and indicate its rating (from the Yearly Program Evaluation) ✔ (somewhat) or ✘ (no). Identify obstacles or difficulties that prevent the goal from being accomplished and describe potential and doable solutions. Present an action plan and a timeline to address the implementation of the goal.

Goal	Problem	Solutions	Action	Timeline
Students ✘ Support for struggling students is offered in L1/L2.	Lack of support staff Funding shortage	Hire more teacher assistants Train parent volunteers Organize cross-age tutoring	Modify budget to hire 1 TA During monthly meetings, recruit and train parents	1 year 2 months
Teachers ✔ New teachers are mentored and given additional staff development.	No mentoring program Lack of time	Develop mentoring program Provide time in the schedule for mentorship	Establish a buddy system Assign a master teacher or coordinator to mentorship	1 month ongoing
Curriculum ✔ Authentic/performance assessment is used to evaluate learner's linguistic and academic progress.	Lack of expertise in alternative assessment	Staff development Monitor and support use of alternative assessment	Organize staff development Create an assessment team	1 year and ongoing
Parents/Community ✘ Parents attend monthly meetings and receive monthly newsletter.	Very few parents attend the parent meetings Newsletter is not sent out consistently	Increase interest in and access to parent meetings Incorporate dual language news in the school newsletter	Alternate day and night meetings and present fun and relevant topics Dual language section	2 months and ongoing
Administration ✔ Sufficient funding is allocated for the program.	Budget cuts Funds are spent on other programs	Allocate a percentage of the budget to dual language Seek grants	Identify 1 or 2 priorities per year and fund those	1 year

69

Aligning the District Standards to the Dual Language Learning Goals

BOX 4.2

At this neighborhood school, even though all the teachers follow the district goals and standards in their instructional planning, in the second year of implementation they realized that they were not incorporating the second language and culture dimensions of the dual language program into their lesson plans. While the lesson plans reflected the curricular activities and the different language groupings for dual language, the learning goals and standards reflected only native language objectives, and no cultural elements. During the dual language teachers' weekly meetings and with the help of the coordinator, they began to discuss ways to align the district's goals and standards with the dual language curriculum, learning objectives, and assessment. The teachers decided to add a second language development component to the lesson plans based on the district's ESL goals and standards and use the same criteria for the Spanish as a second language goals and standards. In addition, multicultural learning goals and standards were included based on the district's foreign language standards' section on culture. The lesson plans and instructional approaches became more aligned with the dual language program goals and objectives. Going through this process helped the teachers become more focused on students' learning outcomes and their own curricular activities and assessment.

district or state mandated standardized testing; therefore, testing issues should be clearly addressed within the program.

School or classroom performance evaluations are also a necessary and much more valuable tool than standardized testing. Teacher-generated, authentic and performance-based assessment provides ongoing information about each student's progress and needs. In addition, this kind of student assessment data helps shape the curriculum by guiding the teacher's instructional content and selection of teaching practices (Hurley & Tinajero, 2001). A more detailed discussion of assessment procedures and techniques is presented in Chapter 5.

Program Description

Outlining the program in the form of a project proposal or as part of the school improvement plan helps greatly in conceptualizing the program's timeline, expectations, needs, benchmarks, and outcomes. Many U.S. schools are required to develop a school improvement plan (SIP) each year. This document, usually created with the input of teachers and parents, identifies the school's top two or three educational priorities and describes how they will be addressed in terms of professional development, instructional designs and programs, student assessment and evaluation, and funding projections and commitments for the coming year. Including the dual language program in the SIP situates it in a formal document that addresses essential program features, curricular and professional needs, and parent and community participation.

PROGRAM MODEL.   The program description should articulate whether the program will be a partial immersion 50–50 model or a total immersion 80–20 or 90–10 model, and it should provide a rationale for the selected model supported by research data and/or school background information. A description of whether the program will be implemented school-wide or by adding one grade level at a time will facilitate the plan of implementation. Also, providing a projection about the grade level the program is intended to reach is critical for long-term planning. Finally, the program description should state at what grade level or levels the program will initially begin.

SCHOOL-WIDE OR STRAND.   The dual language program should clearly articulate whether it will be offered school-wide or be a strand within the school. By offering a school-wide dual language program, the school commits to a comprehensive and collective educational plan that incorporates all teachers, all staff, all students, and all parents. School-wide programs tend to be a better option for three key reasons. First, the entire school community collectively strives to reach the same goals and objectives. Because everyone—from the office staff to the physical education teacher—is on board, a sense of unity and common understanding is created. Second, the tracking and segregation that is inherent in implementing a strand within a school is not present if the program is school-wide. Third, attrition can be problematic for a dual language strand within a school because it is usually not beneficial for students beyond second grade to be accepted into the program, especially if they are native English speakers.

Although school-wide implementation is recommended, sometimes other factors may influence the decision to opt for a dual language strand within the school. A dual language strand can be just as effective as a school-wide program provided certain potential problems are addressed, such as attrition and declining numbers of students after several years, incompatibility or competition for resources with other school programs, and misunderstandings or hostility from non-dual-language participants, including students, teachers, and parents.

CLASSROOM ORGANIZATION.   Decisions about how classrooms are organized depend on teacher availability, expertise, and/or preferences. The two most common arrangements are team-teaching and self-contained classrooms. The program description should state whether the program will be self-contained or team-taught, or a combination of the two. Bilingual teachers have the option of doing self-contained or team-teaching, while monolingual teachers are able to do team-teaching exclusively. Sometimes the option of doing self-contained or team-teaching is presented to bilingual teachers. In Box 4.3, a bilingual teacher reflects on her experiences in teaching under both configurations. Table 4.5 outlines the different components of each classroom arrangement.

ADDITIONAL PROGRAM CONSIDERATIONS

Figure 4.2 poses a number of questions to be considered in the developing stages of program implementation. These are some of the administrative, staff, curricular, and parent and community issues most frequently brought up by educators, parents, and supervisors in schools. Each of these questions, except for the curricular considerations, which are discussed in Chapter 5, is addressed in the following section.

Administrative Considerations

ADMISSION PROCESS.   Admission procedures fall under two categories: new students who are registering in the school for the first time, and existing students who want to participate in the school's dual language program. For students new to the school, dual language programs commonly rely on two admission procedures: a selective or an open admissions process. In the case of selective admissions, usually in private or magnet public schools, selection may be based on a

To Team-Teach or Not to Team-Teach? That Is the Question

Lil began her dual language teaching experience with a partner, whom she viewed as her mentor in teaching terms (since she was a brand new teacher). Lil was also somewhat of a mentor in terms of bilingual education and second language acquisition pedagogy and theory (since she had a master's degree in bilingual education and her partner had no background in the field). Her second team partner was a master teacher with years of experience and expertise and a very open mind who became a staunch supporter of dual language education. They worked well together and learned much from each other. Lil feels that she has been fortunate in her experiences with her two team partners. They complemented each other well, held similar philosophical views on teaching and learning and had similar teaching styles, and were open to one another's ideas.

Due to changes in staff and student enrollment, Lil also taught as a self-contained teacher for several years. Although she enjoyed having her own classroom and having the flexibility to go at her own pace (and not have to be accountable to a partner), she felt that having to cover the curriculum in the two languages and do two language arts lessons each day with thirty-two students and a one-hour-a-day teacher assistant was difficult.

In Lil's eleven years of teaching in dual language programs, she taught both as a team-teacher and a self-contained teacher. Which does she prefer? Lil thinks the answer depends on many factors, one of which is whether one likes to work collaboratively or alone. Another is whether you and your partner get along at a personal level and see eye-to-eye at an educational and philosophical level. For Lil, collaborating with other teachers is very rewarding because she learns from them by seeing other ways of doing things. She also believes that working with others makes life easier because you don't have to find solutions or resources by yourself. On the other hand, with the right conditions (small class size and a teacher assistant), self-contained teaching can also be very gratifying: there is more flexibility; you are responsible for only one classroom; and you can adjust the pace to your students more easily.

variety of criteria, such as academic performance, native language, age, ethnicity, and economic background. Because maintaining a balanced representation of the two languages and cultures is essential for the program, language and ethnicity quotas are sometimes established. In addition, many programs do not admit new students beyond second or third grade unless they can demonstrate sufficient proficiency in the two languages. Other options for admissions are a lottery system and a first-come, first-served basis (Cloud, Genesee & Hamayan, 2000). When the dual language program is a strand within the school, existing students are usually included based on their desire to be in the program. Again, certain restrictions may influence decisions to accept or reject students, such as maintaining a language balance or attempting to increase particular cultural groups, such as African American or Asian students.

Independent of whether the admissions process is selective or open, many schools ask parents to sign a letter of commitment. This document is, of course, not legally binding, but it represents a formal agreement between parents and the school committing to work collaboratively by providing the necessary support for children to meet the dual language program goals and objectives. Figure 4.3 describes some of the components that may be included in a letter of commitment. Box 4.4 presents a sample letter of commitment.

PLACEMENT PROCEDURES.   Regardless of whether the program is schoolwide or a strand within the school, and whether the school has an open or selective admissions policy, a student placement system is needed once students have been accepted into the program, particularly if the school has multiple classrooms at each grade level. The prerequisite to establish and maintain a balanced repre-

■ TABLE 4.5 | Team-Teaching versus Self-Contained

Self-Contained	Team-Teaching
One bilingual teacher provides instruction in both languages.	Two teachers, a minority language and a majority language teacher, provide instruction in one language.
One mixed-language class stays with one bilingual teacher.	Two mixed-language classes alternate between the two teachers.
The two languages are alternated by subject, time, or day within the classroom.	The two languages are alternated by classroom, time, day, teacher, or subject between the two teachers.
If literacy instruction is in the native language, the teacher alternates between the two literacy language groups by day, time, or week.	If literacy instruction is in the native language, the students are grouped by language and receive instruction from the corresponding language teacher daily.
Students from both language groups are integrated for content areas and receive instruction in both languages in all subjects.	Students from both language groups are integrated for content areas and receive instruction in both languages in all subjects from each language teacher.
Instructional materials are in equivalent amounts in the two languages within the classroom.	When there are two classrooms, the instructional materials are in only one language in each classroom.

sentation of the two languages not only in the program but also in each classroom requires careful attention to students' language proficiencies and classrooms assignments.

A common placement tool for English-language learners in schools that provide instruction for non-English speakers is the home language survey. This questionnaire is required by federal mandate and consists of a few questions about language(s) spoken at home. It is completed by parents when registering their children in school. When parents indicate that a language other than English is used in the home, students are referred for further language evaluation to determine English and native language proficiency levels. In some states, when a language other than English is identified in the home language survey, the student is automatically tested for English-language proficiency. Although not always reliable (sometimes parents are reluctant to identify their children as English-language learners, or they simply do not want their children to receive bilingual or ESL instruction), home language surveys are a valuable tool to identify nonnative English-language students.

Merely identifying whether a child speaks a language other than English at home is not enough to determine first and second language proficiency levels. The optimal way to do so is for trained office staff or the program coordinator to screen incoming students' language levels by holding an informal conversation with them in the two languages and filling out a short checklist. Figure 4.4 is a

---

FIGURE 4.2 Questions to Consider before Implementation

Administrative Questions
- How will students be admitted into the program?
- How will student placement be managed and carried out?
- Who will coordinate the program and provide support to the teachers, parents, and students?
- How much time will the coordinator devote to the program?
- How much funding will be available for program implementation?
- How will the program be evaluated, how often, and by whom?

Staff Questions
- How will teachers and teacher assistants be trained on issues related to dual language education?
- How often will follow-up teacher staff development be scheduled?
- In what capacity will teacher assistants support the program?
- How often will teachers have time for curriculum planning and ordering instructional materials?

Curriculum Questions
- In what language will students receive formal initial literacy instruction?
- When will formal literacy instruction in the second language be introduced?
- How will the two languages be separated?
- How will multicultural curriculum be integrated in the program?
- In what language will homework be assigned?
- What assessment measures will be used for evaluating second language acquisition?

Parent and Community Questions
- How will parents be involved in the planning of the program?
- How will parents be consulted and informed about the progress of the program?
- How will parents be involved in the program?
- What support will parents receive in regard to their children's second language acquisition?
- How will the program be promoted in the community?

---

sample checklist that can be used in a Spanish-English dual language program (and can easily be adapted by changing the *S* for *Spanish* to any other language) to informally document a child's approximate language proficiencies in both languages. The adult can begin asking questions or conversing in the student's assumed second language and attend to the student's comfort level based on the answers or the student's body language. The adult can also alternate languages for each question or request, but should not repeat questions in each language.

It might be a straightforward undertaking to determine many students' first and second language proficiency levels. Recent arrivals from other countries probably possess little or no English competency. However, across-the-board assumptions should not be made, since many immigrant children receive English instruction in their home countries. Other students, like those who are at different stages of second language development, require a more in-depth assessment. For these students, language proficiencies may be determined in the classroom after they are in the program for a few weeks, if possible, since, for some students,

---

FIGURE 4.3 Letter of Commitment: Some Suggestions for Inclusion

School Commitments
- Include the dual language vision/mission or philosophy statement
- Clarify the program model, goals, features, and expectations
- Identify the target language and the amount of exposure to each language

Parent Commitments
Parents agree to
- Keep their child in the program for six years
- Maintain a high attendance rate and reduce absenteeism
- Support the continued development of the native language at home
- Support their child's academic, linguistic, and sociocultural development
- Attend monthly dual language parent meetings
- Become involved in the classroom/school functions and events
- Advocate for and support the program

---

being evaluated before establishing a sense of security is often traumatic and may produce unreliable results (Fisher, Lapp, Flood & Suarez, 2001; Peregoy & Boyle, 2001).

Once language proficiency levels have been determined, students can be placed in classrooms according to program needs for maintaining balanced linguistic, gender, and/or ethnic representation. In addition to facilitating student classroom placement, determining students' proficiency levels in each language provides preliminary information for literacy instructional placement, if the literacy instruction is conducted in the native language, or for language grouping within the classroom, such as distribution of students in cooperative groups.

ADMINISTRATIVE SUPPORT. Who makes up the administrative cluster varies widely from school to school. In site-based managed schools, the entire teaching staff is often involved in the decision-making process and is collectively responsible for the effective implementation of educational programs. In other schools, the administrative structure is more traditional, usually composed of the principal, assistant principal, and assigned or elected educators from the school community. Whether a school has an inclusive or selective administrative body, those who have authority and influence over school policy, curricular and funding decisions not only must be well versed in dual language education but must also be staunch supporters and advocates of the program (Castro Feinberg, 2002).

The principal plays a key role by setting the tone for the students, educators, and parents. The convictions and enthusiasm that principals show toward any school program are generally quite evident by the attention they pour into it, often in the form of eager promotion of teacher professional development, significant allocation of funding, and time spent in the development and improvement of the program (Castro Feinberg, 1999). When a program is favored and actively promoted by the principal, a clear message is sent to the entire learning community, including those who may have ambivalent or resistant positions toward it.

One way principals demonstrate their commitment to dual language is to assign a program coordinator or facilitator to oversee the effective implementation of the program and to provide support to teachers, parents, and students. Lindholm-Leary (2001) differentiated between administrative support, normally by the principal who acts as an advocate and guardian of the program, and instructional leadership by the assistant principal or coordinator who facilitates and

Sample Letter of Commitment

BOX
4.4

Parent Letter of Commitment and Consent

I _____ would like my child _____ to
     Parent or Guardian Name   *Child's Name*

participate in the Dual Language Program at this school.

I have been informed about the Dual Language Program's language, academic, and cultural goals, as well as its curriculum, instructional, and assessment approaches. I understand the guidelines and the conditions necessary for the successful participation of my child in the program. I agree to support my child and the program by committing to the following criteria:

1. My child will participate in the program for at least six years.
2. My child will be in a classroom that has a balanced number of English-dominant children and Spanish-dominant [*or another language*] children.
3. In the 90–10 or 80–20 dual language model, my child will initially have the majority of the instruction in Spanish [*or another language*], gradually increasing the amount of English each year until both are used equally for instruction.
4. In the 50–50 dual language model, my child will receive instruction in both languages for equal amounts of time.
5. My child will learn how to read and write in the native language [*or Spanish, Navajo, etc.*] first and then learn to read and write in the second language [*or English*].
6. My child will continue to learn and develop academically, socially, and culturally in his/her first language through the duration of the program.
7. My child will continue to learn and develop academically, socially, and culturally in his/her second language through the duration of the program.
8. My child will develop bilingual (understanding and speaking) and biliterate (reading and writing) competencies in the two languages.
9. My child will maintain a consistent attendance record. I will inform the school of his/her absences due to illness or family emergencies. I understand that my child may be withdrawn from the program due to excessive absences.
10. I will commit to attend the monthly Dual Language Program parent meetings, participate in Dual Language Program events, and support the program and classroom teachers.

_____   _____
     Parent or Guardian Signature   *Date*

_____   _____
     Home Address   *Telephone Number*

guides instructional practices, program organization, and resource selections. Dual language education is a complex and sometimes fluctuating undertaking that requires a solid but flexible organizational structure, knowledgeable and competent leadership, and continual assistance and evaluation. A dual language coordinator can provide the structural supports needed to effectively implement the program. Figure 4.5 summarizes the multiple and vital roles of a dual language program coordinator or facilitator.

FUNDING SOURCES.   A detailed account of the allocation and sources of funding for the program helps in determining an adequate expenditure plan, includ-

FIGURE **4.4** Informal Language Proficiency Level Checklist

Name _____ Grade _____ Second Language _____

Receptive Language (English *E* and Spanish *S*)   **E**   **S**
- Understands and responds to commands or questions   ☐   ☐
- Responds to commands or questions with gestures   ☐   ☐
- Responds to commands or questions with words/phrases   ☐   ☐

Productive Language (English *E* and Spanish *S*)   **E**   **S**
- Uses one word utterances   ☐   ☐
- Uses phrases with some errors   ☐   ☐
- Uses phrases with no errors   ☐   ☐
- Engages in extended conversation   ☐   ☐

Mark approximate language level on the bilingual continuum

SLM   **SLD**   **BB**   **ELD**   **ELM**

SLM Spanish Language Monolingual   **ELM** English Language Monolingual
SLD Spanish Language Dominant   **ELD** English Language Dominant
BB Balanced Bilingual

- Cannot determine at this time

ing provisions for essentials, such as funds for instructional materials, teacher preparation and development, and teacher stipends for planning. When possible, funds should be set aside for hiring teacher assistants and providing stipends to parent volunteers, as well as for field trips and guest speakers. Additional funds should be earmarked for cultural educational experiences, such as artists in residence, children's book authors, cultural ensembles, and other enriching artistic and cultural resources that support the academic, linguistic, and cultural goals of the program.

To search for large school initiative funding, a good starting place is to periodically visit the Office of English Language Acquisition (OELA) at http://www.ed.gov/offices/OELA (formerly the Office of Bilingual Education and Minority Languages Affairs or OBEMLA) and the U.S. Department of Education's Office of Grants and Contracts at http://ed.gov/offices/OCFO/gcsindex.html for information on federal funding and application information. OELA offers funding through Title III (formerly Title VII) for various types of programs that service language minority students, such as the Emergency Immigrant Education Program, Program Development and Implementation Grants, Training for All Teachers, the Comprehensive School Grants (which in 2001 offered the Dual Language Special Competition), and Foreign Language Assistance Grants. The Department of Education administers programs and initiatives that provide funding opportunities for several educational areas, issues, and challenges. Particular emphasis is now given to reading, accountability, standards, and assessment, which are key components of the current national education plan, the No Child Left Behind Act.

Other sources for funding include the Disney Learning Partnership (http://disneylearning.org,) a foundation interested in individual teacher recognition and

FIGURE 4.5 Dual Language Program Coordinator Responsibilities

The Program Coordinator	
■ Helps develop the dual language school handbook ■ Searches for quality instructional materials ■ Promotes the program in educational forums ■ Informs the community about the program ■ Seeks outside funding and grants ■ Coordinates program evaluation and progress ■ Oversees the implementation of the program ■ Becomes a school liaison for visitors and prospective students and parents	**FOR THE PROGRAM**
■ Assists teachers with scheduling ■ Facilitates other school or classroom visitations ■ Informs teachers of available staff developments ■ Provides training on dual language related issues ■ Presents information on best practices for instruction ■ Demonstrates appropriate instructional approaches ■ Organizes monthly dual language teacher meetings ■ Coordinates initial student assessment and placement ■ Provides information and recommendations on available quality instructional materials	**FOR THE TEACHERS**
■ Provides instructional support ■ Helps assess students' progress or needs ■ Offers tutoring services	**FOR THE STUDENTS**
■ Organizes parent meetings ■ Provides information and program support ■ Addresses parent questions and concerns ■ Coordinates second language parent classes ■ Offers training for parent volunteers working in the classroom	**FOR THE PARENTS**

professional development, collaborative school-wide learning initiatives, and strengthened parent-teacher connections. The Pew Charitable Trusts (http://pewtrusts.com) fund K–12 programs that aim to raise the performance of students at all levels of education, especially their abilities to acquire the literacies they need to participate in an increasingly complex society. Junior Great Books and Read Aloud (http://gbf@greatbooks.org) is a program of children's classics, folk and fairy tales, and modern short stories from cultures around the world designed to encourage students from second through twelfth grade to enjoy reading. The grant provides funding for teachers to increase their library collections. Creative Learning Communities (http://disney.go.com/disneylearning/clc/) is a philanthropic initiative of the Walt Disney Company that awards grants to K–5 schools or consortiums to design and implement creative teaching strategies and enriching learning environments.

Given the limited resources that most schools have available to them, a major concern is often the cost of implementing a dual language program. The cost is always relative and dependent on many factors. For instance, if the school and classroom libraries are already well-stocked with quality children's books in both languages, less money may be needed to be allocated for this objective. If the school previously allocated funds for professional development, there is no need to spend additional money, but simply to shift the focus of the training. Thus, the amount of money necessary to implement a dual language program depends on the existing resources of the school (Soltero, 2002). Exemplary schools already allot a large percentage of their budgets to those aspects that support students' high academic, linguistic, and sociocultural attainments, such as investments in smaller class size, an abundance of children's books and quality instructional materials, ongoing professional development for teachers, and supplementary support programs for students and parents, among other features. The resource investments for dual language programs require no more and no less than what any good school that supports high-quality, effective educational programs expects to spend.

Staff Considerations

PROFESSIONAL DEVELOPMENT AND TEACHER PREPARATION. Montague (1997) asserts that the most important aspect of any program is teacher preparation related to pedagogical and theoretical constructs of bilingualism and second language acquisition. Professional development for new dual language teachers should extend beyond programmatic organizational features to include first and second language acquisition theory and pedagogy, first and second language literacy development and instructional practices, multicultural curricular considerations, transactional whole-to-part teaching methods, and authentic assessment techniques.

Most school districts offer professional development in-services that cover many topics pertinent to dual language education, such as literacy and language development, as well as workshops in technology or music, for example. Although these do not specifically address dual language, they are relevant to the program as a whole. School districts, local educational agencies, or consultants who specialize in immersion education may offer educational in-services that focus exclusively on dual language education. Regional and national conferences provide excellent opportunities to acquire the most current information and research data on dual language and related fields (see Appendix C for an extensive listing of educational conferences and seminars). Educators within the school with backgrounds in ESL, bilingual, and/or foreign language education can also share their expertise with their peers and mentor colleagues who are new to the discipline or the program. Internal workshops conducted by resident experienced practitioners tap into the existing resources of the school. Appendix B provides an extensive annotated listing of professional videos that can be used for teacher training and parent informational meetings.

Participation in professional development seminars and education conferences should be ongoing for all those involved in the implementation of dual language programs. Some districts require all their bilingual and ESL teachers to attend at least four professional development conferences a year. Some schools have extended this requirement to include all teachers in dual language programs, both bilingual and general program teachers. Maintaining an effective program means keeping abreast of current research, new theoretical constructs, and innovative instructional approaches. Similarly, a very powerful and effective way to gain experience and develop extended understandings about dual language instruction is to visit existing immersion programs and classrooms. Observing dual language classrooms and talking with experienced teachers provides valuable insights into program application and theoretical foundations. By establishing networks with other dual language schools and programs, educators and parents create a necessary system of support and collaboration.

Teacher assistants should be included in all professional development in-services and should be given opportunities to attend education conferences. The reasons are twofold. First, teacher assistants who are involved in the dual language program are expected to provide considerable support to the teacher and students. Because dual language education requires a good deal of short- and long-term organization and planning, the role of the teacher assistant becomes more involved in the instructional and managerial aspects of the program within the classroom. Thus, teacher assistants should have ample knowledge of dual language education, its philosophical base, and its theoretical and pedagogical foundations (Lessow-Hurley, 2000). Secondly, teacher assistants are potential future teachers. The hands-on classroom practice, together with professional development and conference experiences, offer teacher assistants exceptional opportunities for professional growth.

Teachers, support staff, and administrators who have a solid understanding of the program's philosophy and commitment to its goals are fundamental to the effectiveness of dual language education (Cloud, Genesee, & Hamayan, 2000). Knowledge of issues related to second language acquisition, the use of sheltered instruction and unbiased assessment, and the theoretical and philosophical constructs of dual language education provide the basis for implementation.

CURRICULUM AND ORGANIZATION PLANNING.   Providing time for teachers to plan and discuss organization and curricular issues is of paramount importance. In the preparation stages and after becoming well-informed about dual language education, teachers should have time to meet periodically to discuss daily schedules, language distribution, student grouping, yearly and monthly curricular calendars, parent meetings or conferences, assessment tools and the schedule of evaluations, and teacher planning times. At this time, teachers can also conduct an inventory of existing instructional materials to determine what is needed in the coming years.

The summer prior to the inception of a program is a good time to provide teachers with time to discuss and plan these issues. Once the program is in progress, teachers should have time to continue to plan and discuss issues that may arise. Normally, teachers have at least two or three planning periods a week to meet, discuss, and plan. The program coordinator can facilitate dual language program teacher meetings, either monthly or quarterly, to discuss pressing issues, successes, challenges, and possible solutions or changes.

THE OVERALL SCHOOL COMMUNITY.   A frequently overlooked but essential issue in the initial stages of planning and implementation is the inclusion of *all* teachers and staff in the early information sessions and training seminars. That is, teachers who are not in the dual language program but who will eventually be part of it, as well as teachers and other school staff who may never be part of the program directly (such as the physical education teacher or the librarian), should be informed and have a solid understanding of all the programs in the school, including dual language education. This becomes a critical aspect of effective implementation, since often only those immediately and directly involved in the program are included, usually preK to first-grade teachers. Omitting the rest of the staff may lead to the spread of misinformation and inaccurate views about dual language. In extreme cases, misinterpretations that are based on a lack of information or misunderstandings may result in a slow corrosion of the intentions of the program (Castro Feinberg, 1999). Such has been the case in several schools, where misinformation led teachers and parents to boycott and undermine the program. The doubts and concerns of all teachers should be immediately and openly addressed, especially issues of how the new dual language program will affect their teaching conditions.

INFORMATION DISSEMINATION.   Creating a dual language program newsletter or including a dual language column in the existing school bulletin are good ways to transmit information, updates, and events related to dual language. District and local agencies can also provide an excellent forum for disseminating news and information about the school and the dual language program. Those schools that want or need to recruit students from other schools or areas can also showcase the program's innovative features in local newspapers, television, or radio broadcasts. Special school events, such as assemblies or award ceremonies, can be used to provide information to parents and the community.

PROMOTING THE PROGRAM.   Advertising and marketing the school's dual language program can involve the dissemination techniques discussed above. Also effective is a dual language education brochure or information sheet that provides a program description, highlights accomplishments, and presents future plans. A dual language program section on the school Web site can offer all the information described above and is simple to maintain and update. Any partnerships with universities and businesses that a school has can provide a useful medium for program promotion as well. In particular, collaborations with institutions of higher education and other research centers may very likely augment the program's prestige and reputation in the eyes of the community and potential future students.

SUMMARY

Decisions on educational policies, curricular choices, classroom organization, assessment practices, and parental involvement must always be made in light of the specific needs and characteristics of each school community. This chapter presents a number of possibilities to be considered in the planning stages of creating and implementing a dual language program. It is important to note that the suggestions described here are neither predetermined nor finite. These recommendations and ideas are based on current research on dual language and bilingual education, and they are meant to be used as guidelines for implementation. The preliminary gathering of information on dual language and the creation of a written educational plan that includes curricular, evaluative, administrative, staff, and parent considerations provide the theoretical and pedagogical foundations for a sound dual language program. Aside from the basic factors presented in this chapter, other issues may be considered, depending on the individual needs or goals of the school.

DISCUSSION QUESTIONS

1. If you were interested in starting a dual language program in your school, how would you go about proposing it to your peers, principal, and parents? What rationale and arguments would you use to persuade them to consider implementing the program? What key elements would you tell them should be included in the planning phase? What would the first year of implementation look like?

2. If you and a group of teachers, parents, and administrators were planning to implement a dual language program in your school, what would your program's vision and mission statements include? What fundamental concepts or ideas would the vision and mission incorporate? With a group of your peers, write the vision and mission statements for your ideal dual language program. Brainstorm concepts related to culturally and linguistically responsive education, multicultural and pluralistic perspectives, additive bilingualism, and other issues associated with enriched education.

3. How would you go about determining whether your school should implement a partial immersion (50–50) dual language model or a total immersion (80–20 or 90–10) dual language model? What would be some key considerations in selecting a model?

4. What do you think is more effective: a school-wide dual language program, or a dual language strand within a school? Examine the pros and cons of implementing each.

FIELD-BASED  INQUIRY

1. Visit a school that implements a total immersion (90–10 or 80–20) dual language model and a school that implements a partial immersion (50–50) dual language model. Observe the differences and similarities of the models. Reflect upon the pros and cons of each model. Consider each school's decision to implement a partial or a total immersion program.

2. Interview three or four dual language teachers, and inquire about their perceptions of the program. How

has the program changed or not changed their teaching styles and their curriculum? What do they find most challenging and most rewarding about the program? What are some issues that have not been resolved in the implementation of the program in their school?

FURTHER  READING

Christian, D. (1994). *Two-way bilingual education: Students learning through two languages.* Educational Practice Report No. 12. Washington, DC and Santa Cruz, CA: National Center for Research on Cultural Diversity and Second Language Learning.

Christian, D., Howard, E. R., & Loeb, M. I. (2000). Bilingualism for all: Two-way immersion education in the United States. In *Theory into Practice.* Columbus, OH: Ohio State University.

Cloud, N., Genesee, E., & Hamayan, E. (2000). *Dual language instruction. A handbook for enriched education.* Boston: Heinle & Heinle.

Genesee, F. (1999). *Program alternatives for linguistically diverse students.* Educational Practice Report No.1. Washington, DC and Santa Cruz, CA: Center for Research on Education, Diversity and Excellence.

Lindholm-Leary, K. (2000). *Biliteracy for a global society: An idea book on dual language education.* Washington, DC: The George Washington University.

Montague, N. (1997). Critical components for dual language programs. *Bilingual Research Journal,* (21) 4, 334–342.

5 Dual Language into Practice

The basis for the success of language minority students in two-way bilingual programs might be stated very simply: these students are being treated the same as their more socially prestigious English dominant counterparts. Their language and culture are respected, bilingualism is considered an attainable and desirable goal, the most promising instructional methods are used, and high academic standards are set for them.

Dicker (1996), p. 133

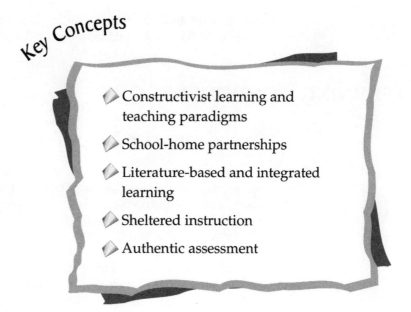

Key Concepts

- ◆ Constructivist learning and teaching paradigms
- ◆ School-home partnerships
- ◆ Literature-based and integrated learning
- ◆ Sheltered instruction
- ◆ Authentic assessment

The kinds of instructional strategies that dual language teachers use and the types of learning activities in which dual language students are engaged underlie the success of all dual language programs. Teaching practices that encourage the active participation of all students in the learning process while they interact in meaningful and purposeful communication provides the optimal forum for the development of the three broad dual language learning goals: bilingual/biliterate, academic, and sociocultural competencies. Figure 5.1 represents a

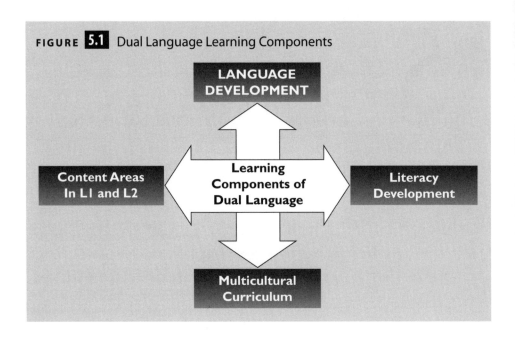

FIGURE **5.1** Dual Language Learning Components

scheme of the basic learning elements found in effective dual language instruction. Each will be addressed in more detail in the following sections.

LEARNING COMPONENTS

Second Language Development

A component that is often, but not always, included in dual language is specialized second language instruction. For part of the day or week, minority language students receive instruction in ESL while majority language students receive instruction in their second language. If the program is Spanish-English, then the target language instruction is referred to as Spanish as a second language (SSL). The same is true for any other minority language, such as Korean as a second language (KSL) or Navajo as a second language (NSL). Although dual language students acquire most of their second language competencies by being integrated while they engage in content learning and social interaction, in some programs students also receive special second language instruction (Zucker, 1995). Through this specialized second language learning time, students are grouped homogeneously by language and receive instruction for short periods (fifteen or twenty minutes) every day or for longer periods (forty-five minutes) two or three times a week, depending on the grade level and the program model.

As discussed in Chapter 1, second language development is best accomplished in content learning, rather than as a discreet language subject. Thus, second language instruction normally emphasizes vocabulary and other linguistic aspects related to the academic content and topics being covered while students are integrated in the mixed language groups. This connection between the language and the academic content provides optimal comprehensible input (Krashen, 1981) because students are actively engaged in acquiring the vocabulary, grammatical structures, and phonologies of the second language by understanding concepts, developing ideas, and learning skills in both languages. Because students are already familiar with the content, acquisition of the second language is facilitated (Ovando & Collier, 1998). This focus on second language instruction is very beneficial for students' second language development because teachers can address specific language objectives and attend to students' errors in the context of meaningful and relevant curricula. In addition, ESL or SSL (or other minority language) can serve as both preview and review of vocabulary and content related to the academic subjects being studied. Thus, this can provide extended scaffolds for students' academic and linguistic development in both languages. In Box 5.1, a second grade teacher explains how he organizes Korean as a second language for his dominant English-speaking students and how he aligns second language instruction with content area learning.

Literacy Development

In dual language education, biliteracy development must be viewed as a critical foundation for students' academic success. Thus, attaining a strong foundation in reading and writing in the first and second language must take center stage for students who will need high levels of literacy to engage in increasingly abstract and context-reduced curriculum. Researchers and educators concur with the notion that a well-developed native oral language correlates to higher reading achievement in both the native language and the second language (Lindholm-Leary, 2001). Hence, students' oral language development in the native and second languages must be continually enhanced and cultivated in both social and academic contexts to provide the foundation for biliteracy.

BOX 5.1

SSL in Second Grade

Twelve of Alexis' twenty-eight students are English dominant speakers with varying degrees of Korean language proficiency, from no knowledge of Korean to high intermediate Korean proficiency. Seven of them have been in dual language since kindergarten, three since first grade, and two are new to the program. Alexis creates an integrated and multileveled Korean as a second language (KSL) curriculum for his students and plans activities that address students' varied levels of second language proficiency and literacy skills, as well as different learning styles and personalities. Some of his students are painfully shy, while others are rowdy extroverts, so Alexis creates ways for all students to participate in forms that are most comfortable for them, including kinesthetic, oral, and visual. He uses total physical response (TPR), dramatizations, and role-playing extensively (kinesthetic). He also uses many visual aids such as posters, transparencies, realia (concrete objects and artifacts), videos, picture books, and photographs (visual), accompanied by classroom discussions and other oral language experiences like listening to audio tapes and computer programs (oral).

Alexis focuses his KSL lessons on vocabulary building and sentence structure related to the theme and topics of study. For example, during a theme on *telling time around the world*, Alexis has integrated math and science concepts, as well as various ways of telling time, using Eric Carle's *The Grouchy Ladybug* (available in English and Korean). Alexis involves students in dramatizations of the story, creation of their own time stories based on the book, building a word wall with related math and science vocabulary, and using graphic organizers, all in Korean. Another activity that students particularly enjoy is creating a Korean version of the rhyme "Hickory, Dickory, Dock." Students work in cooperative learning groups with the help of their cross-age buddies (from seventh grade) to create a Korean version of this familiar nursery rhyme. Alexis thinks that multiple, varied, and multileveled experiences to develop the second language address all students' linguistic, academic, and affective needs.

Whether students are in total or partial immersion, and independent of their primary language competencies, minority language students always receive initial literacy instruction in their native language. For majority language students, decisions on the language of initial literacy instruction depend on the program model as well as the students' level of native language and literacy competencies. For majority language students who are in total immersion programs and come to school with a well-developed literacy foundation in the first language, initial literacy is usually in their second language. However, for majority language students who are still developing language and literacy competencies in their primary language, initial literacy instruction should be in English. Unless the learners are balanced bilinguals (children who have high levels of competencies in both languages), simultaneous initial literacy development is not recommended. Dual language and bilingual education researchers and practitioners agree that second language literacy acquisition should be introduced in third or fourth grade (Lindholm-Leary, 2000; Martínez & Moore-O'Brien, 1993). However, dual language learners should be exposed to second language literacy from preK on in the form of classroom and environmental print and children's books.

Content Areas

In dual language education, students develop content knowledge at the same time they develop first and second language skills. Students initially learn the core curricular subject matter (math, social studies, science) and secondary curricular areas (fine arts, technology, physical education) in the minority language in total immersion programs, and in both languages in partial immersion programs. Occasionally, programs decide to conduct the instruction of one content area in one language and another content area in the second language. When one subject is presented in only one language, particularly in 50–50 programs, teachers should make certain that students who are not proficient in that language are receiving enough comprehensible input to learn and understand the concepts and the language of instruction (Krashen, 1982).

Although students may be learning the subject matter in two languages, the curricular content is never translated or repeated in both languages. Rather, the curriculum is conducted in a spiral approach by building on what was previously learned in either language. For instance, if students are engaged in learning about the water cycle, one day they are learning about evaporation in one language, and the next day they are learning about condensation in the other language, and so on. Figure 5.2 illustrates how the curriculum is covered by building on what has been learned earlier in both languages without using them simultaneously.

Multicultural Curriculum

A major focus of dual language education is the development of positive intersocial and intercultural relationships between the members of the two language groups, including parents, students, and teachers. Thus, raising awareness of and appreciation for the complex social, historical, cultural, and political dynamics involved in linguistic, ethnic, and cultural conflict and harmony becomes a major obligation of dual language education. Nieto (2000) suggests that effective pedagogy in bilingual education is not simply teaching content areas in another language; rather, it is using the languages, cultures, and experiences of the learners in meaningful ways to accomplish linguistic, academic, and affective goals. Nieto adds that programs like dual language education provide powerful ways

FIGURE 5.2 Sample Spiral Curriculum of the Water Cycle

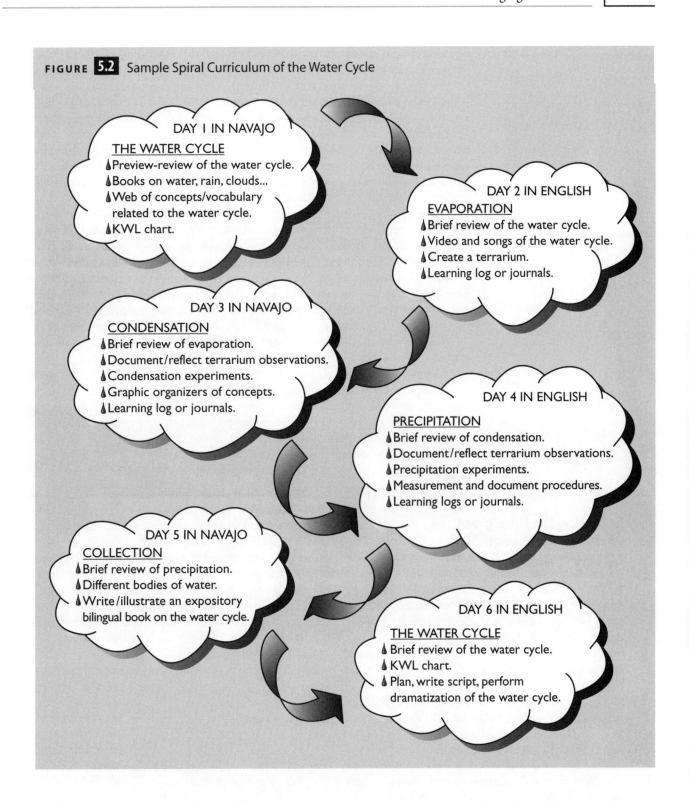

DAY 1 IN NAVAJO

THE WATER CYCLE
- Preview-review of the water cycle.
- Books on water, rain, clouds...
- Web of concepts/vocabulary related to the water cycle.
- KWL chart.

DAY 2 IN ENGLISH

EVAPORATION
- Brief review of the water cycle.
- Video and songs of the water cycle.
- Create a terrarium.
- Learning log or journals.

DAY 3 IN NAVAJO

CONDENSATION
- Brief review of evaporation.
- Document/reflect terrarium observations.
- Condensation experiments.
- Graphic organizers of concepts.
- Learning log or journals.

DAY 4 IN ENGLISH

PRECIPITATION
- Brief review of condensation.
- Document/reflect terrarium observations.
- Precipitation experiments.
- Measurement and document procedures.
- Learning logs or journals.

DAY 5 IN NAVAJO

COLLECTION
- Brief review of precipitation.
- Different bodies of water.
- Write/illustrate an expository bilingual book on the water cycle.

DAY 6 IN ENGLISH

THE WATER CYCLE
- Brief review of the water cycle.
- KWL chart.
- Plan, write script, perform dramatization of the water cycle.

for different linguistic and cultural groups to not only acquire bilingualism, but also to develop favorable views about diversity. Thus, in dual language, multicultural and culturally responsive education makes it possible for students to develop pride and a strong sense of identity in their own cultures as well as an understanding and recognition of the cultures and beliefs of others. These concepts apply to all effective educational programs in an increasingly unpredictable and changing global environment. The goal in understanding conflicting views of the world and how sociohistorical and political perspectives are formed by different groups of people is paramount in building more compatible viewpoints.

Going beyond the traditional curricular topics that include controversial or sensitive issues must be done with responsibility and care. The historical and contemporary relations of power between minority and majority groups cannot be ignored, especially in dual language education in which students from many cultural backgrounds, ethnicities, races, and/or social classes come together. The students themselves bring an abundance of ideas and experiences, both positive and negative. One of the most effective ways to bring authentic multicultural and diverse perspectives into the classroom is to have an extensive collection of children's literature, at all reading levels and in both languages, that depicts subjects relevant to students' lives and is suitable for exploring issues of diversity (Rueda, 1998). Topics such as urban issues, matters of gender, the immigrant experience, historical fiction, cross-cultural relationships, and ethnic folklore can heighten students' interests and provide a medium for rich and meaningful discussion and study. Nao Kao, a third-grade dual language teacher, illustrates how this happens in his classroom in Box 5.2.

Teachers must also make certain that other instructional materials, such as posters, videos, and software, are devoid of racial, ethnic, gender, or disability stereotypes (Sleeter & Grant, 1999). Some educational publishers generate multicultural curricular materials that appear colorful and inoffensive, but in essence perpetuate ethnic, cultural, and gender biases and stereotypes. For example, posters that depict diverse ethnic populations often portray Mexican chil-

BOX 5.2

Exploring the Immigrant Perspective through Children's Books

Nao Kao has been doing extensive thematic units on the immigrant experience for the past four years. His dual language students come from a variety of backgrounds—Colombian, Guatemalan, Jamaican, Korean, Mexican, Filipino, and Salvadoran, as well as different regions of the United States. Consequently, many of his twenty-four third graders have had ample experiences with relocation. For that reason, Nao Kao feels that his students are really hooked on this particular theme of study. At the heart of Nao Kao's thematic unit are children's books on the immigrant experience and urban issues. Since this dual language school is in a large city and many of his students have come from rural areas, Nao Kao feels that including topics on urban issues is particularly relevant and interesting to his students.

Nao Kao begins his theme by brainstorming ideas, topics, and issues written on a web with the whole class and selecting topics of study related to students' interests. He then chooses books that are related to students' topic selections from his classroom library as well as the school and neighborhood libraries. He usually begins the theme by reading Patricia Polacco's *The Keeping Quilt* about a Jewish immigrant family from Russia, Francisco Jiménez' *La Mariposa* about a Mexican migrant worker family in the United States, and Luis Rodríguez' *America Is Her Name* about a young girl who migrated from a small village in Mexico to Chicago. These books provide many bridges to fascinating topics of study that integrate reading, writing listening, and speaking with the content areas, in particular social studies, math, and fine arts. Nao Kao believes that incorporating quality children's literature is an excellent way to scaffold students' linguistic, academic, and sociocultural development.

Over the years, Nao Kao has been building his classroom library with multicultural and cross-cultural books. He has received several small grants to purchase books, and is often in the principal's office petitioning for more money to continue adding to his collection. His passion for children's literature spills over to his students and their parents.

dren in large sombreros and sarapes, Japanese children in kimonos, and American Indian children in traditional headdresses and clothing. The majority of contemporary Mexican, Japanese, and American Indian children do not wear these garments every day, if ever. When children and adults of culturally diverse communities don such attire, it is often in observance of special rituals, celebrations, or cultural passages. In addition, surface aspects of culture, such as dress and food, can be misleading; region, religion, socioeconomic status, levels of education, urban or rural residence, and many other factors differentiate people within groups. Although Latin Americans share many aspects of culture and language, for example, not all follow the same customs, play the same music, dance the same dances, or prefer the same cuisine. Likewise, not all Latin Americans speak Spanish; many speak indigenous languages, Portuguese, English, or French, among other languages, and their languages are intimately connected to different cultural practices.

The inclusion of a well-developed multicultural curriculum goes beyond celebrating typical cultural festivities and studying traditional artifacts. This weak form of multicultural education (Baker, 2001) not only is a diluted and simplified representation of culture, but also tends to perpetuate stereotypes by reducing groups of people to monolithic entities. A case in point is the common and sweeping characterization that all Latinos or Asians have the same traditions, values, beliefs, and experiences. Even within one country those traditions, beliefs and experiences are shaped by many factors; regional differences, urban or rural origin, economic class status, education attainment level, and religious affiliations are some of the elements that influence people's habits and values (Nieto, 2000). Sleeter and Grant (1999) suggest that multicultural education goes beyond improving attitudes about diversity by developing a sound knowledge base that promotes multiculturalism and pluralism. Hence, they argue that teachers should engage students in learning complete concepts related to diverse groups, rather than isolated fragments of information or events. Multicultural education in the context of dual language should provide a forum for students and teachers to explore and scrutinize long-standing stereotypes, prejudices, and injustices, as well as nonmainstream curricular topics, such as exploring the historical context of Columbus's travels from the American Indian perspective.

TEACHING COMPONENTS

Dual language education is framed within a holistic and constructivist pedagogical approach. The student-centered and transactional instructional strategies that dual language teachers practice in their classrooms facilitate academic, linguistic, and sociocultural development by increasing comprehensible input, lowering students' affective filters, and promoting meaningful interactions and experiences. Figure 5.3 is a diagram of the critical teaching elements most commonly found in dual language instruction. In the next section each is addressed in more detail.

Home Connection

Communicating and collaborating with parents are critical elements that greatly enhance any educational endeavor, dual language programs in particular. Because dual language education places high demands on teachers and students, parents play a critical role in assisting and supporting the teaching and learning that goes on in school and that continues at home (Lindholm-Leary, 2001). Collaboration with parents takes many forms and degrees of involvement. For

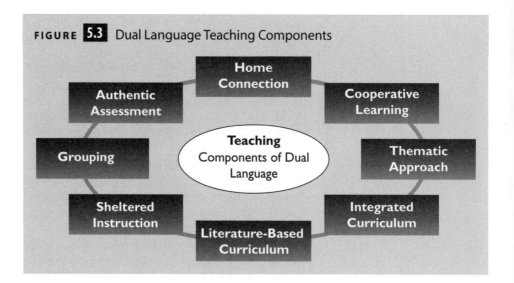

FIGURE **5.3** Dual Language Teaching Components

example, in the planning stages of dual language implementation, parents can take an active part in the decision-making process about the program characteristics that best suit their community and their children. As described in Chapter 4, parents not only need to be informed about educational programs and procedures, but should also be consulted about their views, opinions, and desires on programmatic choices and selections. In Box 5.3, the parent of a child in a dual language program describes her rich and meaningful experiences collaborating with her son's teacher as she shared her expertise and knowledge with the young students.

Parents as Collaborators

**BOX
5.3**

Mrs. Oliver has two children in the dual language program, a daughter in first grade and a son in third grade. Both have been in the program since kindergarten. Mrs. Oliver has been involved with dual language since her son entered the school. She was first a parent volunteer and later became a parent dual language representative in the local parent board. She is a committed supporter and advocate of the dual language program. Because of her enthusiasm for dual language education, she was asked to be part of the Bienvenido/Welcome Wagon, a group of parents who greet new parents and students when they first come to the school and provide them with literature and explanations about the program and the school. This group of parents also welcomes visitors and gives them the official tour of the school.

When Mrs. Oliver's son was in kindergarten, the teacher extended an invitation for parents to come to the classroom and share their expertise, talents, or experiences with the students. Being a native of Jamaica, Mrs. Oliver volunteered to introduce the children to the Jamaican culture. The short presentation was so successful that it extended into a full-blown thematic unit on the Caribbean. Mrs. Oliver and the teacher collaborated in creating meaningful and interesting learning contexts for the children as they engaged in this thematic unit in English and Spanish. The students, the teacher, and Mrs. Oliver found the experience fascinating, educational, and very revealing. They both agreed that everyone involved in the thematic unit was learning: the children and the teacher learned about the Caribbean and Mrs. Oliver learned many new words in Spanish. Mrs. Oliver shared her experience in her son's classroom with other parents, and soon teachers and parents began to collaborate on similar projects. The third-grade teacher invited parents to participate in a thematic unit on dwellings and successfully recruited two fathers who were in the construction business.

Ongoing communication with parents is also essential for effective program implementation. Offering a range of forums for parent-teacher and school-community contact, such as home newsletters, parent meetings, parent-teacher conferences, and even home visits, allows for the inclusion and frequent participation of all members of the learning community (Hewlett-Gómez, 1995). Conducting home visits not only provides opportunities to interact with parents and students in their own environment, but also helps build stronger relationships between the school and the community. Classroom and school activities can also offer excellent vehicles for communication and collaboration (see Table 5.1).

For many minority and majority language parents in dual language programs, one source of concern is their perceived inability to help their children in a language they do not command. Dual language educators must provide parents with clear directions and realistic expectations about their roles in their children's second language growth. The most critical advice is for parents to continue to support their children's academic and linguistic development in the language of the home. The common, but misguided, practice of some educators to encourage non-English-speaking parents to speak English to their children is detrimental and futile. Parents can better support their children's education through the language they know best, not only in a linguistic and academic sense but also in terms of critical affective dimensions. Trying to maintain strong and healthy familial relationships in a language not yet fully acquired in an unfamiliar culture can put enormous strain on family harmony and lead to serious cultural and linguistic gaps between children and parents (Tse, 2001).

Cooperative Learning and Grouping for Academic Instruction

Decisions on how to group students for teaching and learning are also critical in the implementation of dual language education. Table 5.2 delineates the different grouping arrangements (whole group, small group, pairs, and individual) and the specific types of learning and teaching that may occur within each. Thematic

---

■ TABLE 5.1 | Promoting Parent Involvement

School	Classroom
■ Send bilingual school notices	■ Send bilingual newsletters
■ Provide translators	■ Make telephone calls
■ Make telephone contacts	■ Arrange parent conferences
■ Organize school open house	■ Invite parents on field trips
■ Organize social events	■ Conduct home visits
■ Arrange award ceremonies	■ Invite parents as guest speakers
■ Organize assemblies	■ Send biliteracy backpacks home
■ Direct monthly parent meetings	■ Invite parents to be volunteers
■ Provide ESL and literacy parent classes	■ Train parents and organize parent tutoring
■ Provide target language parent classes	■ Invite parents to help create and organize plays, fairs, contests, fund raisers, talent shows …
■ Extend school hours	■ Invite parents to be the audience for plays, fairs, contests, fund raisers, talent shows …
■ Host community events	■ Invite parents to be judges of fairs, contests, talent shows …
■ Organize literacy/math/science family nights	

■ **TABLE 5.2** | **Grouping Organization for Learning Experiences**

Whole Class *heterogeneous*	Small *heterogeneous*	Pairs *heterogeneous*	Individual
■ Read-alouds	■ Guided reading	■ Study buddies	■ Journals
■ Shared reading	■ Projects	■ Peer tutor	■ Free writing
■ Shared writing	■ Study groups	■ Partner reading	■ Individual projects
■ Mini-lessons	■ Cooperative learning	■ Dialog journals	■ Quick writes
■ Field trips	■ Reader's theater	■ Peer editing	■ Free voluntary reading
■ Communicative games	■ Literature circles	■ Cross-age tutors	■ Reading and writing workshop
■ Drama	■ Jigsaw	■ Think-pair-share	
■ Films	■ Numbered heads together	■ Peer editing	
■ Reader's theater	■ Learning centers		
■ Total physical response	■ Role-play		
	homogeneous		
	■ guided reading		
	■ interest groups		
	■ temporary skills		
	■ mini-lessons		

---

approach, cooperative learning, and learner-centered instruction call for students to collaborate in groups most of the time. However, whole group instruction, pairs, and individual work should also be included in the learning experiences of students.

Numerous research studies in K–12 settings have revealed that students who complete learning tasks in cooperative learning groups tend to have more positive self-concepts, better social skills, fewer stereotyped perceptions of others, and greater comprehension of study content and skills (Johnson & Johnson, 1991; Slavin, 1990; Stahl, 1994). Cooperative learning also tends to increase learners' motivation by providing peer support and facilitating the contribution of all students, regardless of their linguistic or academic levels. This instructional approach engages students in small groups by working collaboratively to achieve academic, linguistic, and social learning goals and competencies (Slavin, 1990). Unlike other forms of student group work, where students solve problems together but are responsible for only their individual learning, cooperative learning emphasizes the academic accomplishments of each individual and the learning success of all members of the group (Johnson, Johnson & Holubec, 1993).

Students are commonly grouped in heterogeneous teams that represent varied ranges of academic ability and ethnic diversity, and include both genders and multiple language levels (Cohen, 1994). For brief periods, students may sometimes be grouped homogenously by interest for mini-lessons or because of specific academic needs. All students in the team share the responsibility of accomplishing a group task and making sure they and the other team members learn the academic content (Stahl, 1994). Procedural roles are also assigned to students, such as recorder, illustrator, observer, and reporter, and roles are rotated so that all members have opportunities to experience each role (Peregoy & Boyle, 2001). This teaching and learning approach is highly effective for language development and dual language education because students share and support each other's learning in socially and academically appropriate ways. Cooperative learning is recommended for all grades, from preK to high school, and for all first and second language proficiency levels. Chapter 6 delves into cooperative learning more extensively and outlines a variety of grouping strategies that are effective for collaborative group study.

Thematic Approach

This is an instructional approach that organizes instruction, learning, and assessment around a topic, theme, idea, author, or literary genre; it is aligned to specific student learning goals and outcomes (Pappas, Kiefer & Levstik, 1995). However, Routman (1991) cautions that thematic units are sometimes no more than a series of activities clustered around a central focus or theme which lacks academic, literacy, and linguistic substance. Rather than a collection of activities correlated to a topic or theme, the thematic approach integrates language arts and content area subjects around broad concepts or understandings that are woven throughout the unit.

The thematic approach is integrated and multileveled: the content areas and the four language modes are integrated and not learned as discrete concepts, and students of varying ages and varying academic and linguistic levels are engaged in authentic learning by utilizing problem solving across all academic areas (see Figure 5.4). Themes are also transactional and interactive: the use of scaffolding, assisted performance, cooperative learning, and active learning enhances students' critical thinking skills and facilitates their move toward becoming independent learners. This learning approach works exceptionally well in dual language education because it builds on students' interests and prior knowledge by focus-

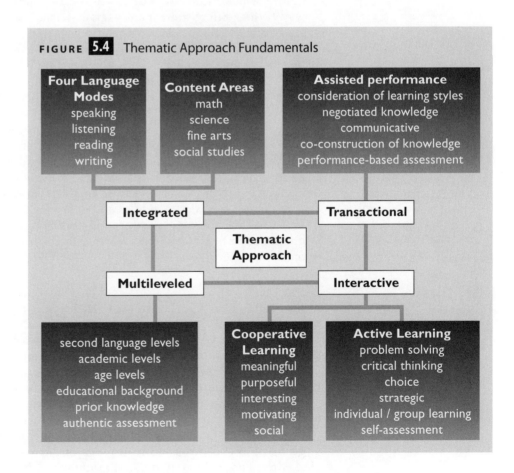

FIGURE 5.4 Thematic Approach Fundamentals

ing on topics that are relevant to them and by linking their background knowledge to new concepts. In addition, thematic instruction supports students' learning styles in a variety of interactive and collaborative ways.

Several considerations must be taken into account in planning a thematic unit: time, topic, learning goals, materials, activities, and assessment. First, the duration and timeline of a theme varies according to students' interest in and the complexity of the subject. Theme cycles can be as short as two weeks and as long as an entire school year. Second, topic selection can be made by the students, teacher, or a team of grade-level teachers. Generally, theme selection is done in collaboration with students; the teacher offers potential topics, usually those in which the teacher has interest or has access to materials and resources; and students make a selection. Third, the teacher identifies the learning objectives by aligning them to the grade-level learning standards. Fourth, materials and resources—such as books, videos, software, magazines, brochures, field trips, guest speakers, artifacts, music, manipulatives, and instruments—are located and collected or contacted. Fifth, activities and learning experiences are selected. These should be meaningful, cognitively demanding, context-embedded, grade-appropriate, integrated, interesting, and engaging. Finally, authentic assessment instruments and performance-based assessments are selected for evaluating students' progress and accomplishments.

Integrated Curriculum

Sheltered instruction, cooperative learning, and thematic instruction provide the most effective means to integrate the curriculum in a cohesive and meaningful way. By integrating content areas (math, science, social studies, fine arts) and language arts (listening, speaking, reading, writing), teachers provide students with opportunities to simultaneously develop academic and language skills and are thus better able to cover the entire curriculum as well as second language objectives. An integrated approach to teaching and learning facilitates students' conceptualizations of the interconnectedness between all content areas and the four language modalities. Thus, students are able to see the big picture and how the parts are connected. This whole-to-part process helps students build background knowledge and vocabulary, links their previous experiences to the learning tasks, and scaffolds their academic and linguistic development. In particular, an integrated approach to learning facilitates comprehensible input, since the learning experiences and objectives are interconnected. Because the concepts and vocabulary are related, activities and strategies that connect several subject areas with listening, speaking, reading, and writing provide optimal academic and language support to all students, whether the instruction is in the native or the second language.

Literature-Based Curriculum

A literature-based approach relies heavily on literary selections as the principal vehicle for teaching and learning academic content, first and second language proficiencies, literacy competencies, and expanded cultural and social knowledge. Using children's literature as the foundation for an integrated curriculum that covers language arts, academic subject areas, and social and cultural dimensions is an effective and vital component of dual language education. Children's literature selections extend from preschool to young adult, include a myriad of genres, and encompass a broad range of interests and readability levels. Thus, children's books offer an optimal forum for addressing the needs of all students, regardless of their academic and second language levels, age, literacy skills, or interests (Hadaway, Vardell & Young, 2002). In the early grades, familiar stories and predictable pattern language books help students acquire literacy skills that are relevant for reading and writing in both languages, as well as support their development of background knowledge.

A balanced literacy approach that incorporates multicultural children's literature addresses all three critical components of dual language education: biliteracy, academic content, and multicultural education. By reading multicultural children's literature, and in particular stories that are based on the cultures of the two languages represented in the program, students become further motivated and interested in learning about one another's backgrounds, experiences, practices, and beliefs. Books that depict traditional and contemporary fables and folktales, cultural poems and songs, and nonfiction accounts of diverse cultures and societies are rich and authentic sources for promoting literacy and linguistic, academic, and cultural development.

Sheltered Instruction

Also known as Specially Designed Academic Instruction in English (SDAIE), sheltered instruction uses special teaching techniques to help students understand English curricular content (Castro Feinberg, 2002). Although this approach was designed to provide comprehensible input in the academic areas for English-language learners, the techniques can easily be applied to other second language learners, such as students learning the target language in dual language programs. Thus, the primary focus in sheltered instruction is to acquire and develop the academic curriculum through comprehensible input in the second language (Freeman & Freeman, 1998). In turn, the development of the second language is achieved as a byproduct of learning the academic content.

The modifications and special techniques used in sheltered instruction include speaking and enunciating clearly, repeating and paraphrasing key points, defining essential vocabulary in context, and combining nonverbal communication cues (such as pictures, objects, and gestures) with spoken or written language (for an in-depth listing of techniques, see Chapter 6.) This method is recommended for second language learners who have achieved intermediate or advanced levels of proficiency in the second language, past the intermediate fluency stage (Krashen and Terrell, 1983). For dual language education, sheltered instruction is well suited for learners in third grade and above. By third grade, students have had several years of academic and social language development, and the content starts to become more complex and abstract.

ENGLISH LANGUAGE DEVELOPMENT.   For students who are at the beginning stages of second language acquisition, in the preproduction, early production, and speech emergence stages (Krashen and Terrell, 1983), English language development (ELD) is more appropriate. This method, also designed for English-language learners, can be used for both minority and majority language learners since it uses many of the same modifications. In contrast to SDAIE, which has a primary focus on academic content through language and is geared toward intermediate and advanced second language learners who are at grade level academically, ELD has a primary focus on language development through content for beginning second language learners who may not be at grade level academically. In sheltered classrooms, instruction is given in a controlled or sheltered format. Linguistic modifications characterize the language used by teachers, such as modified syntactic structures, controlled vocabulary, and shortened sentences (Hamayan & Pearlman, 1990).

MODIFICATIONS.   Sheltered instruction for second language learners involves the use of instructional teacher modifications, or procedures that accommodate the range of abilities and language levels in a classroom. Teacher modifications are particularly important in dual language settings, where all students are at varying degrees of second language acquisition, because they facilitate all learners' linguistic and academic development. That is, teacher modifications address the multileveled needs and multisensory learning styles of all students within a classroom.

Teacher modifications include adjusting speech, using language in context and for meaningful purposes, breaking directions into manageable chunks and regularly verifying for understanding, creating flexible grouping arrangements, shifting from error correction to modeling of correct speech forms, and providing varied multisensory vocabulary building scaffolds (see Table 5.3). When teachers employ language modifications for second language learners, they try to avoid idiomatic expressions (such as "he kicked the bucket" to mean "he died") and language nuances (such as "class is not over until it's over" to mean that class is not over until the person in charge declares that it has concluded). When the teacher or native speakers do use idiomatic expressions or nuances, the teacher must clearly explain the hidden or indirect meanings implied in these utterances.

Environmental modifications are also valuable in scaffolding learners' linguistic and academic development. Environmental modifications may consist of the physical arrangement of the classroom to facilitate students' independent and collaborative work, such as arranging desks in a circle or U-shape, in groups of four, or in rows. The physical arrangement depends on the activity. For instance, a group project is more effective when students are working at a table or when the desks are in a cluster facing each other, but a panel discussion or debate may call for a U-shape desk organization. How the instructional materials (such as books, reference texts, computer software, pencils, and paper) are set up and displayed may also assist or encumber students' access to learning tools. For instance, having reference books close at hand and clearly labeled helps students engage in independent problem solving and promotes initiative. On the other hand, having the reference materials locked up in a closet might deter students from seeking information from these resources. The use and effective display of visual aids, realia, and multimedia are environmental modifications that support and scaffold second language learners' academic, linguistic, and sociocultural growth.

Authentic Assessment

Central to the evaluation of dual language education are the instruments and procedures used to assess and measure students' academic achievement and language proficiency. Katz (2001) suggests that, for assessment to be most effective, educators should follow certain steps: (1) plan assessment; (2) collect and record information; (3) analyze and interpret information; and (4) report and make decisions based on this information and analysis. This assessment cycle repeats as teachers and students progress through the curriculum and the learning standards and goals.

Schools and districts also employ formal assessment measures to determine second language proficiency levels that are commonly used for placement in programs. The most frequently used second language assessment measures for placement are the *Language Assessment Scale* or LAS (Duncan & De Avila, 1977), the *Bilingual Syntax Measure* or BSM (Burt, Dulay & Hernandez-Chavez, 1975), and the *IDEA Oral Language Proficiency Test* (Ballard & Tighe, 1978). These tests should not be used as the sole determinants of students' second language competence levels; teacher evaluative methods and authentic assessment tools should also be used to

■ TABLE 5.3 | **Teacher Modifications for Second Language Learners**

Teacher Speech	■ Use slower but natural rate ■ Paraphrase, repeat, clarify, restate ■ Write new vocabulary, idioms on the board or word wall
Language in Context	■ Use concrete examples with which students are familiar ■ Use pantomime, gestures, facial expressions ■ Use pictures, graphic organizers, props, real-life objects ■ Use films, videos, and software ■ Use demonstrations, role-play, TPR ■ Use manipulatives
Giving Directions	■ Do not translate, do not mix languages ■ Use bilingual students to do minimal translations ■ Break down complex tasks into simpler, shorter steps ■ Ask frequent questions to verify understanding
Student Interaction	■ Use heterogeneous cooperative groups ■ Use the buddy system, partners, heads-together ■ Combine English/Spanish partners
Error Correction	■ Minimize error correction for beginner levels ■ Make students realize that errors are a natural part of learning a second language ■ Function before form: focus on meaning rather than grammatical correctness ■ Model by rephrasing the statement correctly rather than correcting the student directly
Meaningful Dialog	■ Engage in dialog that is negotiated rather than transmitted ■ Engage in discussions rather than straight lecture ■ Ask for open-ended questions: "What do you think?" ■ Personalize the conversation by making reference to students' lives and experiences
Vocabulary Building	■ Classify words by syntactic, semantic, pragmatic functions (suffixes/prefixes, antonyms, synonyms, homonyms) ■ Make connections to cognates (student-estudiante, obscure-obscuro) ■ Color code words, underline, **bold**, CAPITALIZE, box *star*

establish a more comprehensive representation. Multiple forms of assessment, when accumulated over time, can provide a more complete picture of students' learning and progress (Navarrete & Gustke, 1996). Authentic assessment tools are appropriate for dual language programs because they involve students' actual learning processes and performances in specific academic and linguistic tasks (see Table 5.4). Among the most widely used authentic assessment tools are portfolios, teacher observation, anecdotal observations, records and charts, checklists, rubrics, and student self-assessment.

PORTFOLIO.   A portfolio is a systematic and organized collection of work samples, selected by students and/or teachers, that are used to monitor and assess students' progress over time (Burke, 1999). Portfolios provide a comprehensive long-term view of an individual student's learning progress that the student can also use as a self-assessment tool. In addition, parents can see evidence of their child's progress, and teachers can obtain valuable information

■ TABLE 5.4 | Alternative Assessment Techniques

Portfolio	Sample of student's work collected over time that shows growth and development
Observation	Observation of student's academic, linguistic, or social behaviors or performances engaged in alone, in pairs, or in groups
Anecdotal observation	Reflective reports on student's progress based on analysis of the teacher's observation
Anecdotal record	Running account of an observed behavior in real time
Observational chart	List of student's behaviors or criteria that the teacher observes and comments on
Checklist	List used to document academic content, language, and literacy competencies
Rubric	Scoring numerical scale that includes a range of proficiencies, achievements, or benchmarks
Self-assessment	Students monitor their own learning with checklists, anecdotal reflections, or evaluation forms

about students' progress and needs, and in turn adapt and guide the curriculum accordingly. Portfolios can include written samples (narrative stories or expository text) to show process and product, reading samples (student reflections on reading selections or self-evaluations of literature circles) to illustrate literacy progress, and thematic unit work samples (science projects or mathematical problem solving related to the topic of study) to reflect knowledge gain and understanding. Portfolios require a good organizational system that both teachers and students can follow and that can be easily integrated into everyday curricular routines. For example, O'Malley and Pierce (1996) recommend placing a cover sheet or checklist at the front of the portfolio that describes the types of portfolio entries, indicates date of entry, and specifies who has made each entry. They also suggest including an evaluation summary that shows whether students have met the learning standards in various language, literacy, sociocultural, and academic areas. This can take the form of a checklist and/or a narrative summary.

OBSERVATION.   This assessment tool is used to collect information on individual students' progress and achievement. The teacher observes students as they engage in academic, linguistic, or social activities, either alone, in pairs, or in a group, and records the observed behaviors or performance. Although most educators frequently engage in observation as a way to determine students' progress or understanding, teachers often do not document these observations (O'Malley & Pierce, 1996). By keeping a record of who is observed doing what and when, the teacher can maintain a systematic account of students' learning and progress, which is much more reliable than recalling observations from memory. Also, recording observations in different formats provides a more accurate picture of students' actual learning and progress over time. This documented information is readily available and can be shared with other teachers, parents, or the students themselves. Forms of recording observations include anecdotal observations, anecdotal records, observational charts, checklists, rubrics, and rating scales.

ANECDOTAL OBSERVATION.   In this form of documenting students' learning, the teacher writes a reflective report on learners' progress based on an analysis of his or her observations. For example, the teacher may observe three to five different students each day as they engage in literacy, academic, and social activities, and either examine a specific learning area (language development and usage) or observe each student in all aspects of the curriculum. The teacher observes the selected students and writes words or phrases on an observational sheet or on sticky notes. At the end of the day, the teacher writes an interpretive narrative on each student based on the observations and notes taken throughout the day.

ANECDOTAL RECORD.   Unlike anecdotal observations, an anecdotal record is a running account of an observed behavior in real time. That is, the teacher selects a specific behavior to observe over a short period of time and documents in detail all that the learner is doing. A principal difference between anecdotal records and anecdotal observations is that, in anecdotal records, the observations are documented but not interpreted. That is, the anecdotal record contains a description of what the learner did and said, but does not include analysis or reflection on the observed behaviors or language use.

OBSERVATIONAL CHART.   This assessment format combines a checklist or rubric with anecdotal observations. The teacher observes, checks, and comments on a list of students' behaviors, skills, or criteria. The observational chart can take the form of a graphic organizer divided by academic focus (such as math, science, or social studies), language arts categories in the first and/or second language (reading, writing, listening, and speaking), or sociocultural and affective areas (such as group collaboration and turn-taking.) In the L1 and L2 Observation and Rubric sample in Figure 5.5, the teacher documents students' listening, speaking, reading, and writing development in the second language by writing anecdotal records or observations in each box and by scoring each language domain on a 1–5 numerical scale. A numerical scoring rubric would accompany this form and include specific criteria for each number. In the example, the teacher has observed Bruno for one day in his second language, English, while he engaged in different literacy and language arts activities. The teacher wrote short notes on the observed behavior and then circled the number that corresponded to Bruno's level of proficiency or achievement according to the rubric the teacher developed. In the Observation and Checklist sample in Figure 5.5, the teacher has observed Magda once a week during the 3rd quarter of the academic year in geometry. She checked the concepts that Magda has mastered and included observation notes about Magda's success and difficulties, underlining concepts she mastered. Underlining skills or knowledge gained provides information about when each was achieved, something that is not identified in the checklist.

CHECKLIST.   Checklists include specific behaviors, criteria, skills, or content that the learner is to accomplish or learn. They can document academic content, language, social, and literacy competencies. Many textbooks and teacher's manuals include checklists at the ends of chapters or units. However, teacher-created checklists tend to be more effective, since the teacher tailors them to the objectives and goals of the curriculum by including only the items or criteria relevant to instruction. The checklist is completed as the teacher observes behavior and/or students' written work.

FIGURE 5.5 Observational Charts

L1 and L2 Observation and Rubric

Name: _Bruno S._   Date _3-10-04_   Language _L2 English_

LISTENING

listens attentively to peers during coop. learning group acitvity—asks for clarification about the math learning center assignment on fractions

1   2   3   4   ⑤

SPEAKING

uses phrases with correct voc. but sometimes mixes word order (book big)—requests information/clarification often by using phrases/gestures

1   2   ③   4   5

READING

looks for clues in pictures—self-corrects—rereads sentences when not sure—twice substituted a word with another word that did not make sense (dog for dough)

1   2   ③   4   5

WRITING

uses phrases with inconsistent verb tense and word order—uses punctuation appropriately (periods, capitals, commas)—only uses "and then" for all transitional words

1   ②   3   4   5

Observation Checklist

Name: _Magda T._   Date _3rd quarter_   Language _Math—Geometry_

☑ 2-DIMENSIONAL FIGURES
  ☑ RHOMBUS
  ☑ PARALLELOGRAM
  ☑ HEXAGON
  ☑ POLYGON
☐ 3-DIMENSIONAL FIGURES
  ☑ CUBE
  ☐ SPHERE
  ☑ CONE
  ☑ PYRAMID
☐ ATTRIBUTES
  ☑ EDGE
  ☐ FACE
  ☐ BASE
  ☑ CORNER
☑ SYMMETRY
☐ CONGRUENCE
	3-15-04
	uses pattern blocks to create polygons—matches two-dim. figures with correct term—can identify three-dim. figure—having difficulty with cube, sphere, and differentiating between cone/pyramid while using concrete materials
	
	3-22-04
	identifies almost all three-dim. figures and recognizes the difference between cone/pyramid—begins to understand the attributes of geometric figures—can apply the concept of corner to concrete materials in word problems
	
	3-30-04
	continues to have difficulty understanding sphere—identifies edge now and it still developing understanding of base/face—can do basic symmetry activities

RUBRIC.   A numerical scoring scale, known as a rubric, consists of descriptions and criteria for each level associated with standards and learning goals. It includes a range of proficiencies, achievements, benchmarks, or performance levels. The criteria for each performance level are defined in terms of what the learner does to demonstrate skills or proficiency at that level (Law & Eckes, 1995). Teachers can use ready-made rubrics, such as those included in teacher's manuals, textbooks, and assessment resource handbooks like Burke's *How to Assess Authentic Learning* (1999) and O'Malley and Pierce's *Authentic Assessment for English Language Learners: Practical Approaches for Teachers* (1996). Teachers can also design and create their own rubrics based on specific curriculum and learning goals and standards. The length of the continuum usually varies from three to eight, starting at either 0 or 1. That is, the scale can be 0–1–2, 1–2–3, 1–2–3–4, and so on. Burke (1999) suggests using even numbered scales (such as 1–2–3–4 or 1–2–3–4–5–6) because the teacher is then forced to select either the low or the high range. With odd number scales (such as 1–2–3 or 1–2–3–4–5), teachers tend to select the middle number, perhaps making compromises about the student's actual performance.

SELF-ASSESSMENT. According to O'Malley and Pierce (1996), student self-assessment is a critical aspect of authentic assessment and self-monitoring of learning. Self-assessment promotes the immediate and direct involvement of students in their own learning. Furthermore, when students self-regulate their own performance and progress, they have higher levels of control of their learning in that they are much more aware of multiple learning processes and diverse strategies to accomplish learning goals. Students can monitor their own learning through checklists, anecdotal reflections, and evaluation forms.

SUMMARY

The most effective instructional practices that are found in successful dual language programs tend to subscribe to constructivist and transactional modes of teaching and learning (Torres-Guzmán, 2002). These features are highly effective in well-planned and executed dual language programs. Essential dual language instructional and learning components, such as parent involvement, integrated and learner-centered approaches, and multicultural curriculum, become the building blocks for higher academic, linguistic, cultural, and social student outcomes. The learning and teaching elements presented here are compatible with the goals and organization of dual language education. This chapter presents four fundamental learning elements that must be carefully considered in the design and selection of teaching practices: the inclusion of second language learning, literacy acquisition, language development thorough content, and a multicultural curriculum. Based on these key learning components, educators can select appropriate teaching practices that optimize students' learning experiences. These instructional elements include creating a strong and continued collaboration with students' homes, using cooperative learning and grouping strategies, organizing instruction around themes of study, integrating the curriculum, incorporating sheltered instructional techniques, and utilizing varied and authentic measures of evaluation.

DISCUSSION QUESTIONS

1. How would you go about designing a second language (ESL or a minority language) curriculum for your students, and what linguistic objectives would you include? How would you connect these language skills to the content and literacy curriculum? What types of instructional materials would you use?

2. How does multicultural education fit with dual language education? As a dual language teacher, how would you go beyond the weak form of multicultural education and create a multicultural curriculum that addresses issues such as norms, beliefs, and values in diverse populations?

3. Thematic instruction, cooperative learning, authentic assessment, literature-based and integrated curriculum are essential components of dual language education. What other instructional elements would you incorporate in learning experiences for your students?

4. Which forms of assessment would you select for evaluating students' second language development?

How would you go about collecting data, and how would you evaluate and analyze students' progress? Besides the assessment tools presented in this chapter, what other alternative assessment tools would you use in your classroom?

FIELD-BASED  INQUIRY

1. Observe the teaching and learning dynamics of a dual language classroom. Document the instructional practices the teacher employs and the learning environment the teacher creates. Describe the students' learning experiences and how they respond to the instruction and classroom environment. Examine to what extent the instructional practices correlate to the teaching and learning elements presented in this chapter.

2. Select one of the alternative assessment techniques described in this chapter, and apply it in a dual language or bilingual classroom to evaluate students' content learning in the second language. Consider the limitations as well as the positive features of the assessment technique you selected and used.

FURTHER  READING

Faltis, C. J. (1997). *Joinfostering: Adapting teaching for the multilingual classroom.* Upper Saddle River, NJ: Prentice Hall.

Fry, E. B., Kress, J. E., & Fountoukidis, D. L. (2000). *The reading teacher's book of lists.* West Nyack, NY: The Center for Applied Research in Education.

Genesee, F., & Upshur, J. A. (1996). *Classroom-based evaluation in second language education.* New York: Cambridge University Press.

Hurley, S. R., & Tinajero, J. V. (2001). *Literacy assessment of second language learners.* Boston: Allyn and Bacon.

Law, B., & Eckes, M. (1995). *Assessment and ESL: A handbook for K–12 teachers.* Winnipeg, Canada: Peguis Publishers.

Nieto, S. (2000). *Affirming diversity. The sociopolitical context of multicultural education.* New York: Longman.

O'Malley, J. M., & Pierce, L. V. (1996). *Authentic assessment for English language learners: Practical approaches for teachers.* Menlo Park, CA: Addison-Wesley.

Zucker, C. (1995). The role of ESL in a dual language program. *Bilingual Research Journal, 19* (3), 513–523.

6

Instructional Practices and Resources

It is not possible, simply by telling, to cause students to come to have the knowledge that is in the mind of the teacher. Knowledge cannot be transmitted. It has to be constructed afresh by each individual knower on the basis of what is already known and by means of strategies developed over the whole of that individual's life, both outside and inside the classroom . . . it becomes clear that a different model of education is required . . . one that is based on a partnership between students and teachers, in which the responsibility for selecting and organizing tasks to be engaged in is shared.

Wells (1986), p. 3

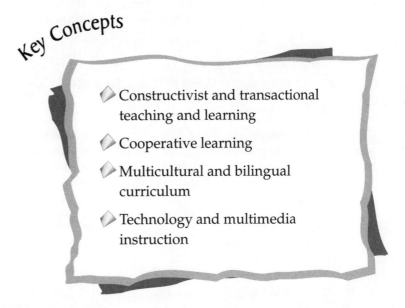

Key Concepts

- Constructivist and transactional teaching and learning
- Cooperative learning
- Multicultural and bilingual curriculum
- Technology and multimedia instruction

TEACHING AND LEARNING PRACTICE

The importance of utilizing transactional modes of teaching and learning as well as learner-centered approaches in dual language programs cannot be stressed enough. Direct instruction and skills-based methods fall short when attempting to develop higher cognitive and linguistic levels as students progress through the academic curriculum. Gonzalez et al. (1993) further assert

103

that the role of the teacher is to enable and guide activities that involve students as reflective learners in socially and academically meaningful tasks. Studies such as those conducted by Díaz, Moll, and Mehan (1986) support the notion that the most effective model of the teacher-learner relationship is not transmission but transaction. The function of teachers shifts from being "dispenser of curricula designed by experts from universities, textbook companies, or their school" (Bissex & Bullock, 1987, p. xi) to being active constructors of their own curricular and pedagogical knowledge.

Transmission-oriented instruction and other traditional approaches, such as memorization of isolated skills and rote learning, greatly inhibit students' potential to develop critical thinking habits and to become independent, strategic learners. Conversely, transactional modes of teaching and learning provide ample opportunities for students to interact in authentic and relevant educational experiences, such as solving problems, creating projects, and scaffolding each other's learning. This constructivist perspective to teaching and learning allows students to use and develop both the native language and the second language by interacting with each other while engaged in developing and making sense of new concepts and ideas. This chapter presents teaching and learning approaches and strategies as well as instructional materials that reflect this authentic learner-centered framework. Table 6.1 delineates the major differences between transaction-oriented and transmission-oriented approaches to teaching and learning.

For dual language education, transactional, developmental, and learner-centered teaching and learning practices (cooperative learning, thematic instruction, and literature-based approaches) are doubly important because all students are second language learners and need comprehensible input in the form of context-embedded learning experiences. This chapter presents specific strategies, methods, and approaches that support students' continual development of their

■ TABLE 6.1	Transmission-Oriented versus Transaction-Oriented Approaches	
	Transaction-Oriented	**Transmission-Oriented**
Curriculum	■ Whole-to-part ■ Top-down approach ■ Builds on what is already known ■ Focuses on meaning and understanding ■ Integrates content areas ■ Integrates the four language modes ■ Problem-solving orientation ■ Negotiable curriculum ■ Authentic learning experiences	■ Part-to-whole ■ Bottom-up approach ■ Ignores learner's prior knowledge ■ Focus on discrete skills ■ Tackles content areas separately ■ Separates each language mode ■ Sequential skills ■ Prescriptive curriculum ■ Drill and practice driven
Teacher	■ Learner-centered ■ Negotiates meanings ■ Relies on cooperative learning ■ Allows for learner choice ■ Focuses on process ■ Teacher as facilitator	■ Teacher-centered ■ Imparts information and facts ■ Relies on direct instruction ■ Teacher makes all the decisions ■ Focuses on product ■ Teacher as sole source of knowledge
Learner	■ Active learner ■ Coconstructs knowledge ■ Ample interaction with peers ■ Relies on background knowledge	■ Learner as passive observer ■ Accepts information as is ■ Interaction only with the teacher ■ Disregards background knowledge

first language, acquisition and progress of their second language, advancement of their academic knowledge, and expansion of their pluralistic and multicultural foundations and understandings. Space and time constraints prevent this text from including all the teaching and learning approaches that are available to teachers in dual language education. However, the methods, strategies, and approaches presented in this chapter represent the types of effective teaching and learning practices that promote academic, linguistic, cultural, and social competencies.

COOPERATIVE GROUPING AND PARTNER STRATEGIES

What children can do together today, they can do alone tomorrow.

Vygotsky (1978)

Cooperative learning subscribes to Vygotsky's (1978) notion that the acquisition of knowledge and development of cognition are socially constructed and shared processes. Vygotsky also maintained that language is the critical link between social and mental cognitive functions. That is, mental processes are initially created collaboratively within social interaction and by means of language. Through collaborative dialogs with more-knowledgeable members of their community, children learn to think and behave in accordance with their sociocultural environment (Berk & Winsler, 1995). This **zone of proximal development** (Vygotsky, 1978), in which learning takes place at the child's level of potential development with the assistance of more capable peers, or adults, reflects the major premises of cooperative learning, particularly for second language learners.

Cooperative learning is quite different from traditional grouping strategies that simply have students work in groups. A group of students sitting at the same table doing their own work is not a structured cooperative effort to solve academic problems or create new knowledge collaboratively (Johnson, Johnson & Holubec, 1993). Likewise, a group of students who are assigned a specific task that only one member completes is not considered to be cooperative learning. Organizing students into groups does not necessarily result in collaborative work. In cooperative learning classrooms, students work together to accomplish shared learning goals and to jointly solve problems and complete assignments or projects. Through cooperative learning, students learn knowledge, skills, strategies, or procedures in group, and then apply the knowledge or perform the skill, strategy, or procedure alone to demonstrate their individual mastery of the material. Students learn it together and then perform it alone (Johnson & Johnson, 1991). Working together for a common goal, when every member is responsible for teammates and his or her own learning, has to be structured and managed by the teacher (Slavin, 1990).

Johnson, Johnson, and Holubec (1998) propose a sequence of steps that teachers can follow when organizing cooperative learning experiences for their students. The role of the teacher is first to identify the learning objectives to be accomplished during and after the collaborative learning activities in which the students are engaged. The learning objectives should include academic and linguistic competencies (for example, understanding the scientific method and using correct punctuation), learning strategies (for example, learning to use inference strategies to get meaning from text), and interpersonal or small group skills (for example, turn-taking or active listening). The teacher then makes decisions on management and organizational issues, such as determining the size of the groups, methods for assigning students to each group, the length of time groups are together, the materials to be used, and the physical arrangement of the classroom. After identifying the learning objectives, determining the arrangement of the groups, and selecting appropriate materials, the teacher describes the project or assignment to the students, explains the cooperative learning strategies to be used, clarifies the learning outcomes, defines the group work expectations, and explains the evaluation procedures for group and individual learning accountability.

Once students are engaged in the collaborative work, the teacher walks from group to group to observe students' interactions and progress, monitors group and individual student learning, and assists each group when necessary. Students' learning and performance are then evaluated as a group and individually. Group evaluations are based on the process and product resulting from the assignment or project. Students are also assessed independently to determine individual understanding and provide evidence of individual learning. This evaluation can be done through varied forms of assessments, such as tests, written or graphic products, and self-assessment. The final stage of cooperative learning should involve some kind of reflective exchange and group self-evaluation about how well the group worked together and what could be improved. In Box 6.1, a self-contained dual language fifth-grade teacher describes how he implements cooperative learning in his classroom and offers his outlook on collaborative work.

In Groups

A primary aim for second language learners in bilingual programs is to acquire the second language for learning literacy skills and academic content, as well as for developing proficiency in that language. In dual language programs, students are expected to continue to progress in the development of their native language, acquire high levels of proficiency in their second language, achieve academically, and develop social and cultural competencies (Lindholm, 1990; Lindholm-Leary, 2001). Effective interaction and communication between students is essential to accomplish these goals (Tinajero, Calderón & Hertz-Lazarowitz, 1993). Cooperative learning is a highly effective instructional practice for second language learners because students work collaboratively in small groups, engage in many meaningful experiences with language and content, and receive more-individualized support from the teacher, who acts as a facilitator. For dual language education, the face-to-face interaction that cooperative learning groups offers is essential for the consistent and daily use of authentic language for meaningful purposes. Students at different levels of academic and second language proficiencies help each other by exchanging knowledge and ideas and by processing information more efficiently and effectively together. In addition, in cooperative learning groups students develop critical cross-cultural and intersocial skills that help them maintain higher levels of interest and motivation and decrease their anxiety and stress (Slavin, 1991). This section presents a sampling of highly effective cooperative grouping and pairing strategies that can be utilized in dual language programs to advance students' linguistic, academic, and sociocultural proficiencies.

Numbered-heads-together is a cooperative learning strategy in which students are grouped in clusters of four to solve a problem or answer questions. The students in the group number off 1 through 4. After students have solved the problem or answered the questions, the teacher calls on one student from each group to report to the class by calling on a particular number. For example, the teacher or students come up with a problem to solve or a question to answer together in the group. The students are given time to research or discuss the solution or answer: then they make sure that all the members of the group understand and can provide the answer or solution to the rest of the class. The teacher ran-

Cooperative Learning in Action

BOX
6.1

Raj has been using cooperative learning in his classroom for as long as he can remember, even before dual language came into his life four years ago. He believes that organizing his classroom for collaborative group work provides the best opportunities for his students to use both languages for academic purposes. He also believes that when cooperative learning is done correctly, students grow into independent learners, have more ownership of their learning, and develop better relationships with their peers.

At the beginning of each year, Raj takes an entire month to explain and model how cooperative learning functions in his classroom, since he has students who have had different or no experiences with cooperative learning in their previous grades. He begins by explaining that students are responsible for their own learning but also for the learning of their teammates. Often this is difficult for students to grasp, so Raj has them do a *fishbowl* exercise, in which four or five students volunteer to role-play in the middle of the classroom as the rest of the students sit in a circle around them as spectators. With Raj's help, students role-play traditional grouping, in which each student does his or her own work and is not concerned for the others in the group. Then students role-play cooperative learning and demonstrate how each student is responsible for the learning of all members of the group. After each-role play, students in the outer circle discuss and brainstorm ideas that emerge, which Raj writes on large chart paper. From these discussions, rules about cooperative learning are created based on students' own understandings of collaboration and community responsibility. Raj has found that the combination of modeling, explaining, role-playing, and discussing cooperative learning is very effective in having students understand the procedures and expectations of group work.

Because he is not familiar with his students at the beginning of the year, he sets up temporary groups that he calls visiting teams for about two weeks. As Raj explains and models the rules and expectations of collaborative projects or assignments, he observes the dynamics of each group and the personalities of each student. With the input of the students, he then assigns them to home teams, where students usually stay for the duration of the thematic unit or the quarter. Once in their permanent groups, students engage in team-building—activities that build trust, respect, and collaborative relationships among the members of the team. They also select a name for their teams, design logos, and create team chants. At the beginning Raj introduces four primary roles to students: discussion leader, presenter, recorder, and organizer. Later, Raj introduces new roles such as illustrator, critic, connector, and historian. Throughout the year, Raj and the students revisit the cooperative learning procedures and responsibilities when conflicts arise or group dynamics start to break down.

domly calls a number between 1 and 4. For example, the teacher calls on all the students who have the number 3 to share the group's solution or answer with the rest of the class. The students who report the correct answer or solution win points for their team. In this cooperative learning variation, all the students in the group are responsible for knowing the answer to the problem because the members of the group do not know what number the teacher is going to call, thus ensuring that all are participating equally. Marta, a third-grade teacher, describes the ways she implements numbered-heads-together in her self-contained dual language classroom in Box 6.2.

Jigsaw is a cooperative learning strategy that engages all the students in a group in increasing their comprehension by discussing the content of the text, setting the purpose, and using problem-solving strategies to understand difficult text (Aronson, 1978). In jigsaw the students are grouped in base teams of four, usually resulting in a range of five to eight teams, depending on the class size. Each member of each base group is given a number from 1 to 4. Each number is responsible for one specific section of the reading or of a topic of discussion. In a

Numbered-Heads-Together

When Marta began using numbered-heads-together in her third-grade dual language classroom, it was exclusively during language arts for reading comprehension. But lately she has been using this group strategy across the content areas and has found it to be particularly effective in math. Since her students do numbered-heads-together at least once a week, they are very familiar with the procedure. During math, Marta usually gives each team several word problems to solve as a group. First she has the team identify and discuss the meanings of all the words in the problems that are related to math, such as *less than*, *sum*, and *compare*. Students then write these words on a dry erase board for reference. This component is especially useful because it helps second language learners understand key vocabulary and concepts. With the use of manipulatives, each team discusses and solves the problems together. After all the teams have finished, Marta likes to do a variation to the traditional numbered-heads-together in which the teacher calls a number and all the students with that number from each team have to explain the answer to the problems. Instead, Marta has Team A call a number of a member of Team B to solve the first problem. If the Team B student whose number has been called gets the problem right, then the team earns points and they get to call a number of a member of Team C to answer the next problem. But if the member of Team B gets the problem wrong, the team does not earn any points and the member with the number on Team C gets to answer the problem. Marta feels that this gives students more control and ownership of the process.

reading example (see Figure 6.1), all the students with number 1s are responsible for reading, understanding, and reporting back on the first paragraph of the text to the base, or original, group; the number 2s for the second paragraph; the number 3s for the third paragraph; and the number 4s for the fourth paragraph. All the students then regroup by numbers in expert groups to read and discuss their section of the text. For example, all the number 1s are grouped to read and talk about the first paragraph and all the number 2s are grouped to read and talk about the second paragraph. After the students in each numbered team become confident or expert about their understanding of the text, they regroup and return to their base groups to explain or report on their assigned sections. This strategy can be adapted for lower or higher levels of second language proficiencies. For example, instead of dividing the text by paragraphs, the reading can be assigned by sentences or by entire pages. In jigsaw, all students are responsible for their own understanding as well as that of their teammates. In Box 6.3, Kenda explains how jigsaw can be adapted to include both short-term and long-term assignments.

Literature circles are clusters of students who are temporarily grouped to read and discuss a book that all the members of the group have chosen to read. As students read the book, they share their responses to the literature and engage in conversations about the reading selection (Harste, Short & Burke, 1988). Literature circles provide excellent opportunities for students who share the same interests in reading a literature selection to talk about their responses to, interpretations of, and ideas about the literature they read. Putting literature circles into practice requires careful organizational structures, good classroom management, and focused instructional guidelines. The teacher's role in literature circles is to organize the procedures, timelines, and reading materials, and to facilitate students' readings and discussions in their groups.

The first steps in organizing literature circles are for the teacher to make preliminary selections of four to six books, briefly introduce each book to the entire class, and invite students to examine the books themselves. In this preliminary overview, the teacher describes the characteristics of the story, such as genre, characters, and plot, and comments on the readability level, interest, and potential

FIGURE 6.1 Jigsaw

Step 1 Students are grouped in teams, and each is designated a number from 1 to 4.

Step 2 A different section of the text is assigned to each number. Students regroup by numbers to read and discuss their designated sections.

Ones read the first paragraph *Twos read the second paragraph*
Threes read the third paragraph *Fours read the fourth paragraph*

Step 3 Students return to their original, or base, teams. Each student reports or explains his or her section to the other members of the base team.

BOX 6.3

Jigsaw

Kenda's seventh-grade dual language students really enjoy doing jigsaw because they are "on a mission to become experts" about a specific topic and, more often than not, it is on something that they are interested in. They also like jigsaw because they don't feel the pressure to understand concepts or topics on their own. Since Kenda implements an integrated curriculum, when students are doing jigsaw in the content areas they are also always engaged in reading and writing. Kenda sometimes has students do jigsaw for a class period or two, such as when she divides reading selections from the science text into five parts and has each member of the home team become knowledgeable about one of these sections. Students from each home team meet with their counterparts from the other teams to discuss and summarize their assigned sections. Then they go back to their home teams and report on what they have learned. At other times, Kenda asks her students to do jigsaw in a much more in-depth manner, such as when they did a theme on the Mayan civilization. In the initial stages of the thematic unit, the whole class brainstormed topics about the Mayan civilization that they would be interested in exploring. Five areas emerged from this discussion: people, history, war, mythology, and religion. Each member of the home team selected one of the areas and regrouped according to each topic. Students stayed in their expert groups for a week while they investigated their areas of specialization by reviewing informational books and software, videos, the Internet, and encyclopedias. Each expert group created graphic organizers, wrote reports, and prepared short presentations about what they learned. Students went back to their home teams and presented their findings and reports to each other. Kenda believes that jigsaw is very effective because students have to understand and process new knowledge at a deeper level, since they have to explain these concepts to their classmates.

audience. For example, the teacher may select books on students' particular interests, such as the immigrant experience, sports, or animal stories. Other selections may be based on an author study (such as books written by Gary Soto or Lois Lowry), the current theme of study (such as ancient civilizations or migration), or a specific literary genre (such as historical fiction or biographies). Book selections should represent a range of interests and difficulty levels so that students have real choices and selections that are appropriate for different reading levels. After students browse through each book, they list their top two or three choices.

Once students have ranked their book preferences, the teacher organizes groups of four to six students based on their selections. When forming the literature circle groups, the teacher should consider students' personalities, perspectives, and learning styles so that the members of the group are diverse but compatible. After the groups have been formed, roles and responsibilities for each member of the group are assigned by the teacher or selected by each member. Group member roles are an integral part of literature circles because they provide a focused structure for reading and group-talks and ensure that all members read the book selections and have responsibilities to fulfill in their team discussion (Daniels, 1994). Group roles can include discussion leader (leads the discussion by posing questions or ideas to the group), illustrator (draws pictures or diagrams of the passages in the story), connector (makes connections to other readings, concepts, prior knowledge, or prior experiences), summarizer (provides a synopsis of the reading selection), literary luminary (chooses a brief passage to read aloud and poses questions for discussion of a particularly interesting, humorous, or profound section of the book), word detective (selects and presents a special word found in the text that is unknown or interesting).

In literature circles, students read sections of the book and meet regularly to discuss key concepts, main ideas, supporting details, story sequence, and plot developments. Students are also encouraged to make connections to other readings and to their background knowledge, pose and answer questions about ambiguous or unclear events or information, and help each other understand unfamiliar or difficult vocabulary. Literature circles are particularly effective for second language learners because the cooperative learning structure provides optimal support and ample opportunities for meaningful and authentic second language and literacy usage.

In Pairs

In addition to the advantages associated with working in cooperative learning groups, second language learners also benefit academically, linguistically, and socially by working with partners (Díaz-Rico & Weed, 2002; Thonis, 1994). Students in dual language programs can simultaneously continue to develop their native language, acquire the second language, and learn academic content through partner work. Partner activities often engage two learners in a range of literacy and language experiences, such as reading to one another, discussing passages or stories, editing one another's writing, or coauthoring a text. Partner learning can be arranged by grade (pairing students who are in the same grade or with cross-age partners), range of abilities (pairing more-proficient or more-competent learners with less-proficient or less-competent learners), student interests (pairing students by their interest in a specific reading topic or theme of study), or student choice (students select their own partners according to their personal preferences.) This section describes three partner teaching and learning strategies: partner reading, think-pair-share, and cross-age buddies.

Partner reading pairs two students to read together, discuss the text, and sometimes answer or create questions about the selection. Students can select their own partners or can be assigned a partner by the teacher. Depending on the purpose of the reading activity, the teacher may pair a stronger reader with a developing reader, or a bilingual proficient student with a still-developing second language learner. The partners then take turns reading parts of the selection aloud and engage in oral and/or written discussion and reflections about the content of the text. Partner reading promotes reading comprehension, fluency, and self-confidence as well as linguistic and cognitive engagement with the partner and the text. The use of reading partners provides comprehension support for the struggling reader or second language learner and opportunities to develop better fluency for the stronger reader. In addition, the bilingual student acts as a language model for the second language learner.

In **think-pair-share** (Lyman, 1981), the teacher poses a thought-provoking or open-ended question and gives students time to think about the question on their own. Students then pair with partners and discuss their ideas about the question for several minutes. After a short time, the teacher invites students to share or comment on possible answers to the question, usually orally but occasionally in written form. This collaborative strategy gives all students the opportunity to discuss their ideas and allows them to confirm or reformulate their responses in partnership with another learner. Students are less inhibited in sharing their responses because they have already discussed their thoughts with a partner.

The think-pair-share strategy improves students' oral communication skills as they talk about their ideas with one another (Gunter, Estes & Schwab, 1999). Think-pair-share engages students first in thinking individually, then pairing with a partner for discussion and reflection, and finally sharing their findings or ideas with the whole class. For example, students individually read a text or listen to the teacher, a video, or other students about a topic or concept. They think, reflect, and may even write about the topic. They then pair up with a partner to discuss and compare notes. Finally, each pair is invited to share their findings, consensus, or disagreement. This technique is particularly effective for second language learners because it provides time for students to think about their responses before answering a question, and to share and confirm ideas with a partner. Second language learners need more time to process a question or a problem because they often translate the question or problem to their native language, formulate a response in the native language, and then translate the response to the second language. Think-pair-share makes them feel safe to process and think about a problem through active learning and collaboration.

Cross-age buddies, sometimes called cross-age tutoring, matches younger students with older, more knowledgeable students. This arrangement can be with younger and older students of the same native language, bilingual students together, or a native speaker with a second language learner. Similar to peer tutoring (Thonis, 1994), in cross-age buddies, older students who have already achieved certain skills and acquired certain knowledge work with younger students to help them acquire and achieve new skills and knowledge (Rosenthal, 1994). For example, in a Chinese-English dual language program, a seventh grader who is a native Chinese speaker may be matched with a second grade native English speaker who is still developing Chinese literacy and language proficiencies. The older student can provide language and literacy support and serve as a language model for the younger student. The teachers schedule weekly encounters between the two classrooms and plan educational activities, such as partner reading or writing and cross-age projects. The teacher of the upper grade is responsible for providing the older students with sufficient training or guidance to work with their younger partners. Cross-age collaborations are usually between a primary grade (preK–3) and an intermediate (4–6) or middle school grade (7–8) within the same school. However, cross-age buddies can also be arranged with a feeder or nearby high school. In Box 6.4, Sofia and Sal describe how

Cross-Age Buddies

BOX 6.4

Sofia and Sal have been teaching partners for several years, though not in the traditional sense: Sofia teaches self-contained dual language kindergarten, and Sam teaches sixth-grade transitional bilingual in the same school. Sofia usually has a range of language proficiencies in her class, from monolingual Spanish to monolingual English to bilingual. Sal has no monolingual English speakers; he does have a range of language proficiencies from monolingual Spanish to bilingual, although most of his students have at least intermediate proficiency in English. These variations in language proficiencies in both classrooms complement very well their cross-age buddy program.

Every year Sofia and Sal organize the cross-age buddies or *amigos* between their students in the two grades. Before school begins, Sofia and Sal meet to arrange the schedule for their get-togethers, plan the curriculum and the learning objectives, and create a list of possible activities and events from which students can select. Although each year students select or design different activities, Sofia and Sal have established a number of routines in which the students participate: partner reading once a week for at least fifteen minutes, lunch together once a week in the cafeteria, a gift exchange between the partners before the winter holidays, one major content area project, a performance at the Mother's Day assembly, at least one field trip during the year, and an end-of-the-year picnic. The older students select the major content area project, which might be a science ex-periment, a social studies drama performance or published book, or a mathematical construction, among other choices. They also brainstorm and come up with other activities they may be interested in doing with their younger partners. The younger students usually choose the reading selections and also have input regarding what kinds of activities they want to do with their partners. Students from both classrooms make selections about the performance, field trip, and picnic. The selection of the cross-age buddies is up to the students. Sofia and Sal facilitate this process by interacting for a few weeks at the beginning of the year so that all students can get acquainted. Once students select their partners, Sofia and Sal schedule one hour a week to get together, usually on Friday afternoons. Because not all the children fit in one classroom, students from both grades break up into two groups. One group stays in the homeroom, and the other group goes to the partner room. The groups take turns going to the partner classroom or staying in their own classroom every other week.

Sal takes responsibility for preparing the sixth graders to work appropriately with their younger partners. He coaches them in tutoring strategies, reading comprehension questioning, and emergent literacy concepts (such as directionality and letter-sound correspondence). He also discusses their responsibilities as role models and the behaviors and topics of conversations that are not suitable for young children. Sal and Sofia believe that both groups benefit immensely from this interaction: socially, academically, linguistically, and culturally.

they implement cross-age buddies in their kindergarten and sixth-grade classrooms.

EFFECTIVE TEACHING AND LEARNING STRATEGIES

The following teaching and learning strategies and methods were compiled from a wide selection of current texts on best practices for second language learners. From this extensive collection, a select number of resources are exceptionally well organized, concise, and comprehensive in regard to instructional practices that are best suited for dual language education. One such book is *Reading, Writing, and Learning in ESL: A Resource Book for K–12 Teachers* by Peregoy and Boyle (2001) which, as the authors aptly state, "is a comprehensive, reader-friendly resource book that provides a wealth of teaching ideas for promoting oral language, reading and writing development" (p. xv). This book presents a myriad of developmentally appropriate and learner-centered instructional approaches and methods, classroom organization suggestions, and assessment tools and techniques that are ideal for dual language programs. A second very practical and useful resource is *Fifty Strategies for Teaching English Language Learners* by Herrell and Jordan (2004). This reader-friendly text clearly presents and describes each of the fifty approaches and accompanies them with classroom vignettes. Although these resources specify practices and approaches for English-language learners, these can easily be adapted for second language learners who are developing a language other than English. The following sections describe some of the most useful and effective strategies, methods, and techniques commonly used in second language classrooms that are highly recommended for dual language education programs.

Anticipation Guides

Anticipation guides (Readence, Bean & Baldwin, 1981) are used to activate students' prior knowledge about a subject or topic, to prepare them to read a story or text, and to set the purpose for reading. Anticipation guides also motivate students and help them make predictions about the text they are about to read. They can be teacher-initiated or student-initiated. Prior to reading a selection, the teacher selects key information or ideas from the text and creates a list of statements with which students agree or disagree in class discussion. After reading, students compare their responses to the information in the text. When anticipation guides are student-initiated, the teacher invites the students to make inferences and predictions about the text through discussion or written responses before reading. After reading the text, students confirm or reformulate their speculations and assumptions (see Figure 6.2). Activating prior knowledge, setting the purpose, and drawing upon students' interests are critical steps before engaging in any educational activity, particularly reading texts or books. Anticipation guides are recommended for native language and intermediate or advanced second language learners who are already reading independently, usually in the third grade and above.

FIGURE 6.2 Anticipation Guide on *Taking Sides* by Gary Soto

Key Vocabulary, Ideas, Concepts before reading	Predictions, Inferences before reading	Agree, Disagree before reading	Confirm, Refute after reading
Concepts Identity Ethnicity Culture Multiculturalism Diversity	The family moves back to the barrio.	✓	✗
	Lincoln is accepted in his new school.	✗	✓
Vocabulary Barrio Suburbs Outcast Immigrant	Lincoln saves the game and gains respect from his coach and peers.	✓	✓

Language Experience Approach

Language experience approach (LEA) is one of the most frequently used approaches for beginning first and second language readers and writers, and it is a highly recommended teaching and learning practice for second language literacy development in dual language education. In LEA, the learners themselves provide the text, which serves as the basis for reading instruction (Lee & Allen, 1963). This approach is very effective because students engage in the reading process by using text that is familiar, concepts or ideas that are of interest, and language and vocabulary that is known.

Prior to dictating the story or narrative to the teacher, learners usually participate in some kind of concrete real-life experience, such as conducting a science experiment, going on a field trip, or engaging in a hands-on activity. The learners then explain or describe the events or experience to the teacher, who records their accounts verbatim. Learners can build on stories dictated individually, in small groups, or as a whole class. Students are able to read their own stories with minimal difficulty because they already know the content and the meaning. In addition, students view reading and writing as purposeful communication about their own interests and concerns. As a result, this approach is tailored to the learners' own interests, background knowledge, and language proficiency level (see Box 6.5). LEA works especially well with emergent and early native language readers as well as with beginner second language learners from first grade and up.

Pattern Language or Predictable Books

Pattern language or predictable books, songs, and poems are particularly effective for beginning readers and second language learners because they allow students

---

BOX 6.5

Language Experience Approach

In his second-grade dual language class, Dumi uses the language experience approach often. He uses it during individual student sessions, in guided reading groups, and in whole group. Last week, Dumi used the language experience approach with his entire group of Navajo and English speaking students. They were involved in a theme on the animal kingdom and had been discussing animal and plant products. To begin the lesson, Dumi brainstormed words and concepts related to dairy products that he wrote on large chart paper, and then read a book about making butter. Dumi showed the students a large glass jar, a quart of cream, and a container of salt. He invited the students to make predictions about the upcoming activity. Dumi talked out loud as he went through the demonstration. He poured the cream and some salt in the jar, closed the jar, and began to shake it. He then passed the jar around the circle and asked each student to continue to shake the jar while counting to twenty in Navajo, and then pass it on to the next student. As the jar was being passed around, Dumi and the students continued to discuss their predictions and make connections to their study on animal and plant products. They also observed how the contents in the jar were changing from liquid to solid. Once the cream and salt mixture turned into butter, Dumi passed crackers around for students to taste their homemade butter. Dumi asked the students to describe in Navajo the procedure for making butter and their experiences as they engaged in this activity. He wrote students' contributions on large chart paper exactly as students described the experience. After the chart was complete, Dumi and the students read the text together several times. Dumi later used the text to do a lesson on punctuation and vocabulary.

to become comfortable with both oral and written language through rhythmic, repeated, and predictable text (Hudelson, 1994). Students hear and use the language patterns in the story, song, or poem and become familiar with its vocabulary and sentence structure. Later, students can replace words or phrases within the pattern of the text to make their own passages or lyrics. Older students can also benefit in reading predictable and pattern language books to younger learners: by reading these types of books to younger children, older students can develop into more effective and fluent readers. Reading routines between older and younger students can be accomplished through cross-age partners, which will increase older students' confidence with reading and greatly decrease any feelings of inadequacy about reading what they perceive as "baby books."

Because fluent and effective reading involves predicting and sampling (Goodman, Goodman & Flores, 1979), predictable and pattern language texts are essential for helping children develop these strategies early on. Learners are able to construct meaning and develop fluency because of the familiarity and predictability of the texts. Pattern language and predictable texts are most commonly used in read-alouds and shared reading, which assists vocabulary growth and reading comprehension (Routman, 1996). In read-alouds, the teacher reads stories to students aloud for enjoyment and to expose them to authentic language and narrative or expository text structures. In shared reading, the teacher and students engage in multiple readings of the same book; students interact with the story and participate in the reading (Holdaway, 1979). Reading to students through read-aloud and shared reading benefits native and second language learners alike because these practices facilitate language acquisition and literacy development in both languages through comprehensible input and rich language experiences (Hadaway, Vardell & Young, 2002).

Many pattern language books are available in English and Spanish, like *Goodnight Moon* by Margaret Wise Brown (1947), *I Went Walking* by Sue Williams (1989), *The Hungry Caterpillar* by Eric Carle (1984), *Brown Bear, Brown Bear* by Bill Martin (1970), and *We Are Going on a Bear Hunt* by M. Rossen (1989). Other popular pattern language books have been translated to other languages, such as Chinese, Hmong, and Korean. Pattern language or predictable books, songs, and poems are highly effective for emergent and early native language readers as well as for beginner second language learners from first grade and up. They are also useful for older readers in cross-age reading.

Preview-Review

Preview-Review is a common strategy used in bilingual classrooms that provides students with comprehensible input by presenting a brief synopsis and review of the lesson in students' native language before and after the concepts are presented in the second language. Although this strategy is intended for bilingual teachers, Freeman and Freeman (1998) maintain that preview-review can be effective even for teachers who do not speak the students' native language, who can rely on bilingual students, paraprofessionals, or parents.

In preview-review, the teacher first previews a lesson by providing a brief synopsis of the content in the students' native language (such as an oral summary, reading a short book about the subject, showing a film, asking key questions, or using anticipation guides). Then the teacher teaches the lesson in the students' second language, and, finally, the teacher reviews the lesson by summarizing key ideas and concepts in the first language (see Figure 6.3). Thus, the teacher takes advantage of the students' first language to provide contextual support for the second language. For example, a dual language Navajo-English teacher uses preview-review to present a lesson in Navajo to the students. The teacher briefly presents the concepts and vocabulary of the lesson, as well as any special procedural instructions in English. The teacher and students then engage in the lesson in Navajo. After the lesson in Navajo has ended, the teacher reviews the concepts, ideas, and vocabulary in English. In dual language programs, the use of preview-review benefits all students, since each language is being used for the actual lesson or for the preview and review sections of the lesson.

In dual language classrooms, there are often students with highly developed proficiencies in both languages who can assist second language learners in using this method. After the teacher has modeled the strategy enough times, these bilingual students can facilitate the preview and review parts of the lesson for learners with beginner or intermediate levels of second language proficiency. When bilingual students conduct the preview and review sections in a collaborative group arrangement, all students benefit academically, linguistically, and socially. For the bilingual student, this provides an authentic opportunity to communicate academic and linguistic knowledge so that the beginner second language learner is able to understand key concepts and vocabulary. For the beginner second language learner, the bilingual student provides an additional language model beyond the teacher. These types of transactions and interdependence between students augment intergroup relations and provide authentic and purposeful forums for interactions. Preview-review is an excellent strategy for students in all grades, and for beginner and intermediate second language learners.

Total Physical Response

Total physical response (TPR) is a method of language teaching that relies on teachers' and students' physical movements to teach and learn vocabulary and concepts in the second language (Asher, 1977). In TPR students listen and physically respond to oral commands that are modeled by the teacher (see Table 6.2). For example, the teacher says "close the door" while closing the door, and the students themselves respond to the command by closing the door. At first, students listen and respond to simple commands given by the teacher, such as "touch your nose" and "stand up." As learners progress in their second language, the commands become more cognitively and linguistically demanding, such as "stand behind a classmate who is taller than you." In order to respond appropriately to this command, students must understand *taller* and *behind*. Commands to which students can respond physically and that are more complex and sophisticated can include a hands-on sequence of instructions, such as following a sequence of commands to make a cup of tea or following a set of instructions to make a candle. Once learners become more proficient and confident with their second language

FIGURE 6.4 Preview-Review

Preview	View	Review
Teacher or more competent student presents a brief preview of the lesson, project, or activity in the students' native language.	Teacher presents the lesson, project, or activity in the students' second language.	Teacher or more competent student reviews the lesson, project, or activity in the students' native language, checking for comprehension.

■ TABLE 6.2 | Total Physical Response (TPR)

Language	Description	Example
Listening	Respond to increasingly more complex commands with physical actions	Close the door Put the pen inside the cup Line up from tallest to shortest
Speaking	Give commands/directions to other students or teacher	Form a parallelogram with six students
Reading	Follow sequential directions from a text with physical actions, drama, realia	The girl tries the hot soup, tries the cold soup, drinks the soup that is just right
Writing	Write a series of commands, directions that have been enacted or are meant to be followed	1. Heat the wax 2. Place the wick in the can 3. Pour the hot wax in the can 4. Let it cool

use, they can generate their own commands to direct their classmates to perform corresponding actions (see Box 6.6).

TPR was initially designed to develop oral language, but recent adaptations have incorporated reading and writing development as well; students perform written commands that they read or they write commands for others to read and perform (Díaz-Rico & Weed, 2002). However, Freeman and Freeman (1998) advise not requiring students to engage in reading and writing commands until after they have developed oral second language proficiency. In addition to reading and writing, other recent adaptations of the method incorporate dialogs, role-play, and storytelling.

TPR provides context-embedded language and ample opportunities for students' active involvement. For dual language education, TPR can be a very effec-

BOX 6.6

Total Physical Response (TPR)

Lil uses TPR so often in her second-grade dual language classroom that by the middle of the year students can create commands and directions for other students to perform or follow. One particular adaptation that Lil's students enjoy is I Spy TPR. She has students engage in this activity for about five to ten minutes during transition times or to give students a break from their usual routines. In I Spy TPR, Lil begins by giving one command related to positional words, using words like *behind, under, east, right,* and *high.* For example, Lil might say, "I spy a ruler left of a pencil" or "I spy all the boys standing at the north wall of the classroom." These words are posted on the word wall and have been already introduced to the class. The first student who responds correctly gets to call the next command by using a different positional word. Close to the end of the year, Lil asks students to write their positional commands on the board, which the students who are responding must read. Lil finds that second language learners get easily confused with positional words, whether in English or Spanish. She thinks that TPR is an excellent technique to have students internalize new meanings in a fun nonthreatening way.

tive method for promoting comprehension and increasing vocabulary. Because students have to demonstrate understanding by responding appropriately to commands, TPR also can serve as an informal assessment on students' progress in the second language. TPR is useful for students in all grades, and usually for beginner second language learners.

 # GRAPHIC ORGANIZERS

Graphic organizers are powerful and effective tools to organize and remember information and concepts. The visual and spatial representations in graphic organizers help students to more concretely conceptualize new ideas and knowledge (Díaz-Rico & Weed, 2002). When presented in books or by the teacher, graphic organizers provide a visual organizational frame for making sense of concepts and knowledge. More importantly, when students themselves utilize graphic organizers as a tool to make connections, summarize, or sequence ideas and concepts, they begin to move toward becoming strategic and independent learners. Graphic organizers can be utilized by a whole class, in small cooperative groups, in pairs, or individually.

Graphic organizers may be used as a study guide; to locate and remember facts; to introduce, arrange, or make connections about text; or to summarize information. Excellent resources for graphic organizers and their potential uses are found at *The Graphic Organizer* Web site (http://www.graphic.org) and the *Write Design Online* Web site (http://www.writedesignonline.com/organizers). This section presents some of the most effective graphic organizers that can be used in all grades and with students from all academic and second language levels. Among the most widely used graphic organizers are maps and webs, semantic feature analysis, Venn diagrams, and dual concept organizers.

Mapping, sometimes called webbing, is an organizing strategy that relies on the graphic representation of connected information, concepts, or ideas. Semantic maps, concept maps, story maps, pictorial maps, cognitive maps, chain maps, and sequential maps are some of the many variations of mapping strategies that can be used to organize, synthesize, and understand new concepts. Figure 6.4 provides actual instructional examples for concept mapping, sequential or chain mapping, story mapping, pictorial mapping, and cyclical mapping.

In semantic or concept maps, the main concept or topic is written in a circle in the middle, with supporting or connected ideas radiating from it. Concept maps can also include details that are connected to the subtopics. Sequential or chain maps are used to organize information in order, either chronologically or by sequential phases. Story mapping is commonly used in the primary grades, but is also very effective with older students who are reading more complex story lines. Story maps can include many more story elements than the ones presented in Figure 6.4. For example, a story map may incorporate supporting characters, subplots, genre, or story message. Pictorial maps utilize drawings or pictures to categorize, classify, or label parts of an idea, object, or event. Pictorial maps are commonly found in science books and journals. Cyclical mapping is also a very useful tool to depict a progression that is repeated, like the water cycle or life cycle.

Semantic feature analysis is another form of graphic organizer that uses a grid to compare a number of characteristics related to concepts or vocabulary. Semantic feature analysis is a very effective tool to categorize and organize ideas, concepts, or literary genres. For example, Table 6.3 depicts a semantic feature analysis of different animals and their habitats. A plus or minus sign is written in each square to indicate the different types of habitats that the animals may or may not

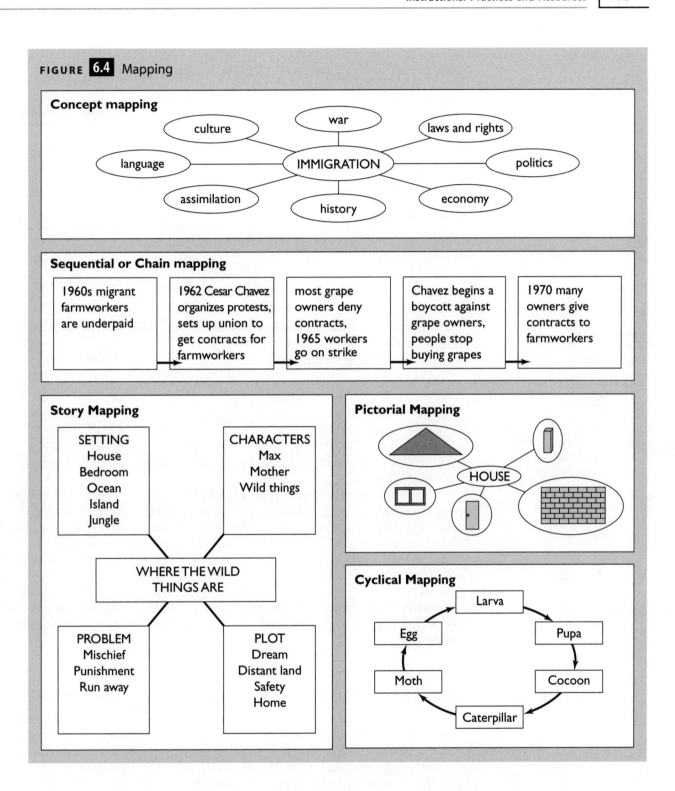

FIGURE 6.4 Mapping

inhabit. The teacher should model semantic feature analysis extensively so that students eventually create their own grids with relevant content and corresponding characteristics or categories.

A Venn diagram is useful tool to compare the similarities and differences between two or three concepts, ideas, or stories. Two or three overlapping circles represent each concept. Details that are not shared by the other concepts are written within the circle. Traits or characteristics that are shared are placed in the

■ TABLE 6.3 | Semantic Feature Analysis Organizer

Animals and Habitats	Jungle	Desert	Ocean	Forest	Mountain	Wetlands
Whale	−	−	+	−	−	−
Lizard	+	+	−	+	+	+
Bear	−	+	−	+	+	−
Monkey	+	−	−	−	+	−
Fox	−	+	−	+	+	−
Birds	+	+	−	+	+	+
Turtle/tortoise	+	+	+	+	−	+
Manatee	−	−	−	−	−	+

middle. This is a teaching and learning tool that can be used and constructed by both teacher and students.

There are countless design varieties and uses of graphic organizers and mapping strategies. Many graphic organizers, such as Venn diagrams and concept maps, are common instructional and learning tools used at all grade levels with all students. Other graphic organizers, such as the fishbone or the step organizer, although less well known (see Figure 6.5), are very useful for students and teachers to arrange, categorize, and classify knowledge. Dual concept organizers are used to represent relationships between ideas or concepts, such as cause and effect, compare and contrast, problem and solution, and fact and proof, and are also effective strategies to help students conceptualize associations or correlations between ideas.

INSTRUCTIONAL RESOURCES

Best practices, such as the ones mentioned above, are contingent on the quality and availability of varied and rich teaching and learning materials and resources. Dual language education does not require any more or any fewer instructional resources than other outstanding and effective education programs. Perhaps the only feature that is exclusive to dual language, which is shared with other additive bilingual education models, is the need for an abundance of quality children's literature and other printed material, as well as videos, music, and software, in both the native and second languages. These instructional materials not only provide vehicles for the teacher to navigate students' development of academic, linguistic, and sociocultural proficiencies, but also provide students with authentic and valued forms of the second language and literacy (Montague, 1997). The final section of this chapter presents a list of key instructional resources and materials for dual language education.

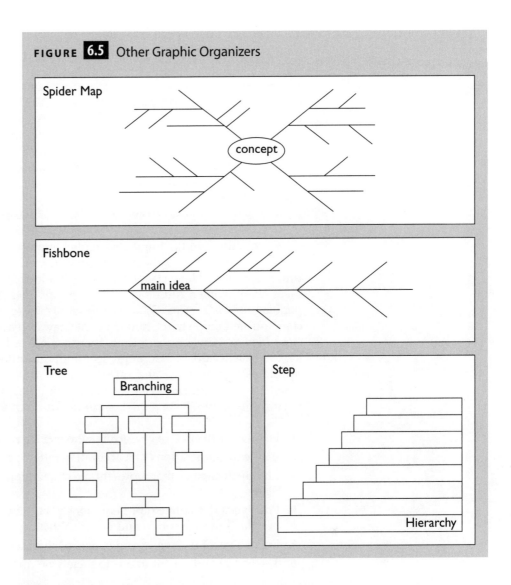

FIGURE 6.5 Other Graphic Organizers

Bilingual and Multicultural Children's Literature

The most significant and essential resource in a dual language classroom is an extensive classroom and school library collection of children's literature. Books, both expository and narrative, are the backbone of any superior educational program (Krashen, 1996). Rigg and Allen (1989) contend that children who engage in listening, speaking, reading, and writing about literature develop a more cohesive knowledge of language in both the native and second languages. In a balanced approach to literacy development, books are the primary instruments for teaching and learning to read and write. After students have developed independent levels of literacy proficiency, it is in books that they find information, concepts, and ideas they need to accomplish academic tasks, solve problems, and acquire new knowledge. In educational programs like dual language that highlight multiculturalism as a major learning goal, multicultural children's literature is a fundamental element for teaching and learning.

MULTICULTURAL CHILDREN'S LITERATURE. Through multicultural children's literature, rich, interesting, and natural language can be used as a medium not only to develop language and academic proficiencies, but also to expand multicultural competencies. Authentic multicultural children's literature develops students' cultural awareness and enhances positive self-concepts for both minority and majority language speakers. Children's literature that accurately portrays the customs, values, beliefs, traditions, practices, and histories of diverse groups has the potential to expand students' understandings of diversity and decrease stereotyping and biases (Hadaway, Vardell & Young, 2002). Books that depict realistic and positive experiences of people who are disabled or elderly, of same-sex parents, and of single-parent families, to name a few, can provide expanded perspectives about diversity and a pluralistic society. Exposure to quality multicultural literature also helps children understand the distinctiveness of other ethnic groups, eliminate cultural ethnocentrism, and develop multiple perspectives. Banks (1994) suggests that literature is a powerful medium for understanding the world because it can be a major carrier of multicultural concepts and ideologies.

In selecting multicultural children's literature, teachers and parents must be keenly aware of overt and covert biases and look for evidence of stereotypes, racism, and sexism. Many classic children's books that have negative or biased messages about women and other diverse groups are still in use today. One such still popular book is *The Five Chinese Brothers* (Bishop & Weise, 1939), which contains a common stereotype that Chinese people have the same physical appearance. The story begins, "Once upon a time, there were five Chinese brothers and they all looked exactly alike." Although seemingly harmless, portraying any group of people as homogenous and one-dimensional is not only misleading but also maintains and reaffirms negative stereotypes. Mei-Yu (1998) recommends the following criteria to selecting quality multicultural children's books.

1. Positive portrayals of characters who engage in realistic behaviors
2. Authentic illustrations that accurately reflect people and their conduct
3. Pluralistic themes that represent the changing faces and trends of the United States
4. Positive and accurate representations of culturally and linguistically diverse people in contemporary and historical fiction
5. Reflections of the values and beliefs of characters from diverse backgrounds
6. The legacy and contributions to society by diverse groups

Children's literature publishers have, in the last decade, increased their selection of books related to multicultural and diverse themes. Books that center on the immigrant experience, such as *La Mariposa* by Francisco Jiménez (1998) about the migrant worker experience and *The Keeping Quilt* (1988) by Patricia Polacco about Jewish immigrants from Russia, are particularly appealing because of their authentic, rich, and diverse content.

BILINGUAL CHILDREN'S LITERATURE. Classroom and school libraries that are equipped with a variety of print genres, such as realistic fiction (adventure, mystery, sports), historical fiction (frontier, war, persecution), fantasy (myths, epics, fables), poetry, and informational books (biographies, encyclopedias, textbooks), as well as magazines, newspapers, and other printed materials, provide students with authentic, purposeful, and meaningful experiences to broaden their literacy and knowledge base (Hudelson, 1994). For dual language education, an abundance of children's books in the two languages that depict cultural diversity can serve as a foundation for all learning. Publishers have responded to the popularity of dual language programs by increasing their selections of bilingual books, particularly in English and Spanish, and books on diversity, multiculturalism, the immigrant experience, and cross-cultural issues (see Appendix A for a sample listing of bilingual books and recommended publishers).

In the primary grades, children's books that contain patterned, rhythmic, and predictable language and events provide critical literacy scaffolding necessary to develop reading and writing skills. These books also offer rich authentic language that promotes vocabulary building and provides models for standard grammatical structures in the second language. Picture books with animal themes, familiar fairy tales, and songs help young learners predict, infer, confirm/disconfirm predication, and connect new information to their prior knowledge (Hudelson, 1994). Building a strong knowledge of vocabulary, text structure, and strategic reading skills allows both first and second language learners to develop into efficient and effective readers and writers (Freeman & Freeman, 2000).

For older students, children's books that include longer, more sophisticated story lines, as well as nonfiction informational text, provide the bridge to tackling and understanding increasingly complex expository text. Because chapter books have more intricate content and fewer contextual clues, such as illustrations, students should engage in collaborative reading and have ample opportunities for discussions in cooperative learning groups or pairs.

Learners should also be encouraged to produce or dictate their own reading materials, regardless of their age, in both languages. Rigg and Allen (1989) argue that having students create their own books produces reading materials for different interests within a classroom and exposes students to an array of different genres. Moreover, student-created reading materials are readable for students because they are familiar with the text and are able to construct meaning from the print. The *Children's Literature Web Guide* provides an abundance of links for teachers and parents that include authors and stories on the Web, book reviews, and links to lesson plans and teaching ideas based on children's literature (http://www.acs.ucalgary.ca/~dkbrown/).

Multimedia Resources

Soska (1994) defines *multimedia instruction* as technology integrating some, but not necessarily all, of the following in an interactive environment: text, graphics, animation, sound, and video. The use of audio and video equipment is especially beneficial and effective for second language learners, since they provide ample auditory and visual contexts for interpreting and learning new concepts in the classroom. Educational videos, video cameras, cassette recorders, and CD players as well as the overhead projector can greatly enhance students' educational experiences by providing optimal means for context-embedded language and comprehensible input. These multimedia resources not only address a range of learning styles (auditory, visual, kinesthetic), but are also multileveled. That is, the use of videos, music, and other media naturally attend to different academic and linguistic levels within one classroom.

Beyond having students view videos and overhead presentations, teachers can invite them to use these multimedia tools themselves. For example, in a learner-centered classroom, students may videotape themselves or their peers while reading, conducting a project, or performing a play. Using computer video editing software with the teacher's assistance, students can edit and add sounds and captions to their video creations. Later, students can check out these student- and teacher-made videos to take home and share with their families.

The overhead projector can be used in multiple ways to enhance teaching and learning in dual language classrooms. Beyond the conventional uses when the teacher writes on transparency sheets or presents transparencies of printed material, overhead projectors can be used by the students themselves to solve problems or present information to their peers, parents, or teachers. For instance, students may work collaboratively on a topic, create their own colored transparencies of their work, and present the project to the class. These student-created transparencies can either be done by hand or on the computer with a color printer and printer transparency film. Also, teachers can purchase an ever-increasing collection of transparency materials, such as overhead maps, clocks, coins, paper money, playing cards, and thermometers. In addition, short picture books can be scanned and printed on transparency films, which are especially handy for shared reading selections that are not available in big book format.

Technology

Computer-based technologies in the classroom and at home, such as educational software, the Internet, and electronic communication, have the potential to be effective and useful educational methods for teaching and learning. This potential is dependent on two major premises: how teachers and students use this technology, and to what extent the technology resources have educational value, substance, and relevance. As with any other curricular resource or material, the varied forms of technology available to schools must be carefully scrutinized for their educational worth. Many educational Web sites and software are not framed around authentic and purposeful learning experiences. Rather, they are rote-learning activities, much like a computer worksheet, that do not promote active learning, critical thinking, or problem-solving behaviors. Thus, teachers must thoroughly examine and select appropriate technological resources in relation to best practices for first and second language learners.

Desktop publishing software programs, such as *AppleWorks* for Macs, *Microsoft Publishing* for PCs, and *Adobe Illustrator* for both systems, are becoming more and more user-friendly, facilitating their use by teachers and students. *PowerPoint* presentations and other programs that can be used with LCD panel projectors not only provide rich context for language, literacy, and academic development for second language learners, but also promote high levels of interest and motivation. Increasingly, educational software companies are producing programs that are interactive and highly motivating to help students develop literacy, language, content area, and problem-solving skills. Healey and Johnson from the TESOL Technology Interest Section have compiled an exhaustive list of educational software programs that can be used with second language learners (http://www.orst.edu/dept/eli/softlist/). Appendix D adapts their list of the most appropriate programs for dual language education in preK–8 and includes additional software products. Other enduring educational software includes *Hyperstudio*, *Kid Pix*, and the *Bilingual Writing Center*. The World Wide Web also offers a multitude of sites related to second or foreign language learning, such as free on-line translation services, foreign-language Web sites, and international electronic pen-pal sites that help create partnerships between U.S. schools and their counterparts around the world.

SUMMARY

This chapter frames dual language teaching and learning practices within constructivist, transactional, and learner-centered theoretical and pedagogical perspectives. Effective education programs subscribe to teaching and learning approaches and strategies that are interactive, developmental, and meaningful. For dual language education, this is doubly important because all students are expected to continue to develop their native language as they meet the challenges inherent in acquiring a second language over an extended period of time. Learning in collaborative groups and pairs within integrated, multicultural themes that make use of scaffolding strategies is critical in assisting students to flourish academically, linguistically, and socioculturally.

DISCUSSION QUESTIONS

1. Examine your beliefs about teaching and learning. What do you think are the optimal circumstances under which learning takes place? What is the role of the teacher in the learning process? What is the role of the learner in the learning process? Do your beliefs about teaching and learning fit in with a transactional or a transmission orientation, and why?

2. Think about specific challenges or difficulties faced by teachers and students when implementing cooperative learning. What may be some obstacles to implementing collaborative group or partner work? Consider structural obstacles (classroom size, furniture, materials), organizational obstacles (number of students, instructional time, time to plan), and managerial obstacles (keeping students on task, discipline, noise levels). How would you address and resolve these challenges?

3. In what ways can instructional materials affect teaching and learning? Consider the types of materials (books, software, periodicals, videos, manipulatives, realia, posters), the language of the materials (balanced amount of quality materials in both languages), the quality of the materials (authentic children's books, basals, worksheets, critical thinking software programs and fill-in-the-blank software programs, black-and-white texts and colorful texts), and the quantity of the materials (number of books per child, amount of reference materials, sufficient texts for each child).

4. How would you go about selecting quality educational software that promotes critical thinking, problem solving, and deductive reasoning and at the same time supports second language development? How would you ensure that the software programs are not above students' language proficiencies? What types of software programs would you avoid considering for use in your classroom, and why?

FIELD-BASED INQUIRY

1. Interview the coordinator of a dual language program. Find out about the guiding principles of the program at his or her school in regard to curriculum, teaching and learning approaches, and instructional materials. Ask how the curriculum is aligned to the state or district standards. Has the school adapted the standards to fit the dual language goals by adding second language goals and standards? What methods, strategies, and approaches does the school consider to be best practices? How are teachers encouraged to use learner-centered and constructivist instructional practices? How are the instructional materials selected, and how much funding is available for teachers to purchase bilingual and multicultural materials? What are the successes and challenges of dual language programs in regard to curriculum, instruction, and materials?

2. Select three multicultural children's books that depict contemporary immigrant experiences (consult a librarian, children's bookstore, the Lectorum Publications catalog, Appendix A, or the Web). Select books that are appropriate for the age level with which you will be working. Read and discuss each book with a group of students in a second language class (dual language or other bilingual classroom, foreign language classroom, or ESL classroom). Ask students to talk about their own experiences or perspectives on immigration as they relate to the stories. Guide the students to think about the similarities and differences between the story and their own experiences. Ask students to write their own stories, either fictional or reality-based. Document and analyze students' discussion responses and narratives.

FURTHER READING

Chamot, A. U., & O'Malley, J. M. (1994). *The CALLA handbook: Implementing the cognitive academic language learning approach.* Menlo Park, CA: Addison-Wesley.

Fry, E. B., Kress, J. E., & Fountoukidis, D. L. (2000). *The reading teacher's book of lists.* West Nyack, NY: The Center for Applied Research in Education.

Herrell, A., & Jordan, M. (2000). *Fifty strategies for teaching English language learners.* Columbus, OH: Prentice Hall.

Herrell, A., & Fowler, J. (1997). *Camcorder in the classroom: Using the videocamera to enrich curriculum.* Upper Saddle River, NJ: Prentice Hall.

New York State Education Department. (2001). *The teaching of languages arts to limited English proficient/English language learners: A resource guide for all teachers.* New York State Education Department, Office of Bilingual Education and the University of the State of New York.

Peregoy, S., & Boyle, O. (2001). *Reading, writing, and learning in ESL: A resource book for K–12 teachers,* 3rd ed. New York: Longman.

Pérez, B., & Torres-Guzmán, M. E. (2002). *Learning in two worlds: An integrated Spanish/English biliteracy approach.* Boston, MA: Allyn and Bacon.

Building and Maintaining a Model Program

Language and communication are at the heart of the human experience. The United States must educate students who are linguistically and culturally equipped to communicate successfully in a pluralistic American society and abroad. This imperative envisions a future in which ALL students will develop and maintain proficiency in English and at least one other language, modern or classical. Children who come to school from non-English backgrounds should also have opportunities to develop further proficiencies in their first language.

Statement of Philosophy, *Standards for Foreign Language Learning* (American Council on the Teaching of Foreign Languages, 1996)

Key Concepts

◆ Enriched education

◆ Professional development

◆ School-community collaboration

◆ Participatory leadership and advocacy

D ual language programs cannot be effectively implemented in all situa- tions with all populations. Certain conditions and structural factors need to be present for a dual language program to be properly carried out, in- cluding a balanced representation of the two language groups, prepared and knowledgeable educators, informed and supportive administrators and parents, and access to quality instructional materials in both languages (Christian, Montone, Lindholm & Carranza, 1997; Lindholm-Leary, 2001). Torres-Guzmán

(2002) warns, "What school districts describe as dual language programs is not always clearly aligned with the technical definition—enrichment education programs that foster language equity and are organized with goals of bilingualism and biliteracy for all children, language minority and mainstream students alike" (p. 1).

In the past decade, the United States has experienced a notable proliferation of dual language immersion and partial immersion programs. Although research and information centers, such as the *Directory of Two-Way Bilingual Immersion Programs in the US*, maintain a listing of existing dual language schools across the country, no data are available regarding the actual number of schools that have terminated their dual language programs and the reasons for their demise. Nonetheless, educators who have participated in failed programs agree that many schools end dual language education after the first few years of implementation. Lack of commitment from teachers, parents, or administrators; limited access to teacher professional development and relevant instructional materials; demographic instability and change; and inadequate leadership are some of the issues that may debilitate and ultimately end a program (Amrein & Peña, 2000).

As discussed in the previous chapters of this book, implementing a dual language program is a long-term commitment that requires continual support from all those involved; appropriate and timely adjustments in response to school changes; and uncompromising advocacy for the program's pedagogical, theoretical, and sociopolitical foundations. Numerous research studies on dual language education have identified key features of effective programs (Amrein & Peña, 2000; Cazabon, Lambert & Hall, 1993; Christian, Montone, Lindholm & Carranza 1997; Lindholm-Leary, 2001; Montague, 1997; Sugarman & Howard, 2001; Torres-Guzmán, 2002). Based on these studies and my own research and observations, this chapter presents a number of conditions that are essential for the preservation and enhancement of existing dual language programs.

CONSIDERATION IN MAINTAINING AN EFFECTIVE PROGRAM

Administrative Support

Dual language education requires visionary, knowledgeable, and committed leadership (Castro Feinberg, 1999). Anything short of this usually results in a weak and ineffectual program. Dual language education is not prescribed or prepackaged and does not offer a one-size-fits-all model in which administrators and teachers are given straightforward directions to follow year after year. Enrichment education programs that focus on high academic standards and the development of bilingualism, biliteracy, and multiculturalism—such as dual language education—are based on clearly established theoretical and pedagogical frameworks and are continually reformulated according to each school's needs and aspirations. Thus, for a dual language program to thrive and for students to successfully accomplish its intended goals, competent and creative leadership is indispensable. The views, attitudes, and expectations of the principal set the tone for the entire school. School principals' priorities and values become readily apparent to teachers, parents, and students alike by the extent to which they are involved in the program and the funding they allocate to its implementation.

Figure 7.1 lists a number of concrete ideas that administrators can use to support and improve dual language in their schools. A critical starting point is for the principal to become informed and knowledgeable about dual language educa-

FIGURE 7.1 Recommendations for Administrators

Administrators
- Become knowledgeable about dual language and related pedagogical issues
- Network with other dual language programs and administrators
- Participate in teacher staff developments
- Seek and lobby for additional funds and support

Staff
- Assign a dual language coordinator
- Hire qualified teachers interested in the program
- Pair new teachers with experienced teachers
- Utilize resource teachers to support students in the program
- Provide ongoing staff development opportunities
- Coordinate weekly and monthly teacher meetings
- Offer guidance and support to struggling teachers
- Provide teacher assistants for the classroom

Instructional Practices
- Require learner-centered and active learning classroom approaches
- Promote thematic and cooperative learning instruction
- Expect teachers to engage students in critical thinking and problem solving
- Discourage direct instruction, rote learning, and the use of worksheets

Parents
- Communicate frequently with parents about the program
- Conduct monthly parent meetings
- Organize dual language assemblies and events
- Invite and train parents to volunteer in classrooms

Resources
- Increase bilingual and multicultural books in the school and classroom libraries
- Augment the school's bilingual and multicultural videos and software collection
- Fund educational field trips and cultural performances
- Increase multimedia and technology resources (computers, Internet, video cameras)

tion, the pedagogical issues related to second language acquisition, and best practices for second language learners (Cloud, Genesee & Hamayan, 2000; Lindholm-Leary, 2001). In particular, the principal and other school leaders must have a thorough understanding of second language acquisition theory and pedagogy, multicultural and bilingual education principles, and instructional practices that are integrative, interactive, and developmental (Hewlett-Gómez, 1995). Administrators who are actively involved in teachers' professional development as participants not only become well informed about dual language education, but their presence also clearly communicates their commitment and enthusiasm. Additionally, administrators' participation in teacher professional development ensures that everyone receives the same information, thus reducing unrealistic expectations or misguided decisions by principals or coordinators. Networking with other schools to share and exchange information and experiences also provides a vital support system.

Enrichment and progressive programs, such as dual language education, need the participation of all members in the decision-making process, which goes beyond the conventional hierarchical administrative structure of most schools. The engagement of all stakeholders (students, parents, teachers, support staff, and administrators) in participatory decision making can lead to school improvement (Cloud, Genesse & Hamayan, 2000). School cultures that promote this sharing of authority and power regard teachers and parents as leaders and decision-makers who have a voice and an active role in the development and implementation of initiatives and the reformulation and transformation of existing programs.

To be effective, teachers must be able to form productive collaborations with colleagues, parents, community agencies, businesses, and others to bring about continuous improvements and positive change. Fullan (1993) contends that teachers will never improve learning in the classroom unless they also help improve conditions that surround the classroom. For dual language education, the participation of teachers and parents, and sometimes students, in the decision-making process is particularly critical. As has been discussed throughout this book, dual language education requires a long-term commitment from all its constituents: teachers, parents, students, administrators, and community. Thus, it is imperative in dual language education to establish forums, committees, and subcommittees to dialog, problem-solve, and make decisions about the program. This school culture organization broadens the decision-making base and enhances student learning by making it possible for educators and parents to make important and informed decisions. In Box 7.1, a principal of a neighborhood urban school describes her role in promoting positive attitudes and continued support for the dual language program.

Most schools have limited funds and resources that must be allocated efficiently in order to address the multiple needs of students and teachers. Administrators and teachers can create lists, in priority order, that include essential and supplemental resources for the effective implementation of the program. Among essential expenditures are professional development in-services for teachers, class size reduction, employment of teacher assistants, and increased instructional resources, in particular children's literature and textbooks. Supplemental costs, which are no less important, may include funds for field trips, cultural and artistic performances, and multimedia/technology software and hardware. Dual language education, as previously mentioned, requires no less and no more than any other highly effective education program. However, decisions on how funds and resources are allocated have to coincide closely with the goals and objectives of the program. For instance, a major goal of dual language education is for students to become bilingual, biliterate, and bicultural. Consequently, a lack or shortage of bilingual and bicultural materials, such as books, music, videos, and software, would significantly hinder attainment of the programs' intended goals and outcomes (Amrein & Peña, 2000).

When teachers are asked what is needed most in the implementation of dual language, the response is common across programs: in addition to money for resources, teachers need more time to meet, plan, and talk to each other. Hence, principals must provide frequent opportunities for teachers to plan together, problem-solve, and share their successes and struggles. In schools that have preparation periods during school hours or have early dismissal days, the principal can coordinate these so that teachers are able to meet at least twice a week. Many schools organize preparation time in a way that allows all the teachers in one grade level to convene and plan from three to five times a week. Principals can also allot time during early dismissal days for teachers to get together, rather than fill these days with meetings and presentations.

Reflections of a Principal on Dual Language Education

BOX 7.1

Barbara has been a principal for fourteen years, six of which have been in a school implementing dual language education in kindergarten through fifth grade. She believes that there are two keys to the success of an innovative, albeit challenging, program such as dual language: high levels of teacher and parent involvement in the decision-making process, and high levels of teacher and parent satisfaction with the program.

Barbara has purposely included teachers and parents in all major decisions about program implementation, such as creating new policies for attendance and homework, and designing new procedures for student placement and report cards. In some instances, she has asked teachers to make decisions without parents' involvement, such as in the selection of instructional materials and the development of scheduling organizations. Because of the intimate knowledge teachers have about their own curricular needs, Barbara feels it is not necessary for parents to be involved in this type of decision making. Based on teacher or parent concerns or needs, Barbara often offers an open invitation to teachers and parents to participate in committees or subcommittees to problem-solve, address needs, or create strategic plans. On occasion, she forms committees based on the nature of the situation and the individuals' expertise. Such was the case when Barbara selected a group of teachers who had attended extensive staff development training on assessment to develop an authentic evaluative tool to determine students' language proficiencies levels in the dual language program.

Barbara believes that teachers are most effective when they are happy and take pride in their teaching, and that parents are most involved with their children's education when they are happy with the education their children are receiving and the progress they are making. Barbara feels that for parents, satisfaction with the dual language program derives from a sense of ownership and pride in the program and the school; evidence that their children are learning and progressing linguistically, academically, culturally, and socially; and ongoing and open communication between home and school. Barbara accomplishes these objectives by organizing parent meetings, sending newsletters, coordinating school and community events, and having a welcoming open-door policy for parents and the community.

To make teachers happy, aside from directly involving them in the decision-making process, Barbara listens to their concerns, provides support, and, whenever possible, honors their requests. Most often, requests include more time to plan, more resources, and help in the classroom. She also tries to keep morale up, especially during particularly stressful times (during report card week, during standardized testing month, and at the end of the year), by organizing cultural potluck lunches, doing team-building activities during staff meetings, and having a school spirit week (during which teachers dress up in silly outfits).

Because parents are an integral part of any good dual language program (Lindholm-Leary, 2001), principals must communicate frequently with them via monthly parent meetings, school newsletters, and other forums like open houses. For a dual language program to maintain its standing and prestige within the school community, it is imperative for principals to be continually visible to parents and students. Administrators' presence in parent meetings, community forums, assemblies, and other parent venues portrays a strong and committed leadership.

Ongoing Professional Development

Teacher preparation ought to extend beyond what is available or offered in the initial phases of program implementation (Sugarman & Howard, 2001). Prior to initiating a dual language program and during its early stages, teachers, administrators, and other support staff need to participate in preservice professional development that address issues specific to dual language pedagogy. Topics that are frequently included are distinctions between dual language and other second language programs, characteristics of the various dual language models, fundamental features in program implementation, language distribution, classroom organization, scheduling, and multicultural curriculum. Although these themes are essential in the beginning stages, they need to be revisited periodically. The two most requested ongoing professional development topics related to dual language education are language distribution and classroom organization.

Other critical teacher preparation topics include first and second language acquisition, biliteracy development, academic content instruction in both languages, and student assessment (see Figure 7.2). In regard to first and second language acquisition and biliteracy development, teacher preparation must include current research and theoretical constructs related to literacy and language development. This knowledge provides the foundation for educators to create optimal learning conditions for their students to develop bilingual and biliterate proficiencies as well as academic and sociocultural competencies. The theoretical and research base guides the selection and use of best teaching and learning practices and appropriate instructional materials. A major focus of teacher professional development rests on pedagogical considerations associated with language acquisition and literacy development (Montague, 1997). Teaching and learning practices, such as balanced literacy approaches that integrate the four language modalities and rely on authentic children's literature, should be at the core of teacher in-services, especially in the early grades.

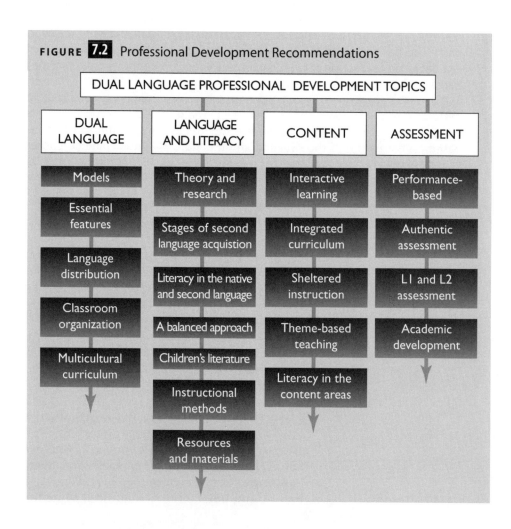

FIGURE 7.2 Professional Development Recommendations

DUAL LANGUAGE PROFESSIONAL DEVELOPMENT TOPICS

DUAL LANGUAGE	LANGUAGE AND LITERACY	CONTENT	ASSESSMENT
Models	Theory and research	Interactive learning	Performance-based
Essential features	Stages of second language acquistion	Integrated curriculum	Authentic assessment
Language distribution	Literacy in the native and second language	Sheltered instruction	L1 and L2 assessment
Classroom organization	A balanced approach	Theme-based teaching	Academic development
Multicultural curriculum	Children's literature	Literacy in the content areas	
	Instructional methods		
	Resources and materials		

In addition to dual language matters and literacy and language development, the teaching and learning of academic content should be an essential component of teacher preparation. Although teachers understand that academic content is a fundamental goal of schooling, sometimes instructional means of delivering subject matter become problematic in the dual language context. This is due to the challenges of teaching and learning in a second language, often with students who are at different levels of language competency and academic proficiency (Howard & Loeb, 1998). In dual language education, it is particularly pressing for the instructional practices and learning arrangements for teaching and learning academic content to employ integrative, interactive, and learner-centered approaches. Sheltered instruction, English language development (ELD), the Cognitive Academic Language Learning Approach (CALLA), and other critical methods for teaching content through the second language require considerable training and opportunities for teachers to discuss and reflect on their applications in the classroom (Christian, 1994; Hewlett-Gómez, 1995; Freeman & Freeman, 1998).

Assessing and evaluating students' progress and growth provides vital information to parents, teachers, administrators, and the learners themselves. In dual language education, measurement of students' progress should include multiple tools and techniques that address various purposes of assessment (Genesee & Upshur, 1996). Assessment covers native and second language proficiency, native and second language literacy development, academic content attainment, and sociocultural competencies. In other words, teachers must have a solid understanding of the best assessment and evaluative means for dual language education. This may be accomplished through comprehensive professional development on varied assessment instruments and interpretation of student data.

Principals, coordinators, resource staff, and classroom teachers must be creative in seeking ongoing quality professional development that encompasses the multiple components of dual language education. Many school districts have excellent teacher professional development programs that address literacy development, bilingual and ESL instructional practices, content teaching, and technology. However, teacher preparation should not be limited to what school districts normally offer, although these certainly fulfill part of the need for dual language teacher preparation. As was discussed in Chapter 2, collaboration with universities can lead to reciprocal arrangements in which university educators, researchers, and graduate students can provide in-services, at no cost, in one or more areas related to dual language education.

Another highly recommended means of continued professional development is to annually allocate funds to send selected teachers or staff to educational conferences, either local or regional (such as California Association for Bilingual Education and CABE's National Two-Way Bilingual Immersion Program Conference), national (such as the National Association for Bilingual Education Conference), or transnational (such as the Dual Language Symposium in Puerto Rico.) These representatives can then conduct workshops for their colleagues (see Appendix C for information on education conferences). In Box 7.2, two resourceful and creative dual language teachers recount their first visit to CABE's National Two-Way Bilingual Immersion Program Conference and how they planned and conducted teacher professional development workshops based on their conference participation.

Within the school, teachers who have expertise or extensive experience in particular areas can also be valuable sources of information and knowledge. Finally, professional videos on dual language and related subjects can provide a good starting point for teacher training and discussion. Videos, such as those listed in Appendix B, portray a broad array of elementary classroom interactions and offer real-life examples of the theories and instructional practices discussed in professional development in-services and program implementation forums. Many of

Attending a National Dual Language Conference

BOX 7.2

After the winter holiday break, Azza and Shailja approached the principal about getting school funding to attend CABE's National Two-Way Bilingual Immersion Program Conference in California. Knowing that it might be a stretch, since they were in Chicago, they armed themselves with information about the nature of the conference, registration fees, and projected travel costs. They also presented a proposal detailing how they would bring back information to share with the teachers and parents and how they would present several staff development workshops based on the sessions they attended at the conference. Although it didn't take much convincing to get the principal's support, getting the funds to attend the conference was more challenging. In the end, the principal paid for the registration fees, the parent council paid for the airfare, and money raised from the school's parking lot evening rental went toward some of the hotel expenses.

Azza and Shailja are dual language teachers who have team-taught in first grade for two years. They wanted to take advantage of a conference that specializes in dual language and hear from other dual language educators. After returning from the conference, Azza and Shailja spent several weeks putting together a booklet with all the information they had gathered. They included pamphlets of vendors and publishers, handouts from sessions they attended, and a summary of information they collected that was most relevant to their school. They then prepared two teacher staff development workshops (literacy instruction and assessment) and one parent workshop (supporting second language acquisition at home). Based on their success in preparing and conducting these workshops, the principal established a special fund to partly subsidize the travel expenses for two teachers to attend the conference each year and follow Azza and Shailja's model for staff development.

these videos include guidelines with suggested timelines, topics of discussion, handouts, and transparencies.

Lindholm-Leary (2001) cautions that teacher preparation should be focused and selective. That is, not all the recommended topics presented here can be addressed at one time. An effective strategy to cope with the vast range of issues that need to be tackled in dual language education is to focus on one category each year. For instance, in the first year of implementation, professional development workshops may address dual language organization and pedagogy. In subsequent years, a school may focus on language and literacy issues, academic content approaches, and assessment issues. Although all these topics should be discussed and addressed from the inception of the program, dual language teachers and administrators may decide to concentrate on one area each year.

Dual Language Teacher and Staff Meetings

Maintaining an effective dual language program or improving a struggling program requires continuous dialog, reflection, and reformulations among teachers, administrators, and support staff. Consequently, designating time and organizing frequent opportunities for faculty to meet is vital to a program's endurance and improvement. Table 7.1 proposes various purposes and grouping arrangements for faculty meetings. For teachers who are team-teaching, weekly gatherings to plan and talk are indispensable to effective collaboration. Teachers from the same grade level, even those who are not in the dual language program, benefit from getting together weekly to plan and discuss curricular issues. In addition, grade-level dual language teachers should also have opportunities to periodically meet with grade-level teachers from the preceding or subsequent grades. For example,

■ TABLE 7.1 | **Sample Schedule of Meetings**

Who	When	Purpose
Team-teachers	*At least twice a week*	■ Plan and organize curriculum
Grade level	*At least once a week*	■ Plan and discuss curriculum
Cross-grade	*Once a quarter*	■ Discuss progress and needs of preceding and subsequent grade levels
Committee (grade-level reps, coordinator, etc.)	*Once or twice a month*	■ Discuss progress and needs ■ Identify focus of improvement ■ Identify and organize staff development and resource needs
Full program	*At least once a month*	■ Discuss progress and needs ■ Disseminate information ■ Share challenges and successes

first-grade teachers meet with kindergarten teachers one quarter and with second-grade teachers another quarter. The purpose of these cross-grade meetings is to communicate and clarify specific grade-level expectations and curriculum to the adjacent grade levels.

For schools that have created dual language committees with one teacher representative from each grade as well as the coordinator, principal, and resource teachers who support the program, committee meetings can be a hub for sharing other teachers' requests, successes, and challenges; making programmatic decisions; and engaging in long-term planning. Similarly, full faculty dual language meetings at which all teachers and supporting staff meet periodically to discuss past, present, and future status of the program are essential to maintaining open and clear communication among the teaching staff and administrators.

Revitalizing the Program

Effective and enduring dual language programs embrace cultural and linguistic diversity and continually endorse the equal status of both languages in and outside of school (Lessow-Hurley, 2000; McCollum, 1999; Nieto, 2000). Preserving this vital premise takes a conscious and deliberate effort from all members of the learning community. One way to ensure a balance of status between the two languages is to create a print-rich environment throughout the entire school that represents the two languages equally. Messages or labels on notices, flyers, bulletin boards, and information panels should be written in both languages. This serves a dual purpose: first, to maintain equality in use of and exposure to the print of each language; and second, to provide access to information and knowledge to all members of the school, regardless of their second language proficiency level. In the total immersion model, a greater emphasis on school environmental print in the minority language may be justifiable, since this immersion model aims at providing maximum exposure to the minority language.

The authentic use of the minority language for everyday communication that does not involve instruction should also be promoted throughout the school. Teachers, secretarial staff, and even cafeteria and custodial personnel who are bilingual should be encouraged to use the non-English language in the school hallways, cafeteria, and offices. This effort to increase the use of the minority language outside the classroom not only elevates the status of the language and its speakers, but also sets a very clear purpose and increases the motivation for majority language students to acquire their second language. However, Valdés (1997) cautions that English language learners in some total immersion schools, especially those with high percentages of minority language students, may be at risk of not developing sufficient English language proficiencies if the programs are not well designed. Thus, the intention is not to eliminate the English language in the school halls, either in written or oral form, but rather to incorporate and increase the minority language so as to create an environment in which the two languages are equally required for communication. While increasing the oral and written use of the minority language in the school, all members of the learning community, including students, must have a clear understanding of language etiquette. That is, the language should not be used to marginalize or exclude those who are not proficient in that language, even if this is not intended.

In addition to continually promoting the minority language in meaningful and authentic ways, a multicultural curriculum that addresses culture from multiple perspectives is essential to a comprehensive and effective dual language program (Sleeter & Grant, 1999). Maintaining a strong cultural component is not an easy feat, given the increasing pressures to cover core curriculum and prepare for standardized tests on curricular content. Program teachers and administrators must periodically revisit the school's dual language mission and vision statements, goals and objectives, and curricular designs to ensure that the cultural component of the program is followed and attains the expected results.

 # TROUBLESHOOTING

Teacher Ambivalence

Particularly during the initial stages of implementation, teachers and other staff unfamiliar with dual language education may have misgivings about participating in the program (Castro Feinberg, 1999). This is especially true in schools in which the decision to start dual language comes from the administration without consultation or inclusion of teachers in the decision-making process. The first and most expedient way to handle teachers' initial hostility toward the program is to provide them with ample and ongoing opportunities to express their concerns and apprehensions. Box 7.3 presents the case of a bilingual teacher who underwent a transformation from self-imposed outsider to enthusiastic participant in the program.

Secondly, since many fears are based on false assumptions and lack of information, teacher in-service professional development is critical in addressing issues related to dual language education. Once teachers are implementing the program, and assuming it has been well designed and thought out, many teachers' uncertainties are replaced by confidence and enthusiasm, such as in the case of Alma. However, even after the program has been in existence for a time, there may still be a number of teachers who simply do not believe in dual language education. This handful of teachers can greatly undermine the program and hinder its effectiveness. More damaging might be their detrimental impact on minority language students' perceptions about their own language and culture as well as majority language students' negative attitudes about the minority language and culture. A drastic way to resolve this situation is for administrators to

BOX
7.3

The Transformation of a Dual Language Disbeliever

When the principal began talking about starting a dual language program at her school, Alma thought, "Here we go again, jumping on the bandwagon of the latest fad." At the time, Alma had been a bilingual primary teacher for sixteen years. She had been teaching transitional bilingual third grade at this school for the past nine years and felt well-prepared to teach the academic and ESL goals and standards to her students.

Alma's negative reaction about dual language came from years of trying new programs, approaches, and instructional series that the school or district administration imposed on teachers, then abandoned. She did not think that the school needed to try another experiment, such as dual language, on them or the students. She expressed her disagreement about starting this program to parents, teachers, and the principal whenever she had the opportunity. But after months of discussions, the majority of the faculty and staff voted in favor of implementing the program, beginning with kindergarten and first grade. Although she would not be part of dual language for a few years, she informed the principal that, when the time came, she would move to the upper grades to avoid participating.

By the time dual language reached third grade, Alma was one of the program's most enthusiastic and committed supporters. What made Alma change so drastically? Many things. With time, Alma became better informed about what dual language is and what it is not. She began to understand that many of her beliefs about language acquisition and pedagogy where very much in tune with the philosophical frameworks behind dual language education. Alma's change of heart was also partly due to feeling that she could ask questions and challenge issues that were unclear or left unanswered. She felt that she could voice her opinion and appreciated the opportunities to find more information or clarification. More importantly, Alma saw first hand how children in the dual language program were progressing academically in their first and second languages, the bonds that were developing between groups of children that had seldom interacted before, and parents' satisfaction with their children's participation in the program. She also noticed something that had bothered her for some time was beginning to disappear: the marked divisions between bilingual and general program teachers were slowly giving way to meaningful collaborations and friendships.

assert their commitment to the program and replace the unreceptive teachers. When circumstances reach this point, both the antagonistic teachers and the dual language schools are more than happy to part ways, given their incompatibility in philosophy and views.

Parent and Community Skepticism

Parents who have reservations about having their children in dual language education should also be given ample opportunities and forums to ask questions, present their concerns, and discuss the issues that are most important to them. In the same way that teachers' ambivalence is addressed, parents' insecurities and doubts are reduced by organizing ongoing parent meetings and providing information, details, and clear explanations about the program. Parents should also be consulted and informed about the progress and status of the dual language program on an ongoing basis.

A proven and effective approach is for teachers to invite apprehensive parents to visit classrooms so that they can see for themselves the supportive and positive learning environments in which their children are involved. At the top of the list of parent concerns is the fear that children will be confused by the two languages and that they will not adequately develop their English language proficiency. Teachers can provide much information to parents by regularly communicating with them; however, for parents there is nothing like seeing with their own eyes what takes place in the classroom. In Box 7.4, two parents recollect their initial misgivings about the dual language program and how teachers, administrators, and the children themselves addressed these doubts.

Shortage of Qualified Teachers

A school that has an established reputation as an outstanding place of learning will likely attract talented and accomplished teachers. Likewise, a successful dual language program with a solid track record will also attract qualified teachers who are interested in dual language and additive forms of bilingual education. Hence, in the long term, the recruitment of qualified and interested teachers and other support staff requires schools and their dual language programs to have a

---

BOX 7.4

Parents' Perspectives on Dual Language Education

When the dual language program was first presented to parents and teachers for consideration, two of the most active parents in the school, Mrs. Heng and Mr. Rivas, reacted with skepticism and concern. Mrs. Heng has three children in the mainstream English program: twins in kindergarten and one child in third grade. Although her family is of Asian descent, everyone in her household speaks English exclusively. Mr. Rivas has two children in the bilingual program: one in kindergarten and one in first grade. His entire family is Spanish dominant, since they arrived from Guatemala only two years ago.

Mrs. Heng and Mr. Rivas were particularly concerned because the program that was being proposed was a total immersion 80–20 model. Mrs. Heng was apprehensive that her kindergarten twins would fall behind academically and not develop strong literacy skills in English. On the other hand, Mr. Rivas felt that his children would not develop English proficiency in a program that devoted so much time to Spanish.

Mr. Rivas and Mrs. Heng voiced their concerns to the principal and teachers. They, among other parents, were invited to participate in several informational sessions on dual language education. They also participated in two program visits to neighboring schools that were implementing dual language education. After the visits and information sessions, they understood the program's philosophy and structure better, but they were still unconvinced about its effectiveness and worried about its potential detriment to their children. The principal and a group of teachers established monthly parent meetings at which more information about the program was shared and parents' questions and concerns were addressed. Experts in the field of dual language education were invited to speak to the parents, as were dual language teachers and parents from neighboring schools. Several videos on dual language classrooms were also viewed and discussed by the parents.

After much discussion and many questions, Mr. Rivas and Mrs. Heng began to feel that the school had the right elements for the program to be effective. They knew that most teachers were very dedicated, used learner-centered instruction, were willing to invest time to plan, and were committed to communicating extensively with parents about their children's progress. Once the program began, Mrs. Heng and Mr. Rivas became parent representatives on the dual language parent committee and the dual language evaluation committee (made up of teachers, parents, and administrators). After three years in the program, Mr. Rivas and Mrs. Heng are very happy about their children's growth in both languages as well as their academic progress. They now talk to incoming parents about the successes of the program and help put new parents' worries at ease.

demonstrated record of high student achievement and strong support for educators in terms of teacher voice, available resources, and continual professional development opportunities. In addition, dual language administrators and teachers can create a replacement strategy: a plan to replace existing educators who voluntarily depart, either for personal (such as retirement or relocation) or professional (such as promotion or continuing education) reasons, with qualified teachers who have a clear interest in dual language education.

In terms of immediate needs for qualified practitioners, particularly in the planning and initial stages of program implementation, schools can employ several strategies. First, individual schools can institute local policies to require all dual language teachers and support staff to complete a determined number of professional development hours or in-services related to dual language education. Districts and schools can also facilitate teachers' efforts to become certified and/or endorsed in bilingual education and/or ESL by either offering full or partial funding for course tuition or by providing information about certification and endorsement procedures and requirements. Second, schools can petition their district offices for increased funding to hire new, qualified teachers to teach in their dual language programs. Third, individual schools can also apply for federal grants specifically aimed at increasing the number of dual language, bilingual, or foreign language programs. Many of these grants require comprehensive teacher professional development and certification for noncertified teachers.

Imbalance of Students from Each Language Group

The representation of both languages must reflect a balanced number of target language and majority language students (Christian, Montone, Lindholm & Carranza, 1997). This is of paramount importance, given that one of the major tenets of dual language education is the social and academic interaction of students from both language groups. This particular component is often a source of concern for many schools that do not have a balanced representation of both languages in the school population.

The recommendation from the Center of Applied Linguistics is that at least two-thirds of students in a school that intends to implement a dual language program should be dominant in either the minority or the majority language. Dual language programs with disproportionate numbers of students from the minority or majority language are compelled to either recruit or retain students from the underrepresented language. This is not easily accomplished, given that the makeup of the student body in many schools is directly dictated by neighborhood demographics. Schools in which almost all students speak the minority language and there is minimal representation of the majority language should reconsider implementing a dual language program and instead consider doing other additive second language program models, such as heritage language and maintenance programs. Schools that have negligible numbers of students of the minority language may consider implementing language enrichment or foreign language programs rather than dual language education.

Student mobility or attrition also hampers efforts to maintain a balanced representation of students from both language groups. Dual language teachers and administrators must continually inform and remind parents about the importance of student attendance. Parents should have a clear understanding that having their children in a dual language program is a long-term commitment, and that transferring children in and out of the program may have adverse effects on their academic and, for some, linguistic development. New students who are admitted into the program in third and fourth grade will likely be at a disadvantage compared to students who have been in dual language since kindergarten or first grade. This is especially challenging for English-dominant students who may have insufficient command of the second language to perform academic tasks and who have no second language support at home. Majority language students who participate in dual language from the early grades have continuous and gradual opportunities to acquire and develop the second language in early childhood contexts that rely heavily on social interaction and focus on language development. These same majority language students who transfer into dual language programs in third grade or above do not have these social and academic linguistic experiences in the second language. Compounding this problem is the fact that content and literacy demands become progressively more complex and abstract beyond third grade.

SUMMARY

For the longevity and continued effectiveness of innovative and enriching educational undertakings, such as dual language education, school practitioners are directly responsible for ensuring permanence and continual improvement. The final chapter of this book delineates some of the recurrent issues with which many dual language educators continue to struggle. As laid out in the preceding chapters as well as in recent research findings, dual language education is not a simple or unproblematic endeavor. On the contrary, in varying degrees, most dual language schools encounter complications and stumbling blocks along the way. The challenge in overcoming these temporary setbacks is lessened when educators, parents, and students have clear understandings of the theoretical, pedagogical, and sociocultural issues involved in the successful implementation of dual language education. Effective and enduring dual language programs require sustained dedication and support from all those involved. A fervent long-term commitment is necessary on the part of parents, students, teachers, and administrators to maintain quality enrichment education for all learners.

DISCUSSION QUESTIONS

1. Why do you think implementing dual language programs requires long-term commitment and advocacy on the part of all participants?

2. How do you think teachers and parents can become more involved in the decision-making process?

3. After several years of implementation, what type of information do you think would be critical in determining the strengths and weaknesses of a dual language program? Once key strengths and weaknesses of a dual language program have been determined, how should this information be used, by whom, and for what purposes?

4. In what ways can dual language schools ensure that the minority language and culture are given equal status with the English language and the mainstream culture?

5. What do you think may be other obstacles or sources of difficulty in dual language education, aside from the ones presented in this chapter? Explain how you might formulate solutions to these challenges.

FIELD-BASED INQUIRY

1. Interview parents whose children participate in dual language education, and inquire about their perceptions of the program. How has the dual language program benefited their children, and how has it benefited them as parents? Have their opinions about the program changed over time? If so, in what ways? Would they recommend this enrichment language program to other parents? Why?

2. Explain the dual language program to a person who is not an educator. Inquire about his or her views of the program, and whether he or she thinks it is a worthwhile educational endeavor. Find out about the person's opinions on minority language students' retaining and developing their native language compared to majority language students' acquiring a second or foreign language.

FURTHER READING

A to ez: Handbook for bilingual teachers staff development guide. New York: Macmillan/McGraw-Hill.

Amrein, A., & Peña, R. A. (2000). Asymmetry in dual language practice: Assessing imbalance in a program promoting equality. *Education Policy Analysis,* 8, 8.

Castro Feinberg, R. (1999). Administration of two-way bilingual elementary schools: Building on strengths. *Bilingual Research Journal,* 23 (1), 234–249.

Sugarman, J., & Howard, E. (2001). *Development and maintenance of two-way immersion programs: Advice from practitioners.* Washington, DC and Santa Cruz, CA: Center for Research on Education, Diversity and Excellence.

Children's Literature and PreK–8 Publishers

A room without books is like a body without a soul.

Cicero

CHILDREN'S LITERATURE

The following collection of children's literature is based on my personal library collection, my experiences using these books as an elementary school teacher and university professor, and my extensive visits to dual language classrooms. This list includes some of the many high-quality fiction books that are used in dual language classrooms (☆ denotes my own special favorites). Although the list presents books in Spanish and English for the most part, publishers are increasingly producing books in other languages, such as Vietnamese, Lao, Khmer, Hmong, Cambodian, Chinese, Korean, French, Persian, Arabic, Japanese, Tagalog, and Russian (see publisher information at the end of this Appendix). In addition, although this list contains fiction books, many high-quality nonfiction books are available in English and Spanish, as well as in other languages.

Bilingual Fiction Books in English and Spanish ~ PreK–2

Text in English and Spanish in the same book

- *Abuelo and the Three Bears ~ Abuelo y los tres osos* (a Latino twist)
  Jerry Tello (1998) New York: Springer
- *America, a Book of Opposites ~ America un libro de contrarios* (multicultural)
  W. Nikola-Lisa (2001) New York: Lee & Low Books
- ☆ *Calor* (native traditions)
  Juanita Alba (1995) Waco, TX: WRS Publishers
- *Carlos and the Squash Plant ~ Carlos y la planta de calabaza* (New Mexico farm)
  Jan Romero Stevens (1993) Flagstaff, AZ: Northland Publishing
- *Hair ~ Pelitos* (a story from the House on Mango Street)
  Sandra Cisneros (1994) New York: Alfred Knopf
- *From the Bellybutton of the Moon ~ Del ombligo de la luna* (poems, Mexico/United States)
  Francisco Alarcón and Maya Cristina González (1998) San Francisco: Children's Book Press
- *Grandmother's Nursery Rhymes ~ Las nanas de abuelita*
  Nelly Palacios Jaramillo (1994) New York: Henry Holt and Company

- *Iguanas in the Snow ~ Iguanas en la nieve* (poems, Latin America/United States)
  Francisco Alarcón (2000) San Francisco: Children's Book Press
- *Little Tortillas for Mama ~ Tortillas para mamá* (Latin American nursery rhymes)
  Margot Griego (1981) New York: Holt, Rinehart and Winston
- *My First Book of Proverbs ~ Mi primer libro de dichos*
  Ralfka González and Ana Ruíz (1995) San Francisco: Children's Book Press
- *Say Hola to Spanish* (rhyming/vocabulary)
  Susan Middleton Elya (1996) New York: Lee & Low Books
- ☆ *Say Hola to Spanish Otra Vez (Again!)* (rhyming/vocabulary)
  Susan Middleton Elya (1997) New York: Lee & Low Books
- ☆ *See What You Say ~ Ve lo que dices* (multicultural)
  Nancy Maria Grande Tabor (2000) Flagstaff, AZ: Northland Publishers
- ☆ *The Bossy Gallito ~ El gallo de bodas* (Cuban folktale)
  Lucía González (1994) New York: Scholastic
- *The Spirit of Tío Fernando ~ El espíritu del tío Fernando* (Mexican folktale)
  Ken Buchanan (1994) Flagstaff, AZ: Northland Publishers
- *Uncle Nacho's Hat ~ El sombrero del tío Nacho* (Mexican folktale)
  Harriet Rohmer (1989) New York: Marwin Productions
- ☆ *We Are a Rainbow ~ Somos un arco iris* (multicultural)
  Nancy Maria Grande Tabor (1995) Watertown, ME: Charlesbridge

Bilingual Fiction Books in English and Spanish ~ 3–5

Text in English and Spanish in the same book

- *Family Pictures ~ Cuadros de familia* (Mexican American/Texas)
  Carmen Lomas Garza (1990) San Francisco: Children's Book Press

■ *Hands across America ~ Manos a través de la Frontera* (United States/Mexico)
Helen West-Rodríguez and Carmen Rodríguez (1999) New York: Brown Books

☆ *Pen Pals: A Friendship in English and Spanish* (Mexico/ United States)
Catherine Bruzzone and Lone Morton (1998) Chicago: Passport Books

☆ *The Flute Player ~ La flautista* (urban/music)
Robin Eversole (1995) New York: Orchard Books

■ *The Gullywasher ~ El chaparrón torrencial* (Southwest)
Joyce Rossi (1995) Flagstaff, AZ: Northland Publishers

FICTION BOOKS AVAILABLE IN ENGLISH AND SPANISH

Pattern and Predictable Language Books ~ PreK–2

■ *Goodnight Moon ~ Buenas noches, luna*
Margaret Wise Brown (1947) New York: Harper & Row

☆ *Guess What? ~ ¿Qué crees?*
Mem Fox (1984) New York: Kane/Miller Book Publishers

■ *I Went Walking ~ Salí de paseo*
Sue Williams (1989) New York: Harcourt Brace Jovanovich

■ *If You Give Mouse a Cookie ~ Si le das una galletita a un ratón*
Laura Joffe Numeroff (1985) New York: Harper & Row

■ *Nicky and the Big Bad Wolves ~ Nico y los lobos feroces*
Valeri Gorbachev (1998) New York: North-South Books

☆ *Olivia*
Aleksei Tolstoy (1998) New York: Blue Sky Press

☆ *Owl Babies ~ Las lechucitas*
Martin Waddell (1992) Cambridge, MA: Candlewick Press

☆ *Pigs Aplenty, Pigs Galore ~ ¡Cerdos a montones, cerdos a granel!*
David McPhail (1993) New York: Scholastic

■ *Rosie's Walk ~ El paseo de Rosie*
Pat Hutchins (1968) New York: Simon & Schuster Books

■ *The Doorbell Rang ~ Llaman a la puerta*
Pat Hutchins (1986) New York: Greenwillow Books

☆ *Where Is My Teddy? ~ ¿Dónde está mi osito?*
Jez Alborough (1992) Cambridge, MA: Candlewick Press

Fiction ~ PreK–2

■ *Ana Banana and Me ~ Ana Banana y yo*
Leonore Blegvad (1989) Boston: Houghton Mifflin

■ *Borreguita and the Coyote ~ Borreguita y el coyote* (Mexican folktale)
Verna Aardema (1991) New York: Scholastic

☆ *Chrysanthemum ~ Crisántemo*
Kevin Henkes (1991) New York: Greenwillow Books

■ *Harold and the Purple Crayon ~ Harold y el lápiz color morado*
Crockett Johnson (1960) New York: Harper

■ *Jamaica's Find ~ El hallazgo de Jamaica* (African American character)
Juanita Havill (1986) Boston: Houghton Mifflin Company

■ *Ruby the Copycat ~ Ruby mono ve, mono hace*
Peggie Rathman (1991) New York: Scholastic

■ *Stellaluna ~ Stelaluna*
Janell Cannon (1993) San Diego, CA: Harcourt Brace

■ *Tell Me Again about the Night I Was Born ~ Cuentame otra vez la noche que nací*
Jamie Lee Curtis (1996) New York: HarperCollins

☆ *The Cow That Went Oink ~ La vaca que decía oink* (bilingual animals!)
Bernard Most (1990) New York: Scholastic

■ *The Button Box ~ La caja de botones*
Margarette Reid (1990) New York: Puffin Unicorn Books

■ *The Rainbow Fish ~ El pez arco iris* (also in Chinese)
Marcus Pfister (1992) New York: North-South Books

■ *The Trek ~ El trayecto*
Ann Jonas (1985) New York: Greenwillow Books

☆ *The Whales' Song ~ El canto de las ballenas*
Dyan Sheldon (1991) New York: Dial Books for Young Readers

■ *Where the Wild Things Are ~ Donde viven los monstrous*
Maurice Sendak (1963) New York: Harper Trophy

■ *Wilfrid Gordon McDonald Partridge ~ Guillermo Jorge Manuel José* (aging)
Mem Fox (1988) Orlando, FL: Harcourt Brace Jovanovich

☆ *This House Is Made of Mud ~ Esta casa está hecha de lodo* (Southwest)
Ken Buchanan (1994) Flagstaff, AZ: Northland Publishers

Fiction Series ~ PreK–2

- *Arthur ~ Arturo Series*
  Marc Brown, New York: Little Brown & Co.
- *Clifford ~ Clifford Series*
  Norman Bridwell, New York: Cartwheel Books
- *Franklin ~ Franklin Series*
  Paulette Bourgeois, New York: Scholastic Trade

Fiction ~ 3–6

- *A Wrinkle in Time ~ Una arruga en el tiempo*
  Madeleine L'Engle (1962) New York: Farrar, Straus, and Giroux
- *Abel's Island ~ La isla de Abel*
  William Steig (1976) New York: Farrar, Straus and Giroux
- ☆ *Bunnycula ~ Bonícula*
  Deborah and James Howe (1996) New York: Aladdin Paperbacks
- *Charlotte's Web ~ Las telarañas de Carlota*
  E. B. White (1952) New York: Harper
- *Freckel Juice ~ Jugo de pecas*
  Beverly Cleary (1971) New York: Four Winds Press
- *Hatchet ~ El hacha*
  Gary Paulsen (1987) New York: Trumpet Club
- *Shiloh*
  Phyllis Reynolds Naylor (1991) New York: Maxwell Macmillan International
- *The Hundred Dresses ~ Los cien vestidos* (Polish theme)
  Eleanor Estes (1944) New York: Harcourt-Brace
- *The Indian in the Cupboard ~ La llave mágica*
  Lynne Reid Banks (1981) Garden City: Doubleday

Fiction Series ~ 3–6

- *Ramona Series*
  Beverly Cleary, New York: Harper Trophy
- *C. S. Lewis Series*
  New York: Harper Collins
- *Roald Dahl Series*
  New York: Puffin
- *Goosebumps ~ Escalofríos Series*
  R. L. Stine, New York: Scholastic Trade
- *Harry Potter Series*
  J. K. Rowling, New York: Scholastic Trade

- *Laura Ingalls Wilder Series*
- *Ghosts of Fear Street ~ Fantasmas de Fear Street Series*
  R. L. Stine, New York: Aladdin books

Latino Culture ~ PreK–2

- *Abuela* (urban)
  Arthur Dorros (1991) New York: Dutton Children's Books
- *Abuela's Weave ~ El tapiz de la Abuela* (Guatemala)
  Omar Castañeda (1993) New York: Lee & Low Books
- ☆ *Let's Eat! ~ ¡A comer!* (Spain)
  Ana Zamorano (1996) New York: Scholastic
- *Salsa* (Afro-Caribbean in New York)
  Lillian Colón-Vilá (1998) Houston, TX: Piñata Books
- *The Tortilla Factory ~ La tortillería*
  Gary Paulsen (1995) San Diego, CA: Harcourt Brace

Latino Culture ~ 3–5

- *Atariba & Niguayona* (Puerto Rican fable, bilingual)
  Harriet Rhomer and Jesús Guerrero Rea (1988) San Francisco: Children's Book Press
- *In My Family ~ En mi familia* (Mexican American, bilingual)
  Carmen Lomas Garza (1996) San Francisco: Children's Book Press
- *Miguel Vicente the Wanderer ~ Miguel Vicente, pata caliente* (Venezuela)
  Orlando Araujo (1992) Caracas, Venezuela: Ekaré-Banco del Libro
- *The Most Beautiful Place in the World ~ El lugar más bonito del mundo* (Guatemala)
  Ann Cameron (1996) Miami, FL: Santillana
- *The Red Comb ~ La peineta colorada* (Puerto Rico)
  Fernando Picó (1991) Mahwah, NJ: Bridgewater Books
- ☆ *The Streets Are Free ~ La calle es libre* (Venezuela)
  Karusa (1981) Caracas, Venezuela: Ediciones Ekare
- *The Weeping Woman ~ La llorona* (Latin American folktale, bilingual)
  Joe Hayes (1987) El Paso, TX: Cinco Puntos Press
- *Tell Me a Cuento ~ Cuentame una Story* (Latin American folktales, bilingual)
  Joe Hayes (1998) El Paso, TX: Cinco Puntos Press
- *Vejigante* (Puerto Rico)
  Lulu Delacre (1993) New York: Scholastic

The Immigrant Experience ~ 3–5

☆ *Amelia's Road ~ El camino de Amelia* (migrant worker experience)
Linda Jacobs Altman (1993) New York: Lee & Low Books

▬ *Calling the Doves ~ El canto de las palomas* (migrant worker poetry, bilingual)
Juan Felipe Herrera (1995) San Francisco: Children's Book Press

▬ *Friends from the Other Side ~ Amigos del otro lado* (Mexico, bilingual)
Gloria Anzaldúa (1993) San Francisco: Children's Book Press

☆ *La Mariposa* (migrant worker experience)
Francisco Jiménez (1998) Boston: Houghton Mifflin

▬ *Molly's Pilgrim ~ Molly y los peregrinos* (Russian)
Barbara Cohen (1983) New York: Lothrop, Lee & Shepard Books

▬ *My Name Is Jorge on Both Sides of the River* (Mexico, bilingual)
Jane Medina (1999) Honesdale, PA: Wordsong/Boyds Mills Press

▬ *Pie-Biter ~ Comepasteles* (Chinese, trilingual)
Ruthanne Lum McCunn (1998) Acadia, CA: Shen's Books

▬ *The Keeping Quilt ~ La colcha de los recuerdos* (Russian)
Patricia Polacco (1988) New York: Simon & Schuster Books for Young Readers

☆ *The Magic Shell ~ El regalo mágico* (Dominican Republic)
Nicholasa Mohr (1995) New York: Scholastic

▬ *When Jessie Came across the Sea ~ Cuando Jessie cruzó el océano* (Eastern Europe)
Amy Hest (1997) Cambridge, MA: Candlewick Press

Diversity and Multiculturalism ~ PreK–2

☆ *Bein' with You This Way ~ La alegría de ser tú y yo* (diversity)
W. Nikola-Lisa (1994) New York: Lee & Low Books

▬ *Crow Boy ~ Niño cuervo* (Native American)
Taro Yashima (1983) Harmondsworth, England: Puffin Books

▬ *Elizabeti's Doll ~ La muñeca de Elizabeti* (Tanzanian)
Stephanie Stuve-Bodeen (1998) New York: Lee & Low Books

☆ *Frida* (Mexican artist Frida Kahlo)
Jonah Winter (2002) New York: Arthur Levin Books

▬ *Stevie* (African American)
John Steptoe (1969) New York: Harper & Row

▬ *The Shepard Boy ~ El niño pastor* (Native American)
Kristine Franklin (1994) New York: Atheneum

Diversity and Multiculturalism ~ 3–5

▬ *Annie and the Old One ~ Ani y la anciana* (Native American)
Miska Miles (1971) Boston: Little, Brown

▬ *Brother Eagle, Sister Sky ~ Hermana águila, hermano cielo* (Native American)
Chief Seattle (1991) New York: Dial Books

▬ *The Ballad of Mulan ~ La balada de Mulán* (Chinese fable, available in Spanish, Chinese, Hmong, Vietnamese)
Song Nan Zhang (1998) Union City, CA: Pan Asian Publications

▬ *The Best of Friends ~ Los mejores amigos* (disabilities)
Pirkko Vainio (2000) New York: North-South Books

Urban Issues ~ 2–5

☆ *America Is Her Name ~ La llaman América* (immigrant, Chicago, urban life)
Luis Rodríguez (1997) Willimantic, CT: Curbstone Press

▬ *It Doesn't Have to Be This Way: A Barrio Story ~ No tiene que ser así. Una historia del barrio* (gang life)
Luis Rodríguez (1999) San Francisco: Children's Book Press

☆ *Smoky Night ~ Noche de humo* (Los Angeles riots)
Eve Bunting (1994) San Diego, CA: Harcourt Brace

▬ *The Lady in the Box ~ La señora de la caja de cartón* (homelessness)
Ann McGovern (1997) New York: Turtle Books

CROSS-CULTURAL AND MULTICULTURAL BOOKS IN ENGLISH

Picture Books

☆ *Big Jimmy's Kum Kau Chinese Take Out* (Chinese in Brooklyn)
Ted Lewin (2002) New York: Harper Collins

▬ *Everybody Bakes Bread* (multicultural)
Norah Dooley (1996) Minneapolis: Carolrhoda Books

☆ *Everybody Cooks Rice* (multicultural)
Norah Dooley (1991) Minneapolis: Carolrhoda Books

▬ *Everybody Serves Soup* (multicultural)
Norah Dooley (2000) Minneapolis: Carolrhoda Books

▬ *How My Parents Learned to Eat* (Chinese)
Ina Friedman (1984) Boston: Houghton Mifflin

- *I Speak English for My Mom* (immigration)
  Muriel Stanek (1989) Morton Grove, IL: Albert Whitman and Company

☆ *Kente Colors* (African)
  Debbie Chocolate (1996) New York: Walker and Company

☆ *Mama Provi and the Pot of Rice* (urban/multicultural)
  Sylvia Rosa-Casanova (1997) New York: Aladdin Paperbacks

☆ *Market!* (multicultural)
  Ted Lewin (1996) New York: Harper Collins

- *Mario's Mayan Journey* (Mexico)
  Michelle McCunney (1997) New York: Mondo

☆ *My House Has Stars* (multicultural)
  Megan McDonald (1996) New York: Scholastic

☆ *Uncle Rain Cloud* ~ (Mexican-American in Los Angeles)
  Tony Johnston (2001) Watertown, ME: Charlesbridge Publishing

☆ *Somewhere in the World Right Now* (global/multicultural)
  Stacey Schuett (1995) New York: Alfred Knopf

- *The Name Jar* (immigrant/Korean)
  Yangsook Choi (2001) New York: Alfred Knopf

☆ *The Talking Cloth* (United States/African traditions)
  Rhonda Mitchell (1997) New York: Orchard Books

- *Throw Your Tooth from the Roof: Tooth Traditions from around the World*
  Sally Beeler (1998) Boston: Houghton Mifflin

Wordless Picture Books

☆ *The Snowman* ~ *El muñeco de nieve*
  Raymond Briggs (1978) New York: Random House

- *Looking Down*
  Steve Jenkins (1995) Boston: Houghton Mifflin

- *People*
  Peter Spier (1980) Garden City, NY: Doubleday

- *Time Flies*
  Eric Rohman (1994) New York: Crown

- *Zoom*
  Istvan Banyai (1995) New York: Viking

BILINGUAL AUTHOR SETS IN ENGLISH AND SPANISH

Alma Flor Ada ~ PreK–5

- *Gathering the Sun: An Alphabet in Spanish and English* (migrant workers)
  (1997) New York: Lothrop, Lee & Shephard Books

☆ *I Love Saturdays y Domingos* (Mexican American)
  (2002) New York: Atheneum Books

- *My Name Is María Isabel* ~ *Me llamo María Isabel* (immigrant experience)
  (1993) New York: Aladdin Paperbacks

- *The Gold Coin* ~ *La moneda de oro* (Latin America)
  (1994) New York: Maxwell Macmillan Canada

- *The Lizard and the Sun* ~ *La lagartija y el sol* (Mexican folktale, bilingual)
  (1997) New York: Doubleday Book for Young Readers

Helen Cowcher in English, Spanish, and Chinese

- *Antártica* ~ *Antarctica*
  (1991) New York: Farrar, Straus and Giroux

- *Jaguar*
  (1997) New York: Scholastic

- *Nan chi ta lu* ~ *Antarctica* (Chinese)
  (1997) London, England: Milet

☆ *Rain Forest* ~ *El bosque tropical*
  (1988) New York: Farrar, Straus and Giroux

- *Tigress* ~ *Tigresa*
  (1991) New York: Farrar, Straus, and Giroux

Eric Carle ~ PreK–2

- *The Grouchy Ladybug* ~ *La mariquita malhumorada*
  (1996) New York: HarperCollins

- *The Hungry Caterpillar* ~ *La oruga muy hambrienta*
  (1987) New York: Philomel Books

Tomie de Paola ~ K–3

☆ *Erandi's Braids* ~ *Las trenzas de Erandi* (Mexican)
  (1999) New York: Putnam

- *Oliver Button Is a Sissy* ~ *Oliver Button es una nena*
  (1979) New York: Harcourt Brace Jovanovich

- *Strega Nona*
  (1975) Englewood Cliffs, NJ: Prentice-Hall

- *The Art Lesson* ~ *La clase de dibujo*
  (1989) New York: Putnam

- *The Legend of the Poinsettia* ~ *La leyenda de la nochebuena* (Mexican)
  (1994) New York: Putnam

Ezra Jack Keats ~ PreK–2

- *Peter's Chair* ~ *La silla de Pedro*

(1967) New York: Harper & Row

▥ *The Snowy Day* ~ *El día de nieve*
(1962) New York: Viking Press

▥ *Whistle for Willy* ~ *Sílbale a Willy*
(1964) New York: Viking Press

Pat Mora ~ PreK–3

▥ *Delicious Hullaballoo* ~ *Pachanga deliciosa* (Southwest, bilingual)
(1998) Houston, TX: Piñata Books

▥ *Listen to the Dessert* ~ *Oye al desierto* (Southwest, bilingual)
(1994) New York: Houghton Mifflin

▥ *One, Two, Three* ~ *Uno, dos, tres* (Mexican, bilingual)
(1996) New York: Clarion Books

☆ *The Desert Is My Mother* ~ *El desierto es mi madre* (Southwest, bilingual)
(1994) Houston, TX: Piñata Books

☆ *Tomas and the Library Lady* ~ *Tomás y la señora de la biblioteca* (Mexican American)
(1997) New York: Dragonfly Books

Robert Munsch ~ PreK–3

▥ *Angela's Airplane* ~ *El avión de Angela*
(1988) Toronto, Canada: Annick Press

▥ *David's Father* ~ *El papá de David*
(1983) Toronto, Canada: Annick Press

▥ *Love You Forever* ~ *Siempre te querré*
(1986) Buffalo, NY: Firefly Books

☆ *Moira's Birthday* ~ *El cumpleaños de Moira*
(1987) Toronto, Canada: Annick Press

▥ *Murmel, Murmel, Murmel* ~ *Agu, agu, agu*
(1982) Toronto, Canada: Annick Press

☆ *Pigs* ~ *Los cochinos*
(1989) Toronto, Canada: Annick Press

▥ *Purple, Green and Yellow* ~ *Verde, violeta y amarillo*
(1992) Toronto, Canada: Annick Press

▥ *The Boy in the Drawer* ~ *El muchacho en la gaveta*
(1990) Toronto, Canada: Annick Press

▥ *The Fire Station* ~ *La estación de bomberos*
(1991) Toronto, Canada: Annick Press

☆ *The Paper Bag Princess* ~ *La princesa vestida con una bolsa de papel*
(1980) Toronto, Canada: Annick Press

Shel Silverstein ~ K–up

☆ *A Light in the Attic* ~ *Una luz en el desván*
(1981) New York: HarperCollins

▥ *Falling Up* ~ *Batacazos*
(1996) New York: HarperCollins

▥ *The Giving Tree* ~ *El árbol generoso* (also in Chinese)
(1964) New York: Harper & Row

☆ *Who Wants a Cheap Rhinoceros?* ~ *¿Quién quiere un rinoceronte barato?*
(1983) New York: Macmillan

Gary Soto ~ K–8

▥ *Baseball in April and Other Stories* ~ *Béisbol en abril y otras historias* (Latino)
(1990) San Diego, CA: Harcourt Brace Jovanovich

☆ *Chato's Kitchen* ~ *Chato y su cena* (Mexican American, East Los Angeles)
(1995) New York: Putnam

▥ *Pacific Crossings* ~ *Cruzando el Pacífico* (Mexican American, Japan)
(1992) San Diego, CA: Harcourt Brace Jovanovich

▥ *Taking Sides* ~ *Tomando partido* (Mexican American)
(1991) San Diego, CA: Harcourt Brace Jovanovich

▥ *Too Many Tamales* ~ *¡Que montón de tamales!* (Mexican American)
(1993) New York: Putnam

Chris Van Allsburg ~ 1–5

▥ *Jumanji*
(1981) Boston: Houghton Mifflin Company

▥ *The Mysteries of Harris Burdick* ~ *Los misterios del Señor Burdick*
(1984) Boston: Houghton Mifflin

▥ *The Polar Express* ~ *El expreso polar*
(1985) Boston: Houghton Mifflin

▥ *The Sweetest Fig* ~ *El higo más dulce*
(1993) Boston: Houghton Mifflin

☆ *The Widow's Broom* ~ *La escoba de la bruja*
(1992) Boston: Houghton Mifflin

Audrey and Don Wood ~ PreK–2

☆ *Quick as a Cricket* ~ *Veloz como el grillo*
(1982) New York: Child's Play (International)

- *The Big Hungry Bear ~ El ratoncito, la fresa roja y madura y el gran oso hambriento*
  (1990) New York: Child's Play (International)

☆ *The Napping House ~ La casa adormecida*
  (1984) San Diego, CA: Harcourt Brace Jovanovich

Dr. Seuss ~ PreK–6

☆ *Green Eggs and Ham ~ Huevos verdes con jamón*
  (1960) New York: Beginner Books

- *How the Grinch Stole Christmas ~ Como el Grinch robó la navidad*
  (1957) New York: Random House

- *Oh, the Places You'll Go! ~ ¡Oh, cuán lejos llegarás!*
  (1990) New York: Random House

- *The 500 Hats of Bartholomew Cubbins ~ Los 500 sombreros de Bartolomé Cubbins*
  (1990) New York: Random House

- *The Cat in the Hat* (bilingual)
  (1985) New York: Random House

- *The Lorax ~ El Lórax*
  (1971) New York: Random House

PUBLISHERS

Trade Books and Collections

- ChildBook.com—Chinese Children's Books
  P.O. Box 8266, Rowland Heights, CA 91748
  http://www.childbook.com/index.html
  Chinese children's books and bilingual Chinese-English books, PreK–12.

- Iranbooks
  P.O. Box 30087, Bethesda, MD 20824
  http://iranbooks.com
  Persian language books and English books about Iran. Includes bilingual materials for children, PreK–12.

- Lectorum Publications, Inc.
  111 Eighth Ave., New York, NY 10011-5201
  http://www.lectorum.com
  Children's literature in English and Spanish, mostly fiction, but includes some nonfiction, classroom reference materials, big books, music, videos, and software, PreK–8.

- Many Cultures Publishing
  1095 Market St., Suite 602, San Francisco, CA 94103
  http://www.studycenter.org/mcp.html
  Bilingual storybooks with audiocassettes and teacher's guides in Vietnamese, Lao, Khmer, Hmong, Cambodian, and Mien, K–12.

- Perma-Bound Books
  617 Vandalia Rd., Jacksonville, IL 62650
  http://www.perma-bound.com
  Extensive collection of fiction and nonfiction children's literature in hard cover, including reference materials, K–12.

- Pan Asian Publications
  29564 Union City Blvd., Union City, CA 94587
  http://www.panap.com
  Asian educational and reference materials in Chinese, Vietnamese, Japanese, Korean, Thai, Khmer, Lao, Hmong, Tagalog, English, Spanish, and Russian, K–12.

- Scholastic Inc.
  557 Broadway, New York, NY 10012-3999
  http://www.scholastic.com
  Collection, series, and trade books, mostly in English, but a significant number of materials in Spanish. Also includes nonfiction, classroom reference materials, professional teaching books, big books, music, videos, and software, K–12.

- Shen's Books
  8625 Hubbard Road, Auburn, CA 95602-7815
  http://www.shens.com
  Extensive collection of books with Asian themes, as well as Latino and African children's literature. Features different versions of several traditional fairy tales from around the world, such as over sixty Cinderella titles.

Series, Readers and Textbooks

- Hampton-Brown Books
  P.O. Box 369, Marina, CA 93933
  http://www.hampton-brown.com
  Series and collections in English and Spanish for literacy and ESL instruction. Holistic, with a strong language development focus, K–8.

- Houghton-Mifflin
  222 Berkeley St., Boston, MA 02116
  http://www.hmco.com
  Textbooks, instructional technology, assessments, and other educational materials; includes curriculum materials in Spanish, K–12.

- McGraw-Hill Children's Publishing
  8787 Orion Place, Columbus, OH 43240
  http://www.mcgrawhill.com
  Series and collections in English and Spanish for literacy, ESL, math, science, and social studies instruction. Includes software and videos for curriculum areas, K–8.

- Scott Foresman/Addison Wesley
  1900 East Lake Ave. Glenview, IL 60025
  http://www.scottforesman.com or http://www.aw.com/aw/
  Scott Foresman offers series and collections in English and Spanish for literacy, ESL, math, science, and social studies

instruction for K–6. Addison Wesley offers materials for ESL, K–12.

CHILDREN'S LITERATURE WEB SITES

- The Association of Library Services to Children
  http://www.ala.org/alsc

- The Children's Literature Web Guide
  http://www.ucalgary.ca/~dkbrown/index.html

- The Internet Public Library Youth Division
  http://www.ipl.org/youth/

- National Association to Promote Library and Information Services to Latino and the Spanish-Speaking
  http://www.csusm.edu/csb/english/

- Barahona Center for the Study of Books in Spanish for Children and Adolescents
  http://clnet.ucr.edu/library/reforma/resources/

FEATURING DUAL LANGUAGE EDUCATION

Learning in Two Languages. Freedom, CA: Migrant Media Productions, 1999.

Introduces two-way bilingual immersion programs in San Francisco and includes footage of students, teachers, and parents working together in Cantonese, Korean, and Spanish immersion programs.

Learning Together: Two-Way Bilingual Immersion Programs. Santa Cruz, CA: National Center for Research on Cultural Diversity and Second Language Learning, Regents of the University of California, 1996.

Presents the rationale for two-way bilingual immersion and discusses its goals and effectiveness by showcasing classroom scenes depicting bilingual students engaged in challenging academic activities.

Many Voices, Many Dreams. Oak Brook, IL: NCREL, 1995.

Portrays how three schools, teachers, and students engage in multicultural and language pluralism. Students' prior culture, language, and experiences provide the foundation for learning and for understanding and accepting cultural differences. Features two dual language schools.

Profile of Effective Bilingual Teaching: Kindergarten. Santa Cruz, CA: National Center for Research on Cultural Diversity and Second Language Learning, Regents of the University of California, 1994.

Shows how an educator in a dual language kindergarten uses methods, techniques, and practices to promote effective bilingual teaching, with an emphasis on language development.

Profile of Effective Bilingual Teaching: First Grade. Santa Cruz, CA: National Center for Research on Cultural Diversity and Second Language Learning, Regents of the University of California, 1994.

Shows how a first-grade bilingual teacher uses methods, techniques, and practices to promote effective bilingual teaching in this dual language classroom, with an emphasis on early literacy development.

Profile of Effective Two-Way Bilingual Teaching: Sixth Grade. Santa Cruz, CA: National Center for Research on Cultural Diversity and Second Language Learning, Regents of the University of California, 1996.

Demonstrates how a sixth-grade dual language teacher uses methods, techniques, and practices to promote effective bilingual teaching, with an emphasis on critical thinking, problem-solving, and communication.

FEATURING FIRST AND SECOND LANGUAGE THEORIES AND PRACTICES

Communicative Math and Science Teaching: Enriching Content Classes for Secondary ESOL Students. Washington, DC: Center for Applied Linguistics, 1998.

Profiles middle and high schools that integrate language learning and academic learning in math and science for culturally and linguistically diverse students in three U.S. cities. Teachers demonstrate effective classroom practices, such as cooperative learning, communication, peer tutoring, problem solving, and positive uses of competition and games.

Developing the Young Bilingual Learner. Cincinnati, OH: NAEYC, 1996.

Explores the importance of supporting children's home language while also helping them learn English, and provides strategies for supporting young children in becoming bilingual learners.

English as a Second Language. ProServ Television and the Master Teacher. Port Chester, NY: National Professional Resources, 1998.

1. Legal and Practical Issues of Fair Assessment
2. Discovering Language Proficiencies of Culturally Diverse Students
3. Making the Right Choice: Distinguishing between ESL and Special Education
4. Authentic Assessment: Holistic Approaches for Assessing Progress

Designed to help educators understand appropriate evaluation that meets the learning needs and progress of ESL students and to make them better able to help students acquire the language skills necessary for success in English-based instruction. Classroom assessment, parental involvement, and techniques that respect individual student ability are discussed.

First and Second Language Literacy: From Research to Practice. Voices from the Pacific Islands. Honolulu, Hawaii: Pacific Resources for Education and Learning, 1999.

Features educators from the United States and Pacific Islands exploring research-based practices for teaching reading to multicultural student populations. Classroom footage shows various strategies for literacy development in linguistically diverse settings.

Instructional Conversations: Understanding through Discussion. Santa Cruz, CA: National Center for Research on Cultural Diversity. Regents of the University of California. Washington, DC: Center for Applied Linguistics, 1995.

Demonstrates how collaborative talk is used in the classroom to negotiate meaning between students and teacher in bilingual settings.

Multiple Intelligences and the Second Language Learner. Port Chester, NY: National Professional Resources, 1998.

Presents pioneering programs in California that integrate multiple intelligences with second language learning. It demonstrates how to teach in creative ways that focus on educational environments and account for learners' multiple intelligences.

Nourishing Language Development in Early Childhood. Davis, CA: Davidson Films, 1996.

Discusses the basic aspects of language, how language is acquired by young children, and strategies for nourishing early language acquisition.

Profile of Effective Teaching in a Multilingual Classroom. Santa Cruz, CA: National Center for Research on Cultural Diversity and Second Language Learning, Regents of the University of California, 1994.

Showcases an educator teaching in a middle school class composed of students from various linguistic backgrounds.

Teaching the Language of Print: Second Language Learning with Jim Cummins. Classroom Impact: An Early Literacy Staff Development Series. Bothell, WA: The Wright Group, 1998.

Presents theoretical and pedagogical implications for teaching and learning practices of English-language learners. First and second language proficiencies, literacy acquisition, and academic development are discussed.

Whisper and Smile: A Study in Verbal and Non-Verbal Communication Styles. Northbrook, IL: InService Works, 2000.

Highlights and discusses various cultural differences in verbal and nonverbal communication styles.

FEATURING MULTICULTURAL EDUCATION

In Our Classroom. Berkeley, CA: University of California, Extension Center for Media and Independent Learning, 1992.

Highlights a sixth-grade multilingual and multicultural classroom in a Los Angeles school in which students from fifteen countries are represented and nine different languages are spoken.

Educating Everybody's Children. Alexandria, VA: Association for Supervision and Curriculum Development, 2000.

1. *Attitudes and Beliefs*
2. *Capitalizing on Students' Strengths*
3. *Matching Instructional Methods to Students' Instructional Needs.*

Describes numerous teaching approaches that can be used across subject areas for grades K–12. The strategies and practices are effective for culturally and linguistically diverse students from a wide range of ability levels.

Storytelling as a Cultural Bridge. Instructional Support Services. Bloomington, IN: Indiana University, 1998.

Introduces the use of folktales, urban legends, and ballads with students learning English as a second language. Identifies words within the stories that may be unfamiliar to students, and discusses meanings and metaphors that reflect U.S. life and culture.

Diversity in the Elementary Classroom: Implications for Teaching. National Association of Elementary School Principals. Livingston, NJ: Instructivision, 1995.

Describes the ideological shift in the United States from the concept of the melting pot to that of the salad bowl. Promotes cultural pluralism by explaining how understanding cultural diversity helps in understanding classroom dynamics; why curriculum should be inclusive, holistic, and integrated; and the significance of having multiethnic and diverse educators.

FEATURING BEST PRACTICES

Teacher's Tool Kit for Beginning Reading: Applying Reading Research to Classroom Practices, with Marilyn Adams. Classroom Impact: An Early Literacy Staff Development Series. Bothell, WA: The Wright Group, 1998.

Shows how to link instructional practices with research on word recognition skills that include orthographic, phonologic, and semantic knowledge. Sound-symbol relationships, context, decoding, spelling-sound correspondence, and phonemes are also discussed.

A Balanced Approach to Reading: Becoming Successfully and Joyfully Literate, with Constance Weaver. Classroom Impact: An Early Literacy Staff Development Series. Bothell, WA: The Wright Group, 1998.

Literacy researcher Weaver examines balanced literacy approaches that integrate skills and strategies in context with reading, writing, listening, and speaking. Footage illustrates how to use flexible grouping and scaffolding strategies to reach the individual needs of all students.

Developing Oral Language and Phonemic Awareness through Rhythm and Rhyme, with Babs Bell Hajdusiewicz. Classroom Impact: An Early Literacy Staff Development Series. Bothell, WA: The Wright Group, 1998.

Overview of how rhythm and rhyme are used to build oral language and phonemic awareness through poetry. The video demonstrates how to use reading aloud and focus talk, and how to select poems for classroom use.

Reading Strategies and Skills, with Margaret Moustafa and Constance Weaver. Classroom Impact: An Early Literacy Staff Development Series. Bothell, WA: The Wright Group, 1998.

Instructional strategies for teaching students to read with understanding and fluency are presented. Whole-to-part techniques for phonics instruction are demonstrated through classroom footage. Shows what good readers do to predict and monitor comprehension of text.

Planning Integrated Units: A Concept-Based Approach. Alexandria, VA: Association for Supervision and Curriculum Development, 1997.

Examines the theory of concept-based instruction and outlines a planning process for creating integrated units.

What Is Visual Literacy? with Steve Moline. York, ME: Stenhouse Publishers, 1996.

Demonstrates a number of ways to teach visual literacy by using graphic organizers, diagrams, illustrations, drawings, graphs, and other visual techniques in a classroom with fourth graders.

Using Literacy Centers to Strengthen Your Reading and Writing Program, Grades K–3. Bellevue, WA: Bureau of Education & Research, 1999.

Discusses how literacy centers are used to enhance literacy development, how to maximize classroom space, how to effectively manage a literacy center, and how to design literacy centers to meet students' needs while reducing preparation and maintenance.

Child-Centered Classroom. Crystal Lake, IL: Rigby, 1994.

Examines dynamic classroom environments across the country and gives a practical guide for establishing and managing a balanced literacy classroom.

Learning through Literature, Grades 4–6. Jefferson City, MO: Scholastic, 1988.

Highlights teaching and learning experiences with reading and examines ways to integrate literature across the curriculum. Examples also include using English language materials with non-English-speaking students.

APPENDIX
C

Professional Organizations and Research Centers

PROFESSIONAL ORGANIZATIONS

AAAL   The American Association for Applied Linguistics
http://www.aaal.org/

BEN   Bilingual/ESL Network
http://www.cde.ca.gov/cilbranch/bien/bien.htm

IRA   International Reading Association
http://www.ira.org

NABE   National Association for Bilingual Education
http://www.nabe.org

NAEYC   National Association for the Education of Young Children
http://www.naeyc.org

NCTE   National Council of Teachers of English
http://www.ncte.org

NAME   National Association for Multicultural Education
http://www.inform.umd.edu/EdRes/Topic/multicultural/NAME/

TESOL   Teachers of English to Speakers of Other Languages
http://www.tesol.edu/index.html

INFORMATION/RESEARCH CENTERS

CAL   Center for Applied Linguistics
http://www.cal.org

CARLA   Center for Advanced Research on Language Acquisition
http://carla.acad.umn.edu

CBER   Center for Bilingual Education and Research
http://www.asu.edu/educ/cber

CMMR   Center for Multilingual/Multicultural Research
http://www.bcf.usc.edu/~cmmr

CLMER   Center for Language Minority Education and Research
http://www.csulb.edu/~clmer/clmer.html

CREDE   Center for Research on Education, Diversity, and Excellence
http://www.crede.ecsc.edu/homepage/home/html

ERIC   Educational Resources Information Center
http://www.accesseric.org/index.html

LMRI   Linguistic Minorities Research Institute
http://lmrinet.gse.ucsb.edu

LPRC   Language Policy Research Center
www.biu.ac.il/hu/lprc/

NCELA   National Clearinghouse for English Language Acquisition and Language Instruction Educational Programs
http://www.ncela.gwu.edu/

NLRC   National Language Resource Center
http://carla.acad.umn.edu/NLRClinks.html

OELA   The Office of English Language Acquisition, Language Enhancement, and Academic Achievement for Limited English Proficient Students
http://www.ed.gov/offices/OELA/

SIL   Summer Institute of Linguistics
http://www.sil.org

TESL   The Internet TESL Journal
http://www.aitech.ac.jp/~iteslj/

Dave's ESL Café
http://www.pacificnet.net/~sperling/eslcafe.html

Directory of Two-Way Bilingual Immersion Programs in the U.S.
http://www.cal.org/crede

James Crawford's Language Policy Website and Emporium
http://ourworld.compuserve.com/hompages/jwcrawford/

NATIONAL CONFERENCES AND SEMINARS

Dual Language Education Annual Conferences and Seminars

- Dual Language Symposium in Puerto Rico
1870 College Dr., Baton Rouge, LA 70808

- Dual Language Institute: Dual Language Education in the New Millennium
  http://www.hartfordschools.org
- La Cosecha: Dual Language Education of New Mexico
  http://www.duallanguagenm.org/
- CABE National Two-Way Bilingual Immersion Program Summer Conference
  http://www.bilingualeducation.com
- Summer CARLA Institute for Second Language Teachers
  http://carla.acad.umn.edu/summerinst.html

Language and Multicultural Annual Education Conferences and Seminars

- China-U.S. Conference on Education
  http://www.globalinteractions.org
- Conference on Teaching Diverse Learners
  http://www.alliance.brown.edu/
- National Association for the Education and Advancement of Cambodian, Laotian, and Vietnamese Americans Conference (NAFEA)
  http://www.nafea.org
- National Association of Bilingual Education Conference (NABE)
  http://www.nabe.org
- National Association for Multicultural Education Conference (NAME)
  http://www.name.org
- National Association for Asian and Pacific American Education Conference (NAAPAE)
  http://sphsu@aol.com

- National Association of Native American Studies Conference
  Morehead State University, 212 Rader Hall, Morehead, KY 40351
- National Indian Education Association (NIEA)
  Suite 800, 1819 H Street NW, Washington, DC 20006
- National Council of La Raza Conference (NCLR)
  http://www.nclr.org
- National Council of Teachers of English Conference (NCTE)
  http://www.ncte.org
- National Network for Early Language Learning: Summer Seminar in California
  http://www.coedu.usf.edu/mecastan/
- TESOL Annual Convention
  http://www.tesol.edu/conv/

Other Annual Education Conferences and Seminars

- American Educational Research Association Conference (AERA)
  http://www.aera.net
- National Association for the Education of Young Children Conference (NAEYC)
  http://www.naeyc.org/conferences
- International Reading Association Conference (IRA)
  http://www.ira.org

The following listing of educational software programs is a sampling of the products available from these software distributors. Due to space restrictions, not all distributors or available software products can be listed in this appendix. Excellent information on other available products and distributors, including free downloadable sites like translation programs, can be found on the NCELA technology site at http://www.ncela.gwu.edu/links/tech.htm.

ADDISON-WESLEY
FOR MAC/WIN

One Jacob Way, Reading, MA 01867-3999

(http://www.aw.com ~ 800-322-1377)

Word Stuff. Spanish and English ~ Beginning ~ PreK–3

Students learn words in various thematic contexts. Focuses on nouns, opposites, and action words, and also includes interactive graphics, animation, songs, and music.

BRODERBUND
FOR MAC/WIN

500 Redwood Blvd., Novato, CA 94948

(http://www.broderbund.com ~ 800-548-1798)

Arthur's Teacher Trouble. Spanish and English ~ Beginning, Intermediate ~ PreK–6

Students read and listen to the story of Arthur the Aardvark and build language and literacy skills through games and activities (contains sound effects and dialog.)

Green Eggs and Ham. Spanish and English ~ Beginning, Intermediate ~ PreK–6

Students read and listen to the Dr. Seuss's story Green Eggs and Ham and build language and literacy skills through games and activities (contains sound effects and dialog.) Other Dr. Seuss titles available are The Cat in the Hat and Dr. Seuss ABC.

Just Grandma and Me. Spanish, French, German and English ~ Beginning ~ PreK–1

Students experience the popular Mercer Mayer book through interactive reading and games that aim to develop vocabulary and reading comprehension.

The Tortoise and the Hare. Spanish and English ~ Beginning, Intermediate ~ PreK–6

Students read and listen to the story of The Tortoise and the Hare and build language and literacy skills through games and activities (contains sound effects and dialog.)

EDMARK CORPORATION
FOR MAC/WIN

P.O. Box 97021, 6727 185th Ave. NE, Redmond, WA 98073-9721

(http://www.edmark.com ~ 800-691-2986)

The following list is a sampling of the many selections from their Elementary Software Collection for PreK–8.

Bailey's Bookhouse. Beginning, Intermediate~ PreK–2

Seven reading and writing centers reinforce emergent readers' concepts of letter recognition, words, word families, rhyming, adjectives, and storytelling. Students can create greeting cards and stories.

Mighty Math Zoo Zillions. Beginning, Intermediate ~ PreK–2

Five math centers introduce students to addition, subtraction, story problems, number facts, shapes, and value of money. Several characters, such as Ryan the Lion and the Otter Twins, guide students through the enriching activities.

Millie's Math House. Spanish and English ~ Beginning, Intermediate ~ PreK–3

Seven math centers provide students with activities to learn numbers, shapes, sizes, quantities, patterns, sequencing, addition, and subtraction. Students build, create, count, and find answers to problems.

Mind Twister Math. Intermediate, Advanced ~ 3–4

This program reinforces third-grade math concepts such as addition, subtraction, multiplication, and division, and problem-solving skills such as visualization, deduction, sequencing, estimating, and pattern recognition. Aligned to the national math standards.

Sammy's Science House. Beginning, Intermediate~ K–2

Five science centers build basic concepts about science skills and processes and expand science vocabulary about seasons, weather, animals, and plants.

Talking Walls. Intermediate, Advanced ~ 4–8

Students explore the historical, political, and cultural issues related to some of the most famous and interesting walls.

Books, interactive software, Web sites, and classroom activities supplement this series.

Thinking Science ZAP. Intermediate, Advanced ~ 3–6

Students acquire and practice thinking skills and scientific processes, such as observation, prediction, deductive reasoning, conceptual modeling, theory building, and hypothesis testing by working with laser beams, electrical circuits, and visible sound waves. Aligned to the national science standards.

Thinking Things Tooney the Loon's Lagoon. Beginning, Intermediate ~ PreK–2

Students engage in critical thinking, creativity, and problem solving through this adventure theme program. Students become acquainted with several interesting characters such as Oranga Banga.

Travel the World with Timmy. Multiple Languages ~Beginning, Intermediate ~ PreK–2

Through stories, songs, games, crafts, and number and word activities, students explore the cultures of Argentina, France, Japan, Kenya, and Russia. Cross-curricular activities cover language arts, math, and art. Students can hear words in Spanish, French, Japanese, Swahili, and Russian.

HARMONY INTERACTIVE
FOR MAC/WIN

4936 Yonge Street, Suite 702, Toronto, Ontario, Canada M2N 6S3

(http://www.discis.com ~ 416-225-6771)

Interactive stories in English and Spanish. The reading can be slowed to make it more comprehensible for second language learners. The narrations are accompanied by music and sounds. The programs also have an on-line glossary of key words that include pronunciation, part of speech, and the meaning of the word in context. Among the stories are several books by Robert Munsch and other noted authors:

1. *A Promise Is a Promise* by R. Munsch and M. Kusugak, illustrated by Vladyana Krykorka (a story about an Inuit girl and her adventures), 1–6
2. *Anansi* by J. Adam and L. Darrach, illustrated by S. Murata, (a fable about a trickster that is half man and half spider), 1–4
3. *Mud Puddle* by R. Munsch, illustrated by M. Martchenko (a story about a girl who is attacked by a mud puddle and how she reacts), 1–4
4. *Scary Poems for Rotten Kids* by S. O. Huigin, illustrated by J. Fraser and S. Hughes (humorous and imaginative poems), 1–8
5. *The Paper Bag Princess* by R. Munsch, illustrated by M. Martchenko (a story about a young princess

whose encounters with a dragon make her a heroine), 1–4
6. *The Tale of Benjamin Bunny* by B. Potter (one of the Peter Rabbit series), 1–4
7. *Thomas' Snowsuit* by R. Munsch, illustrated by M. Martchenko (a story about a boy who does not want to wear his snowsuit), preK–2

HEARTSOFT
FOR MAC/WIN

3101 North Hemlock Circle, Broken Arrow, OK 74012

(http://www.heartsoft.com ~ 800-285-3475)

Heartsoft Bestseller. Spanish and English ~ Beginning, Intermediate ~ PreK–8

A series of twelve computer programs that engage the learner in language and content activities.

1. *Billiards 'n' Homonyms* (vocabulary game homonyms, synonyms, antonyms), 2–8
2. *Bubblegum Machine* (sight words, rhyme, vocabulary building), 2–8
3. *Coin Changer* (practice recognizing the value of coins and bills), 2–4
4. *Electric Math Chalkboard* (addition, subtraction, multiplication, division), K–4
5. *Electric Coloring Book* (alphabet, numbers, words, keyboarding skills), K–1
6. *Great American States Race* (social studies game about U.S. regions and states), 4–8
7. *Memory Master* (concentration game with letters and numbers), K–4
8. *Reading Rodeo* (literacy game matching pictures to words), K–1
9. *Sleuth Master* (logical thinking game, problem solving), 4–8
10. *Spinner's Choice* (version of Wheel of Fortune, guessing words and phrases), 2–8
11. *Tommy the Time Turtle* (practice in telling time), 2–4
12. *Word Capture* (wordsearch puzzles), 2–8

KNOWLEDGE ADVENTURE
FOR MAC/WIN

6060 Center Drive, 6th Floor, Los Angeles, CA 90045

(http://www.knowledgeadventure.com ~ 888-221-0802)

Chicka Chicka Boom Boom. Beginning ~ PreK–1

Based on the popular alphabet book. Young children build

reading readiness skills, phonemic awareness, and rhyming in English.

Jump Start Languages. Spanish, French, Japanese, and English ~ Beginning, Intermediate~ PreK–3

Students engage in interactive activities, lessons, games, and quizzes to develop language and cultural concepts at three levels of difficulty.

Jump Start Reading Series. Beginning~ PreK–2

Consists of three programs: JumpStart Kindergarten Reading, JumpStart 1st Grade Reading, and JumpStart 2nd Grade Reading. Multimedia game elements designed to promote literacy.

Primary Steps to Comprehension. Multiple languages ~Beginning, Intermediate ~K–3

This is an interactive reading program with thirty-six original stories written at six different reading levels. Each story includes comprehension questions, can be customized to meet different students' needs, and is designed to track student progress through the lessons. Students can hear the text in any of eight different languages.

Steps to Comprehension. Multiple languages ~ Beginning, Intermediate ~ K–6

This is an interactive reading program with ninety original stories written at eleven different reading levels. Each story includes comprehension questions, can be individualized to different students' needs, and is designed to track student progress through the lessons. Students can hear the text in any of eight different languages.

Bilingual Reading Comprehension. Spanish and English ~ Beginning ~ K–6

This is a reading comprehension program in Spanish and English that features immediate on-screen translation of stories into either language. It features thirty-six stories with colorful graphics. Includes audio capability for students to hear key words translated into either language.

MINDPLAY
FOR MAC/WIN

160 W. Ft. Lowell Rd., Tucson, AZ 85705

(http://www.mindplay.com ~ 800-221-7911)

Easy Street. Spanish and English ~ Beginning ~ K–3

This is an early learning program that builds reading and math readiness, and covers counting, classification, and vocabulary.

Word Hound. Spanish and English ~ Beginning, Intermediate ~ K–6

This is a word-building program in the form of a game of matching words with pictures (instructions are spoken).

NATIONAL GEOGRAPHIC SOCIETY EDUCATIONAL SERVICES
FOR MAC/WIN

6160 Summit Drive N., Minneapolis, MN 55430-4003

(http://www.learningco.com ~ 800-395-0277)

National Geographic Society Wonders of Learning CD-ROMs. Spanish and English ~ Beginning, Intermediate ~ PreK–up

This program contains thirty-six books on eight CDs. The stories are read and are accompanied by music and sound effects. Students can explore and learn concepts about the solar system, Earth, animals, plants, the human body, holidays, and seasons.

OPTIMUM RESOURCES
FOR MAC/WIN

18 Hunter Rd., Hilton Head Island, SC 29926

(http://www.stickybear.com ~ 888-784-2592)

Stickybear's Early Learning Activities. Spanish and English ~ Beginning~ PreK–3

Introduces students to the alphabet, counting, shapes, colors, and opposites through six different activity settings.

Stickybear's Reading Room. Spanish and English ~ Beginning, Intermediate ~ PreK–6

Introduces students to prereading and emergent reading skills by matching words to pictures, finding words, and creating sentences.

SCHOLASTIC SOFTWARE
FOR MAC/WIN

555 Broadway, New York, NY 10012-3999

(http://www.scholastic.com ~ 800-541-5513)

I Spy Spooky Mansion. Intermediate, Advanced ~ 1–5

Picture riddles and multileveled games build essential language and literacy skills and develop creativity and critical thinking skills such as cause and effect, logic and reasoning, classifying and sorting, following directions, visual discrimination, and memory skills.

WiggleWorks. Beginning ~ PreK–2

Introductory program for reinforcing listening, speaking, reading, and writing through interactive software program and supplemental materials and stories.

SUNBURST COMMUNICATIONS
FOR MAC/WIN

101 Castleton Street, Pleasantville, NY 10570

(ftp.sunburst.com/index.html ~ 800-321-7511)

Curious George Pre-K ABC. Spanish and English ~ Beginning ~ K–6

Engages young children in multilevel activities about letter names and shapes, initial sounds, letter pronunciation, the order of the alphabet, and vocabulary words.

Spanish/English Literacy Skills. Spanish and English ~ Beginning ~ K–6

Engages students in multiple writing activities. Topics include English for You; My First Sentences; Class Journals; Chant, Chant, Chant; Poetry for Young Poets; The Me Disk I, Sentence Writing I, Sentence Combining with Aesop; Sentences to Paragraphs I.

SYRACUSE LANGUAGE SYSTEMS
FOR MAC/WIN

4100 W. 190th St., Torrance, CA 90504

(http://www.syrlang.com, 800-542-4240)

All in One Language Fun! English, Spanish, Japanese, German, and French ~ Beginning ~ PreK–6

Introductory teaching of vocabulary in each language through games such as Bingo, jigsaw puzzles, Concentration, and Simon Says

THE LEARNING COMPANY
FOR MAC/WIN

6160 Summit Drive N., Minneapolis, MN 55430-4003

(http://www.learningco.com ~ 800-395-0277)

The Art Lesson. Intermediate, Advanced ~ PreK–4

Tomie dePaola reads the story, which is accompanied by rich illustrations. Students can read the story themselves and create stories with the author. Also includes activities, video clips of the author's studio, and the author talking about his life.

Math Keys. Spanish and English ~ Intermediate, Advanced ~ PreK–6

Five separate software programs that cover whole numbers, probability, geometry, measurement, fractions and decimals.

Reader Rabbit Reading 1. Beginning ~ K–2

Emergent readers recognize letter and words through colorful graphics. Students match letters with sounds.

Reader Rabbit's Interactive Reading, Journey 2. Beginning, Intermediate ~ K–2

Presents stories and games that promote the development of phonics, word recognition, and reading comprehension.

Reader Rabbit 3. Beginning, Intermediate ~ 2–4

Students create their own stories by writing their own words or choosing from a selection of phrases.

Storybook Weaver. Spanish and English ~ Beginning, Intermediate ~ K–6

Students write and illustrate their own storybooks by selecting from a wide range of sceneries and images combinations, music and sounds, animation, and narrations.

TOM SNYDER PRODUCTIONS
FOR MAC/WIN

80 Coolidge Hill Rd., Watertown, MA 02172

(http://www.teachtsp.com ~ 800-342-0236)

Reading Magic Library. Intermediate, Advanced ~ PreK–3

Using interactive storybook software, students create their own adventures and choose what will happen next. Students can record themselves reading or create movies of their stories. Stories include Jack and the Beanstalk, Hansel and Gretel, Flodd the Bad Guy, Fidd and Martina in Tough Kudd, *and* Hilary and the Beast.

Bilingual Graph Club. Spanish and English ~ Beginning, Intermediate, Advanced ~ K–6

Students construct, organize, and describe data with a variety of graphs. Includes a library of over 150 icons, and will count numbers aloud as the graph is created.

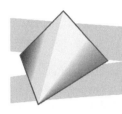

Glossary of Terms and Acronyms

ACRONYMS

BICS	Basic interpersonal communicative skills	**L2**	Second language
CALLA	Cognitive academic language learning approach	**LAD**	Language acquisition device
CALP	Cognitive academic language proficiency	**LEA**	Language experience approach
CUP	Common underlying proficiency	**LEP**	Limited English proficient
EFL	English as a foreign language	**PEP**	Potential English proficient
ELD	English language development	**SLA**	Second language acquisition
ELL	English language learner	**SLL**	Second language learner
ESL	English as a second language	**TBE**	Transitional bilingual education
ESOL	English for speakers of other languages	**TESL**	Teaching English as a second language
FEP	Fluent English proficient	**TEFL**	Teaching English as a foreign language
FES	Fluent English speaking	**TPI**	Transitional program of instruction
FLES	Foreign language in the elementary school	**TPR**	Total physical response
L1	First language, native language, mother tongue	**ZPD**	Zone of proximal development

TERMINOLOGY

additive bilingual education: Bilingual education program models that aim to maintain and develop students' native language, as well as develop students' second language. The primary goal of these program models is high levels of bilingualism and biliteracy by adding another language to the students' linguistic and cognitive repertoire. Additive bilingual programs include *dual language, maintenance, developmental,* and *heritage language* programs.

basic interpersonal communicative skills (BICS): Everyday conversational social language that is heavily supported by contextual clues. Second language learners commonly acquire conversational language in six months to two years (Cummins, 1984, 2000).

bilingual education: The use of two languages for instruction to facilitate students' academic, linguistic, and literacy development in both the native and the second language, or in only the second language. Program models are characterized as either *additive* or *subtractive.* Additive models use and promote two languages (*maintenance, developmental, heritage language, dual language/two-way immersion*). Subtractive models foster only monolingualism in English, the students'

second language (*transitional bilingual education,* either *early-exit* or *late-exit*).

bilingual enrichment: See *dual language education.*

bilingual immersion: See *dual language education.*

bilingualism: The ability to use two languages along a continuum (Hornberger, 1994) that includes variations in proficiency in expressive (speaking and writing) and receptive (listening and reading) language; differences in proficiencies between the two languages; variations in proficiency between the two languages according to the functions and purpose of use of each language; and changes in proficiency of each language over time. Individuals who use two languages may be simultaneous bilinguals (those who develop the two languages at the same time) or sequential bilinguals (those who first acquire one language and later acquire the second language). Bilinguals can also be characterized as circumstantial (those who learn a second language because of their circumstances, such as immigrants, and whose first language is at risk of being replaced by the second language) or elective (those who chose to learn a second language and who do not risk losing their native language).

biliteracy: The ability to read and write with high levels of proficiency in two languages through the appropriate and effective use of the grammatical, syntactic, graphophonic, semantic, and pragmatic systems of the two languages.

codeswitching: The alternate use of two languages interchangeably or simultaneously that occurs among bilinguals and developing bilinguals. Codeswitching includes any switch between the two languages at the level of words, sentences, or blocks of speech.

cognate: Words that are related in meaning and form to words in one or more languages due to their common historical morphemic sources, usually from a Latin origin, such as *obscure* in English and *obscuro* in Spanish from the Latin word *obscurus*. Certain words in different languages that sound alike but have unrelated meanings are known as false cognates (such as *embarrassed* in English and *embarazada* in Spanish, which means *pregnant*.)

cognitive academic language proficiency (CALP): Academic language, which is increasingly highly decontextualized, needed by second language learners to engage in abstract and cognitively demanding academic tasks. Second language learners commonly acquire academic language in five to seven years (Cummins, 1981).

common underlying proficiency (CUP):   The notion that cognition and language skills that are learned in the first language form the basis for subsequent learning in a second language. The second language and the native language share a common foundation. This linguistic interdependence allows the transfer of ideas, concepts, knowledge, and skills from one language to another when the learner understands the second language (Cummins, 1989).

communicative competence: The ability to interact with others by using language effectively in social situations to convey meaning (Hymes, 1972).

comprehensible input: Language that a learner can understand with the aid of contextual clues such as gestures, body language, visuals, context, or prior knowledge (Krashen, 1981).

content-based instruction: Second language programs that base language instruction around themes, topics, or subject matter, rather than on the language system itself.

critical period hypothesis (CPH):   The notion that there is a specific and limited period for language acquisition. CPH holds two related positions: first, that after puberty biological mechanisms that assist in the acquisition of language are no longer available and the learner has to resort to other mechanisms not designed for language development; and second, that after puberty a learner has less time and motivation to develop the high levels of second language acquisition that children can attain.

developmental bilingual education: An additive bilingual education model that aims to develop and maintain the native language while developing the majority second language. Also known as *maintenance* bilingual education.

dominant language: The language in which the speaker has greater proficiency and/or that the speaker uses most often.

double immersion: See *dual language education.*

dual language education: An additive bilingual education model that consistently uses two languages for instruction and communication, with a balanced number of students from two language groups who are integrated for instruction at least half of the school day. Also known as *immersion, two-way bilingual education,* and *two-way immersion.*

early-exit bilingual education: A subtractive transitional bilingual education model that provides native language instruction for one to three years while students acquire sufficient English language proficiency to function in mainstream classes.

English as a second language (ESL):   The field of study that addresses theoretical and pedagogical applications to the teaching and learning of English as a second language. ESL is an educational approach designed to provide specialized instruction in English to English-language learners. ESL may take the form of the traditional grammar-based approach (teaching the syntax and morphology of the English language through practice) or the content-based method of instruction (teaching the English language through the learning of subject matter, such as math or science).

English language development (ELD):   An instructional approach that focuses on second language development through content for beginner second language learners who may not be at grade level academically.

English language learner (ELL):   The term used to describe students who are acquiring English as a second language. ELL, a more developmental and positive term, is currently replacing the traditional and more commonly used deficit-oriented term *limited English proficient (LEP).*

first language: See *native language.*

heritage language bilingual program: An additive bilingual education model that aims to develop and maintain the native language and culture of second language learners in conjunction with their acquisition of

English. Sometimes referred to as *maintenance* or *developmental bilingual* education.

home language: See *native language.*

immersion: A term derived from the Canadian French-English additive form of bilingual education, which provides academic and language instruction to students from two language groups in both languages to achieve bilingual, biliterate, bicultural, and academic competencies. Also known as *dual language* and *two-way immersion.* English-only immersion in the United States is a subtractive model of instruction for English language learners (see *structured English immersion*).

language: The systematic use of syntactic, semantic, pragmatic, phonological, and morphological symbols for communication within a community by engaging in listening and speaking, and sometimes reading and writing.

language acquisition: The unconscious process of acquiring a language (the native language and maybe the second language) in a natural, meaningful, and developmental way through social interaction with native speakers of that language.

language acquisition device (LAD):   The innate knowledge of the "universal" principles common to all languages. This innate knowledge permits learners to discover the structure of a language on the basis of relatively small amount of input. Chomsky (1959) claimed that all children are born with this ability to discover the underlying rules of a language system.

language learning: The conscious process of learning a language (usually the second language) through formal instruction (Krashen, 1981).

language majority students: Students whose native language is the high-status language usually (but not always) spoken by the majority of the population. (In the case of the United States it is English; in the case of Canada's province of Quebec it is French.)

language minority students: Students whose native tongue is considered a low prestige language that is usually spoken by a subjugated or lower status group. (In the case of the United States it might be Spanish, Yaqui, or Urdu.)

late-exit bilingual education: A subtractive transitional bilingual education model that offers native language instruction while second language learners acquire English for a longer period of time than early-exit bilingual education, usually for more than three years. English language learners continue to develop their native language for a period of six to eight years even after they have acquired English.

limited English proficient (LEP):   Refers to individuals who speak a language other than English and are still in the process of learning English as their second language. This term is used for beginner, intermediate, and advanced students of English. Due to its deficit-oriented connotation, it has been replaced by the more developmental term *ELL (English language learner).*

maintenance bilingual education: An additive bilingual education model that supports and aims to develop students' native language, heritage, and culture, as well as the English language and culture. Also known as *developmental bilingual education.*

majority language: The language of high prestige used by the mainstream or those in power. The language usually (but not always) used by the majority population.

minority language: The language of low status used by those with less power. The language usually (but not always) used by the minority of the population.

morphology: The study of word structures and formations: the lexicon of a language that includes bound and free morphemes (words, compound words, suffixes, and prefixes).

mother tongue: See *native language.*

native language (L1):   The first language acquired by a child. Also known as *mother tongue, home language, primary language, first language,* or *heritage language.*

newcomer programs: A program designed for English language learners with limited formal schooling who are behind academically and have little or no literacy skills in their native language. Usually short-term and offered in upper elementary and high school.

partial immersion: A dual language or two-way bilingual program in which students receive instruction in the target language 50 percent of time and in the majority language the other 50 percent of the time. Also known as the 50–50 or balanced model.

phonology: The study of speech sounds in a language, including intonation, pronunciation, graphophonics, and phonemic awareness.

pragmatics: The knowledge of how language is used in context, or the meaning of sentences in terms of the speaker's or writer's intentions in using them.

primary language: See *native language.*

productive language: Language that is generated in the form of speaking, writing, or signing.

receptive language: The ability to understand a message aurally (listening) or visually (reading print or sign language).

scaffolding: The temporary structures of support provided by adults or more capable peers that permit learners to participate in complex processes before they are able to do so unassisted.

second language (L2):   The second language acquired by a child or adult after the native language. May sometimes be defined as the weaker language or the lesser-used language. It may be the individual's native language, especially when the native language has been abandoned or underused.

second language acquisition (SLA):   The process of acquiring a second language that occurs subconsciously as a result of meaningful and natural communication.

second language learner (SLL):   A term used to refer to anyone learning another language in addition to her or his native language. Usually refers to learners who are acquiring the language of their host country.

semantics: The understanding of meaning based on the knowledge of words, intonation, context, and word order.

silent period: A stage of about one to twelve months in which the second language learner opts to focus on receptive competencies rather than on producing the second language.

sink or swim: This term is used in reference to situations when second language learners are placed in mainstream classrooms with no specialized assistance, either in the native language or in the form of ESL support, and are expected to function like their majority language peers.

structured English immersion: A subtractive model of instruction in which second language learners are placed in English classrooms with little or no first language support and minimal ESL assistance, usually in the form of pullout second language instruction. The teacher uses a simplified form of the second language and the curriculum. Also known as *structured immersion* education.

submersion: See *sink or swim.*

subtractive bilingual education: Bilingual education program models that aim to replace students' native language with a second language. The primary goal is monolingualism in the second language. This is accomplished by subtracting the home language from the students' linguistic and cognitive repertoire. Subtractive program models include *transitional, structured English immersion,* and *newcomer centers.*

syntax: The knowledge and understanding of the order of words in a language, or rules of grammar.

target language: A second language that is being acquired or learned. For English language learners in the United States, the target language is English. For English dominant students in dual language programs, the target language might be Spanish, Korean, or Navajo.

threshold hypothesis: The notion that first language literacy transfers to a second language only when a learner has reached a critical level of competency in the first language. Only when this native language competency is reached does the learner obtains cognitive benefits from knowing the two languages.

total immersion: A dual language or two-way bilingual program in which students receive instruction in the minority language 90% or 80% of the time initially and 10% or 20% of the time in the majority language, increasing the amount of the majority language gradually until a balance of the two languages is used for instruction by 5th or 6th grade.

transitional bilingual education: See *early-exit* and *late-exit* bilingual education.

two-way immersion: See *dual language education.*

zone of proximal development (ZPD):   Vygotsky's (1978) notion that there is a specific distance between the actual development level, which is determined by independent problem solving, and the level of potential development, as determined through problem solving under adult guidance or in collaboration with more capable peers: the zone between what the student can do alone and what the student can do with the help of an adult or more knowledgeable peer.

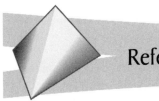

References

A to ez: Handbook for bilingual teachers staff development guide. New York: Macmillan/McGraw-Hill.

Ada, A. F. (1995). Creative education for bilingual teachers. In O. Garcia & C. Baker (Eds.), *Policy and practice in bilingual education: Extending the foundations* (pp. 237–243). Clevedon, England: Multilingual Matters.

American Council on the Teaching of Foreign Languages. (1996). *Standards for foreign language learning: Preparing for the 21st century.* National Standards in Foreign Language Education Project. American Council on the Teaching of Foreign Languages.

Amrein, A., & Peña, R. A. (2000). Asymmetry in dual language practice: Assessing imbalance in a program promoting equality. *Education Policy Analysis, 8,* 8.

Aronson, E. (1978). *The jigsaw classroom.* Beverly Hills, CA: Sage.

Asher, J. (1977). *Learning another language through actions: The complete teacher's guide.* Los Gatos, CA: Sky Oaks Publications.

August, D., & Hakuta, K. (1998). *Improving schooling for language minority children.* Washington, DC: National Academy Press.

Baker, C. (2001). *Foundations of bilingual education and bilingualism.* Clevedon, England: Multilingual Matters.

Ballard, W., & Tighe, P. (1978). *IDEA oral language proficiency test.* San Rafael, CA: Ballard & Tighe.

Banks, J. (1994). *Multiethnic education: Theory and practice.* Boston: Allyn and Bacon.

Bartolomé, L. I. (1994). Teaching strategies: Their possibilities and limitations. In B. Mcleod (Ed.), *Language and learning: Educating linguistically diverse students* (pp. 199–223). New York: State University of New York Press.

Bean, M. S. (1997). Talking with Benny: Suppressing or supporting learner themes and learner worlds? *Anthropology and Education Quarterly, 28,* 50–69.

Berk, L. E., & Winsler, A. (1995). *Scaffolding children's learning: Vygotsky and early childhood education.* Washington, DC: National Association for the Education of Young Children.

Bishop, C., & Weise, K. (1939). *The five Chinese brothers.* New York: Sandcastle.

Bissex, G. L., & Bullock, R. H. (1987). *Seeing for ourselves: Case study research by teachers of writing.* Portsmouth, NH: Heinemann.

Brisk, M. E. (1998). *Bilingual education: From compensatory to quality schooling.* Mahwah, NJ: Lawrence Erlbaum.

Brisk, M. E., & Harrington, M. M. (2000). *Literacy and bilingualism: A handbook for all teachers.* Mahwah, NJ: Lawrence Erlbaum.

Britton, J. (1992). *Language and learning: The importance of speech in children's development.* New York: Penguin Books.

Brown, H. D. (2000). *Principles of language learning and teaching.* New York: Addison Wesley Longman.

Brown, M. W. (1947). *Goodnight moon.* New York: Harper & Row.

Bruner, J. S. (1996). *The culture of education.* Cambridge, MA: Harvard University Press.

Burke, K. (1999). *How to assess authentic learning.* Arlington Heights, IL: Skylight Professional Development.

Burt, M., Dulay, H., & Hernandez-Chavez, E. (1975). *Bilingual syntax measure.* Orlando, FL: Harcourt Brace Jovanovich.

Carle, E. (1984). *The hungry caterpillar.* New York: Philomel Books.

Castro Feinberg, R. (1999). Administration of two-way bilingual elementary schools: Building on strengths. *Bilingual Research Journal, 23* (1), 234–249.

Castro Feinberg, R. (2002). *Bilingual education: A reference handbook.* Santa Barbara, CA: ABC CLIO.

Cazabon, M., & Lambert, W. E., & Hall, G. (1993). *Two-way bilingual education: A progress report on the Amigos program.* Washington, DC and Santa Cruz, CA: National Center for Research on Cultural Diversity and Second Language Learning.

Cazabon, M., Nicoladis, E., & Lambert, W. E. (1998). *Becoming bilingual in the Amigos two-way immersion program.* Research Report No. 3. Washington, DC, and Santa Cruz, CA: National

Center for Applied Linguistics. Director of Two-Way Bilingual Immersion Programs in the U.S. http://www.cal.org/twi/directory/.

Center for Research on Cultural Diversity and Second Language Learning.

Chamot, A. U., & O'Malley, J. M. (1994). *The CALLA handbook: Implementing the cognitive academic language learning approach.* Menlo Park, CA: Addison-Wesley.

Chomsky, N. (1957). *Syntactic structures.* The Hague: Mouton.

Chomsky, N. (1959). A review of B. F. Skinner's verbal behavior. *Language, 35* (1), 26–58.

Christian, D. (1994). *Two-way bilingual education: Students learning through two languages.* Educational Practice Report No. 12. Washington, DC, and Santa Cruz, CA: National Center for Research on Cultural Diversity and Second Language Learning.

Christian, D., Howard, E. R., & Loeb, M. I. (2000). Bilingualism for all: Two-way immersion education in the United

States. *Theory into practice*. Columbus, OH: Ohio State University.

Christian, D., Montone, C., Lindholm, K., & Carranza, I. (1997). *Profiles in two-way immersion education*. Washington DC: Center for Applied Linguistics.

Cloud, N., Genesee, E., & Hamayan, E. (2000). *Dual language instruction: A handbook for enriched education.* Boston: Heinle & Heinle.

Cohen, E. G. (1994). *Designing groupwork: Strategies for the heterogeneous classroom*. New York: Teachers College Press.

Corson, D. (2001). *Language diversity and education*. Mahwah, NJ: Lawrence Erlbaum.

Council on Inter-Racial Books for Children. (1994). 10 quick ways to analyze children's books for racism and sexism. In *Rethinking our classrooms: Teaching for equity and justice* (pp. 14–15).

Crawford, J. (1999). *Bilingual education: History, politics, theory and practice.* Los Angeles: Bilingual Education Services.

Crawford, J. (2001). *At war with diversity*. Clevedon, England: Multilingual Matters.

Cummins, J. (1980). The construct of language proficiency in bilingual education. In J. E. Alatis (Ed.), *Georgetown University Round Table on Language and Linguistics*. Washington, DC: Georgetown University Press.

Cummins, J. (1981). *Bilingualism and minority language children*. Ontario, Canada: Ontario Institute for Studies in Education.

Cummins, J. (1984). *Bilingualism and special education: Issues in assessment and pedagogy.* Clevedon, England: Multilingual Matters.

Cummins, J. (1989). Language and literacy acquisition in bilingual contexts. *Journal of Multilingual and Multicultural Development*, 10, 17–31.

Cummins, J. (1992). Heritage language teaching in Canadian schools. *Journal of Curriculum Studies*, 24 (3), 281–286.

Cummins, J. (1995). Empowering minority students: A framework for intervention. In O. Garcia & C. Baker (Eds.), *Policy and practice in bilingual education: Extending the foundations* (pp. 103–117). Clevedon, England: Multilingual Matters.

Cummins, J. (2000). *Language, power and pedagogy: Bilingual children in the crossfire.* Clevedon, England: Multilingual Matters.

Cummins, J. (2001). *Negotiating identities: Education for empowerment in a diverse society.* Los Angeles: California Association for Bilingual Education.

d'Anglejan, A. (1994). Language and literacy in Quebec: Exploring the issues. In B. M. Ferdman, R. Weber, & A. G. Ramírez (Eds.), *Literacy across languages and cultures* (pp. 273–291). New York: State of New York Press.

Daniels, H. (1994). *Literature circles: Voice and choice in the student-centered classroom.* York, ME: Stenhouse.

Darder, A. (1997). Creating the conditions for cultural democracy in the classroom. In A. Darder, R. D. Torres, & H. Gutiérrez (Eds.), *Latinos and education: A critical reader* (pp. 331–350). New York: Routledge.

Darder, A., Torres, R. D., & Gutiérrez, H. (1997). *Latinos and education: A critical reader.* New York: Routledge.

Day, E. M., & Shapson, S. M. (1996). *Studies in immersion education*. Clevedon, England: Multilingual Matters.

Delgado-Gaitán, C. (1991). Involving parents in the school: A process for empowerment. *American Journal of Education*, 100 (1), 20–46.

Delgado-Gaitán, C. (1993). Relating experiences and text: Socially constituted reading activity. In O. Garcia & C. Baker (Eds.), *Policy and practice in bilingual education: Extending the foundations* (pp. 190–199). Clevedon, England: Multilingual Matters.

Díaz, S. Moll, L. C., & Mehan, H. (1986). Sociocultural resources in instruction: A context specific approach. In C. E. Cortés & D. Holt (Eds.), *Beyond language: Social and cultural factors in schooling language minority students* (pp. 187–230). Los Angeles: Evaluation, Dissemination and Assessment Center, California State University.

Díaz-Rico, L. T., & Weed, K. Z. (2002). *The crosscultural, language, and academic development handbook: A complete K–12 reference guide.* Boston: Allyn and Bacon.

DiCerbo, P. A. (2000). *Framing effective practices: Topics and issues in educating English language learners.* A Technical Assistance Synthesis by the National Clearinghouse for Bilingual Education. Washington, DC: Center for the Study of Language and Education.

Dicker, S. J. (1996). *Languages in America: A pluralistic view.* Clevedon: Multilingual Matters.

Dicker, S. J. (2000). Official English and bilingual education: The controversy over language pluralism in U.S. society. In J. K. Hall & W. G. Eggington (Eds.), *The sociopolitics of English language teaching* (pp. 45–66). Clevedon, England: Multilingual Matters.

Duncan, S. E., & DeAvila, E. A. (1977). *Language assessment scales*. Larkspur, CA: De Avila, Duncan and Associates.

Durán, L. (1994). Toward a better understanding of codeswitching and interlanguage in bilinguality: Implications for bilingual instruction. *The Journal of Educational Issues of Language Minority Students*, 14, 69–88.

Edelsky, C. (1986). *Writing in a bilingual program: Había una vez.* Norwood, NJ: Norwood.

Epstein, J. L. (1987). Parent involvement: What research says to administrators. *Education and Urban Society*, 19 (2), 119–136.

Escamilla, K. (1993). Promoting biliteracy: Issues in promoting English literacy in students acquiring English. In J. V.

Tinajero & A. F. Ada (Eds.), *The power of two languages: Literacy and biliteracy for Spanish-speaking students* (pp. 220–233). New York: Macmillan/McGraw Hill.

Faltis, C. J. (1997). *Joinfostering: Adapting teaching for the multilingual classroom*. Upper Saddle River, NJ: Prentice Hall.

Ferdman, B. M., & Weber R. (1994). Literacy across languages and cultures. In B. M. Ferdman, R. Weber, & A. G. Ramírez (Eds.), *Literacy across languages and cultures* (pp. 3–29). New York: State of New York Press.

Fisher, D., Lapp, D., Flood, J., & Suarez, L. (2001). Assessing bilingual students: When policies and practices meet in the classroom. In S. R. Hurley & J. V. Tinajero (Eds.), *Literacy assessment of second language learners* (pp. 104–114). Boston: Allyn and Bacon.

Freeman, D. E., & Freeman, Y. S. (1997). *Teaching reading and writing in Spanish in the bilingual classroom*. Portsmouth, NH: Heinemann.

Freeman, D. E., & Freeman, Y. S. (2000). *Teaching reading in multilingual classrooms*. Portsmouth, NH: Heinemann.

Freeman, R. (1998). *Bilingual education and social change*. Clevedon, England: Multilingual Matters.

Freeman, Y. S., & Freeman, D. E. (1998). *ESL/EFL teaching: Principles for success*. Portsmouth, NH: Heinemann.

Freire, P., & Macedo, D. (1987). *Literacy: Reading the word and the world*. South Hadley, MA: Bergin and Garvey.

Fry, E. B., Kress, J. E., & Fountoukidis, D. L. (2000). *The reading teacher's book of lists*. West Nyack, NY: The Center for Applied Research in Education.

Fullan, M. (1993). *Change forces: Probing the depths of educational reform*. London: Falmer Press.

Gallimore, R., & Tharp, R. (1990). Teaching mind in society: Teaching, schooling, and literate discourse. In L. C. Moll (Ed.), *Vygotsky and education: Instructional implications and applications of sociohistorical psychology* (pp. 175–205). Cambridge: Cambridge University Press.

García, E. E. (1985). *Early childhood bilingualism*. Albuquerque, NM: University of New Mexico Press.

García, E. E., & Curry-Rodríguez, J. E. (2000). The education of limited English proficient students in California schools: An assessment of the influence of Proposition 227 in selected districts and schools. *Bilingual Research Journal*, 24 (1-2), 1–21.

Garcia, O. (1985). Bilingualism in the US: Present attitudes in the light of past policies. In S. Greenbaum (Ed.), *The English language today* (pp. 147–158). Oxford: Pergamon Institute of English.

Genesee, F. (1987). *Learning through two languages*. Cambridge, MA: Newbury House.

Genesee, F. (1999). *Program alternatives for linguistically diverse students*. Educational Practice Report No. 1. Washington, DC, and Santa Cruz, CA: Center for Research on Education, Diversity and Excellence.

Genesee, F., & Gándara, P. (1999). Bilingual education programs: A cross national perspective. *Journal of Social Issues*, 55 (4), 665–685.

Genesee, F., & Upshur, J. A. (1996). *Classroom-based evaluation in second language education*. New York: Cambridge University Press.

Giroux, H. A. (1989). *Schooling for democracy: Critical pedagogy in the modern age*. London: Routledge.

Glenn, C., & LaLyre, I. (1991). Integrated bilingual education in the USA. In K. Jaspaert & S. Kroon (Eds.), *Ethnic minority languages and education*. Amsterdam: Swets & Zeitlinger.

Goble, P. (2001). "The rise in bilingualism." Radio Free Europe/Radio Liberty. http://www.rferi.org.

González, N., Moll, L. C., Tenery, M. F., Rivera, A., Rendón, P., González, R., & Amanti, C. (1993). *Teacher research on funds of knowledge: Learning from households*. National Center for Research on Cultural Diversity and Second Language Learning, Office of Education Research and Improvement of the U.S. Department of Education.

Goodman, K. S., Goodman, Y. M., & Flores, B. (1979). *Reading in the bilingual classroom: Literacy and biliteracy*. Rosslyn, VA: National Clearinghouse for Bilingual Education.

Goodman, Y. M., & Goodman, K. S. (1990). Vygotsky in a whole language perspective. In L. C. Moll (Ed.), *Vygotsky and education: Instructional implications and applications of sociohistorical psychology* (pp. 223–250). New York: Teachers College Press.

Gunter, M. A., Estes, T. H., & Schwab, J. H. (1999). *Instruction: A models approach*. Boston: Allyn and Bacon.

Hadaway, N. L., Vardell, S. M., & Young, T. A. (2002). *Literature-based instruction with English language learners*. Boston: Allyn and Bacon.

Hakuta, K. (1986). *Mirror of language: The debate on bilingualism*. New York: Harper Collins.

Hakuta, K. (1990). Language and cognition in bilingual children. In S. Padilla et al. (Eds.), *Bilingual education: Issues and strategies* (pp. 66–72). Newbury Park, CA: Sage.

Hakuta, K., Butler, Y. G., & Witt, D. (2000). *How long does it take English language learners to attain proficiency?* Santa Barbara, CA: University of California Linguistic Minority Research Institute.

Halliday, M. A. K. (1975). *Learning how to mean: Explorations in the development of language*. Wheeling, IL: Edward Arnold.

Halliday, M. A. K. (1978). *Language as social semiotics: The social interpretation of language*. New York: Routledge.

Halliday, M. A. K. (1994). The place of dialogue in children's construction of meaning. In R. Ruddell, M. Ruddell, & H. Singer (Eds.), *Theoretical models and processes of reading* (pp. 163–182). Newark, DE: International Reading Association.

Hamayan, E., & Pearlman, R. (1990). *Helping language minority students after they exit from bilingual/ESL programs: A handbook for teachers*. NCBE Program Information Guide Series, #1.

Harman, S., & Edelsky, C. (1989). The risk of whole language literacy: Alienation and connection. *Language Arts*, 4, 392–405.

Harste, J. C., Short, K. G., & Burke, C. (1988). *Creating classrooms for authors: The reading-writing connection*. Portsmouth, NH: Heinemann.

Heath, C. B. (1983). *Ways with words*. New York: Cambridge University Press.

Herrell, A. (2000). *Fifty strategies for teaching English language learners*. Columbus, OH: Prentice Hall.

Herrell, A., & Fowler, J. (1997). *Camcorder in the classroom: Using the videocamera to enrich curriculum*. Upper Saddle River, NJ: Prentice Hall.

Hewlett-Gómez, M. R. (1995). Dual language instruction design for educating recent immigrant secondary students on the Texas-Mexico border. *The Bilingual Research Journal*, 19 (3-4), 429–452.

Holdaway, D. (1979). *The foundations of literacy*. New York: Ashton Scholastic.

Hornberger, N. H. (1990). Creating successful learning contexts for bilingual literacy. *Teachers College Record*, 92 (2), 212–229.

Hornberger, N. H. (1994). Continua of biliteracy. In B. M. Ferdman, R. Weber, & A. G. Ramírez (Eds.), *Literacy across languages and cultures* (pp. 103–139). New York: State of New York Press.

Howard, E. R., & Loeb, M. I. (1998). *In their own words: Two-way immersion teachers talk about their professional experiences*. Washington, DC: ERIC Clearinghouse on Languages and Linguistics.

Howard, E. R., & Sugarman, J. (2001). *Two-way immersion programs: Features and statistics*. ERIC Clearinghouse on Languages and Linguistics. http://www.cal.org/ericcll/dogest/0101twi.html.

Hudelson, S. (1994). Literacy development of second language children. In F. Genesee (Ed.), *Educating second language children: The whole child, the whole curriculum, the whole community* (pp. 129–158). New York: Cambridge University Press.

Huerta-Macías, A., & Quintero, E. (1992). Code-switching, bilingualism, and biliteracy: A case study. *Bilingual Research Journal*, 16 (3-4), 69–90.

Hurley, S. R., & Tinajero, J.V. (2001). *Literacy assessment of second language learners*. Boston: Allyn and Bacon.

Hymes, D. (1971). Competence and performance in linguistic theory. In R. Huxley & E. Ingram (Eds.), *Language acquisition: Models and methods* (pp. 78–97). London: Academic Press.

Hymes, D. (1972). Models of the interaction of language and social life. In J. J. Gumperz & D. Hymes (Eds.), *Directions in sociolinguistics: The ethnography of communication* (pp. 35–71). New York: Holt, Rinehart and Winston.

Jacobson, R., & Faltis, C. (1990). *Language distribution issues in bilingual schooling*. Clevedon, England: Multilingual Matters.

Jiménez, F. (1998). *La Mariposa*. Boston: Houghton Mifflin.

Johnson, D. W., & Johnson, H. (1991). *Learning together and alone: Cooperation, competition, and individualization*. Englewood Cliffs, NJ: Prentice Hall.

Johnson, D. W., Johnson, R. T., & Holubec, E. J. (1993). *Circles of learning: Cooperation in the classroom*. Edina, MN: Interaction Book.

Johnson, D., Johnson, R., & Holubec, E. (1998). *Cooperation in the classroom*. Boston: Allyn and Bacon.

Johnson, R. K., & Swain, M. (1997). *Immersion education: International perspectives*. New York: Cambridge University Press.

Katz, A. (2001). Weaving assessment into a standards-based curriculum. *NABE News*, 24 (6), 13–15.

Krashen, S. (1981). *Second language acquisition and second language learning*. Oxford, England: Pergamon Press.

Krashen, S. (1982). *Principles and practices in second language acquisition*. New York: Pergamon Press.

Krashen, S. (1993). *The power of reading*. Englewood, CO: Libraries Unlimited.

Krashen, S. (1996). *Every person a reader: An alternative to the California task force report on reading*. Culver City, CA: Language Education Associates.

Krashen, S., & Terrell, T. (1983). *The natural approach*. New York: Pergamon Press.

Krashen, S., Tse, L., & McQuillan, J. (1998). *Heritage language development*. Culver City, CA: Language Education Associates.

Lambert, W. E., & Tucker, R. (1972). *Bilingual education of children: The St. Lambert experiment*. Rowley, MA: Newbury House.

Law, B., & Eckes, M. (1995). *Assessment and ESL: A handbook for K–12 teachers*. Winnipeg, Canada: Peguis Publishers.

Lee, D. M., & Allen, R.V. (1963). *Learning to read through experience*. New York: Meredith.

Lessow-Hurley, J. (2000). *The foundations of dual language instruction*. New York: Longman.

Lightbown, P. M., & Spada, N. (2000). *How languages are learned*. Oxford, England: Oxford University Press.

Lindholm, K. (1990). Bilingual immersion education: Criteria for program development. In A. Padilla, H. H. Fairchild, & C. M.Valdéz (Eds.), *Bilingual education: Issues and strategies* (pp. 91–105). Newbury Park, CA: Corwin Press.

Lindholm, K. (1991).Theoretical assumptions and empirical evidence for academic achievement in two languages. *Hispanic Journal for Behavioral Sciences*, 13 (1), 3–17.

Lindholm-Leary, K. (2000). *Biliteracy for a global society: An idea book on dual language education.* Washington, DC: The George Washington University.

Lindholm-Leary, K. (2001). *Dual language education.* Clevedon, England: Multilingual Matters.

Lyman, F. (1981). The responsive classroom discussion. In Anderson, A. S. (Ed.), *Mainstreaming digest.* College Park, MD: University of Maryland College of Education.

Mackey, W. F. (1978). The importation of bilingual education models. In J. Alatis (Ed.), *Georgetown University roundtable: International dimensions of education.* Washington, DC: Georgetown University Press.

Martin, B. (1970). *Brown bear, brown bear.* New York: Harcourt Brace Jovanovich.

Martínez, J., & Moore-O'Brien, J. A. (1993). Developing biliteracy in a two-way immersion program. In J.V. Tinajero & A. F. Ada (Eds.), *The power of two languages: Literacy and biliteracy for Spanish-speaking students* (pp. 276–293). New York: Macmillan/McGraw Hill.

McCarty, T. L., & Watahomigie, L. J. (1998). Language and literacy in American Indian and Alaska Native communities. In B. Perez (Ed.), *Sociocultural contexts of language and literacy* (pp. 69–99). Mahwah, NJ: Lawrence Erlbaum.

McCollum, P. (1999). Learning to value English: Cultural capital in a two-way bilingual program. *Bilingual Research Journal,* 23 (2-3), 113–134.

McLaughlin, B. (1984). *Second language acquisition in childhood: Preschool children.* Mahwah, NJ: Lawrence Erlbaum.

McLaughlin, B. (1995). *Fostering second language development in young children: Principles and practices.* Educational Practice Report 14. National Center for Research on Cultural Diversity and Second Language Learning. Office of Education Research and Improvement of the U.S. Department of Education.

Mcleod, B. (1994). *Language and learning: Educating linguistically diverse students.* New York: State University of New York Press.

Mei-Yu, L. (1998). *Multicultural children's literature in the elementary classroom.* Bloomington, IN: ERIC Clearinghouse on Reading English and Communication.

Moll, L. C., & Díaz, S. (1987). Teaching writing as communication: The use of ethnographic findings in classroom practice. In D. Bloome (Ed.), *Literacy and schooling* (pp. 55–65). Norwood, NJ: Ablex.

Moll, L. C., Tapia, J., & Whitmore, K. F. (1993). Living knowledge: The social distribution of cultural resources for thinking. In G. Salomon (Ed.), *Distributed cognition: Psychological and educational considerations* (pp. 139–163). New York: Cambridge University Press.

Montague, N. (1997). Critical components for dual language programs. *Bilingual Research Journal,* 21 (4), 334–342.

Montone, C., & Loeb, M. (2000). *Implementing two-way immersion programs in middle and high schools.* Washington, DC, and Santa Cruz, CA: Center for Research on Education, Diversity and Excellence.

Mora, J. K., Wink, J., & Wink, D. (2001). Dueling models of dual language instruction: A critical review of the literature and program implementation guide. *Bilingual Research Journal,* 25 (4), 417–442.

Navarrete, C., & Gustke, C. (1996). *A guide to performance assessment of linguistically diverse students.* Albuquerque, NM: EAC West, New Mexico Highlands University.

New York State Education Department. (2001). *The teaching of languages arts to limited English proficient/English language learners: A resource guide for all teachers.* New York State Education Department, Office of Bilingual Education and the University of the State of New York.

Nieto, S. (2000). *Affirming diversity: The sociopolitical context of multicultural education.* New York: Longman.

Nieto, S. (2002). *Language, culture and teaching: Critical perspectives for a new century.* Mahwah, NJ: Lawrence Erlbaum.

O'Malley, J. M., & Pierce, L.V. (1996). *Authentic assessment for English language learners: Practical approaches for teachers.* Menlo Park, CA: Addison-Wesley.

Ovando, C. J., & Collier, V. P. (1998). *Bilingual and ESL classrooms: Teaching in multicultural contexts.* Boston: McGraw-Hill.

Ovando, C. J., & Pérez. R. (2000). The politics of bilingual immersion programs. In C. J. Ovando & P. McLaren (Eds.), *The politics of multiculturalism and bilingual education: Students and teachers caught in the crossfire* (pp. 149–165). Boston: McGraw-Hill.

Pappas, C. C., Kiefer, B. Z., & Levstik, L. S. (1995). *An integrated perspective in the elementary school: Theory into action.* New York: Longman.

Peal, E., & Lambert, W. E. (1962). The relationship of bilingualism to intelligence. *Psychological Monographs,* 76 (27), 1–23.

Peregoy, S., & Boyle, O. (2001). *Reading, writing, and learning in ESL: A resource book for K–12 teachers* 3rd ed. New York: Longman.

Pérez, B. (1998). *Sociocultural contexts of language and literacy.* Mahwah, NJ: Lawrence Erlbaum.

Pérez, B., & Torres-Guzmán, M. E. (2002). *Learning in two worlds: An integrated Spanish/English biliteracy approach.* Boston: Allyn and Bacon.

Polacco, P. (1988). *The keeping quilt.* New York: Simon & Schuster Books for Young Children.

Ramírez, A. (1994). Literacy acquisition among second language learners. In B. M. Ferdman, R. Weber, & A. G. Ramírez (Eds.), *Literacy across languages and cultures* (pp. 75–101). New York: State of New York Press.

Ramírez, J. D. (1992). Executive summary. *Bilingual Research Journal,* 16 (1), 1–62.

Readence, J., Bean, T., & Baldwin, R. (1981). *Content area reading: An integrated approach.* Dubuque, IA: Kendall-Hunt.

Rigg, P., & Allen, V. G. (1989). *When they don't all speak English: Integrating the ESL student into the regular classroom.* Urbana, IL: National Council of Teachers of English.

Riley, R. W. (2000). *Excelencia para todos—excellence for all: The progress of Hispanic education and the challenges of a new century.* Speech presented at Bell Multicultural High School, Washington, DC, March 15. http://www.ed.gov/speeches/03-2000/000315.html.

Romero, A. A. (1999). Two-way bilingual programs: The demand for a multilingual workforce. *Intercultural Development Research Association Newsletter, 26,* 5.

Rosenthal, S. (1994). Students as teachers. *Thrust for Educational Leadership, 23* (6), 36–38.

Rossen, M. (1989). *We're going on a bear hunt.* New York: Margaret K. McElderry Books.

Routman, R. (1991). *Invitations: Changing as teachers and learners K–12.* Portsmouth, NH: Heinemann.

Routman, R. (1996). *Literacy at the crossroads: Crucial talk about reading, writing and other teaching dilemmas.* Portsmouth, NH: Heinemann.

Rueda, R. (1998). Addressing the needs of a diverse society. In T. E. Raphael & K. H. Au (Eds.), *Literature-based instruction: Reshaping the curriculum* (pp. 349–354). Norwood, MA: Christopher Gordon Publishers.

Ruiz, R. (1997). The empowerment of language-minority students. In A. Darder, R. D. Torres, & H. Gutiérrez (Eds.), *Latinos and education: A critical reader* (pp. 320–328). New York: Routledge.

Savignon, S. J. (1983). *Communicative competence: Theory and classroom practice: Text and contexts in second language learning.* Los Angeles: Addison Wesley.

Schifini, A. (1985). *Sheltered English.* Los Angeles: Los Angeles County Office of Education.

Short, D. J. (2002). Newcomer programs: An educational alternative for secondary immigrant students. *Education and Urban Society, 34* (2), 173–198.

Skinner, B. F. (1968). *The technology of teaching.* New York: Appleton-Century-Crofts.

Skutnabb-Kangas, T. (1981). *Bilingualism or not: The education of minorities.* Clevedon, England: Multilingual Matters.

Skutnabb-Kangas, T. (1995). *Multilingualism for all.* Netherlands: Swets & Zeitlinger.

Skutnabb-Kangas, T. (2000). *Linguistic genocide in education: Or worldwide diversity and human rights?* Mahwah, NJ: Lawrence Erlbaum.

Slavin, R. E. (1990). *Cooperative learning: Theory, research and practice.* Boston: Allyn & Bacon.

Slavin, R. E. (1991). Synthesis of research on cooperative learning. *Educational Leadership, 48* (1), 71–82.

Sleeter, C. E., & Grant, C. A. (1999). *Making choices for multicultural education: Five approaches to race, class, and gender.* New York: John Wiley & Sons.

Soltero, S. W. (1997). Biliteracy: The connection between language, culture and literacy. *Educación y Ciencia,* 77–91.

Soltero, S. (2002). Key programmatic decisions in dual language education. *Illinois Association for Multilingual Multicultural Education Bulletin, 27* (1), 7–11.

Soska, M. (1994). An introduction to educational technology. *Direction in Language Education, 1* (1), 1–8.

Soto, G. (1991). *Taking sides.* San Diego, CA: Harcourt Brace Jovanovich.

Stahl, R. J. (1994). *Cooperative learning in social studies: A handbook for teachers.* Menlo Park, CA: Addison-Wesley.

Sugarman, J., & Howard, E. (2001). *Development and maintenance of two-way immersion programs: Advice from practitioners.* Washington, DC, and Santa Cruz, CA: Center for Research on Education, Diversity and Excellence.

Swain, M., & Lapkin, S. (1982). *Evaluating bilingual education: A Canadian case study.* Clevedon, England: Multilingual Matters.

Swain, M., & Lapkin, S. (1991). Heritage language children in an English-French immersion program. *Canadian Modern Languages Review, 47* (4), 635–641.

Teachers of English to Speakers of Other Languages. (1997). *ESL standards for preK–12 students.* Alexandria, VA: Teachers of English to Speakers of Other Languages.

Tharp, R. G., & Gallimore, R. (1988). *Rousing minds to life: Teaching, learning, and schooling in social context.* New York: Cambridge University Press.

Thomas, W., & Collier, V. (1997). Two languages are better than one. *Educational Leadership, 55* (4), 23–24.

Thomas, W., & Collier, V. (1998). *School effectiveness for language minority students.* Alexandria, VA: National Clearinghouse for Bilingual Education.

Thomas, W., & Collier, V. (2002). *A national study of school effectiveness for language minority students' long-term academic achievement.* Center for Research on Education, Diversity and Excellence. http://www.crede.ucsc.edu/research/llaa/1.1es.html.

Thonis, E. W. (1994). The ESL student: Reflections on the present concerns for the future. In K. Spangenberg-Urbschat & R. Pritchard (Eds.), *Kids come in all languages: Reading instruction for ESL students* (pp. 207–216). Newark, DL: International Reading Association.

Tinajero, J. V., & Ada, A. F. (1993). *The power of two languages: Literacy and biliteracy for Spanish-speaking students.* New York: Macmillan/McGraw Hill.

Tinajero, J. V., Calderón, M. E., & Hertz-Lazarowitz, R. (1993). Cooperative learning strategies: Bilingual classroom applications. In J. V. Tinajero & A. F. Ada

(Eds.), *The power of two languages. Literacy and biliteracy for Spanish-speaking students* (pp. 241–253). New York: Macmillan/McGraw Hill.

Torres-Guzmán, M. E. (2002). *Dual language programs: Key features and results*. Directions in Language and Education, 14. National Clearinghouse for Bilingual Education.

Trueba, H. T. (1989). *Raising silent voices: Educating the linguistic minorities for the 21st century.* New York: Newbury House.

Trueba, H. T. (1991). The role of culture in bilingual instruction: Linking linguistic and cognitive development to cultural knowledge. In O. Garcia (Ed.), *Bilingual education: Focusschrift in honor of Joshua A. Fishman on the occasion of his 65th birthday* (pp. 43–55). Philadelphia: John Benjamins Publishing Company.

Tse, L. (2001). *Why don't they learn English? Separating fact from fallacy in the US language debate.* New York: Teachers College Press.

Valdés, G. (1996). *Con respeto: Bridging the distance between culturally diverse families and schools.* New York: Teachers College Press.

Valdés, G. (1997). Dual-language immersion programs: A cautionary note concerning the education of language-minority students. *Harvard Educational Review, 67* (3), 391–429.

Valdés, G. (1998). The world outside and inside school: Language and immigrant children. *Educational Researcher, 27* (6), 4–18.

Valdés Fallis, G. (1976). Social interaction and codeswitching patterns: A case study of Spanish/English alternation. In G. Keller, R. Teschner, & S. Viera (Eds.), *Bilingualism in the bicentennial and beyond* (pp. 53–85). New York: Bilingual Press.

Vygotsky, L. S. (1978). *Mind in society*. Cambridge, MA: Harvard University Press.

Wells, G. (1986). *The meaning makers: Children learning language and using language to learn.* Portsmouth, NH: Heinemann.

Williams, S. (1989). *I went walking.* New York: Harcourt Brace Jovanovich

Wong Fillmore, L. (1991). Second language learning in children: A model of social language learning in social context. In E. Bialystock (Ed.), *Language processing in bilingual children* (pp. 49–69). Cambridge, MA: Cambridge University Press.

Wong Fillmore, L., & Snow, C. E. (2000). *What teachers need to know about language.* Washington, DC: Center for Applied Linguistics.

Wong Fillmore, L., & Valadéz, C. (1986). Teaching bilingual learners. In M. C. Wiltrach (Ed.), *Handbook of research on teaching* (pp. 648–685). New York: Macmillan.

Woods, P., Boyle, M., & Hubbard, N. (1999). *Multicultural children in the early years: Creative teaching, meaningful learning.* Clevedon, England: Multilingual Matters.

Zucker, C. (1995). The role of ESL in a dual language program. *Bilingual Research Journal, 19* (3), 513–523.

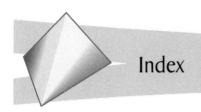

Index